I Should've Been Nicer to Quentin Tarantino

and Other Short Stories
of Epic Fails and Saves

Kathleen Kinmont

McNae, Marlin & Mackenzie, Ltd.
BOOK AND PERIODICAL PUBLISHERS
GLASGOW • NEW YORK • LOS ANGELES
QUEENS ROAD, GLASGOW, LANARKSHIRE G42 800 SCOTLAND

1

ISBN-13: 978-1-64921-577-2
ISBN-10: 1-64921-577-0

For more information on Kathleen Kinmont
Please visit www.kathleenkinmont.com and
visit us at www.m3publishers.com

For
my daughter, Ayden Grace, my princess

For
my mom, Abby Dalton, my queen

For
my dad, Jack Smith, my humble hero

And for everyone whose name is placed in a book title
without their permission

With love,
Your loyal subject

Acknowledgements

I want to thank my amazing daughter, Ayden Grace, for the inspiration to write this book and the insight to live my best life.

I would like to thank the super brave souls who read this book from start to finish before I had a publisher, editor or any idea of what I was doing. There were only a few who I could trust to read this mosh pit of turbulent Hollywood faire in its unedited version. Their care and unconditional love encouraged me to finish and continue this quest to completion.

My glass is eternally raised to the kindness of Tom Sheeter, a wildly gifted comedic and dramatic actor, who left us too soon but will remain forever in my heart. His uplifting notes and incitement were a tremendous gift that will never be forgotten. I also bow to the unflinching friendship of Karen Pillot, a perceptive, insightful reader and champion of morale-boosting, with the most contagious laugh on the planet.

When it finally came time to put this creation into readable, understandable pulp non-fiction, Mali Monae became my superhero. Without Mali's proficient help, brilliant guidance and tireless questions delving deeper into my psyche, I don't think I would have finished as swiftly. Mali is a stunning actor from Norway and the fact that English is her second language is astounding. I raise my glass to these brave three who toured my skull and I say to you all "Skal!"

Translation ~ I salute you; my admired group of friends and I cheers to your good health and our cherished companionship.

I want to thank poet, philosopher and artist Kahlil Gibran for his most enlightened book, *The Prophet*. I have been highly transformed by his masterpiece and was inspired by his template for my own musings and meanderings on life and its endless subject matters. I have the greatest respect for his achievement and his words are a part of my soul.

I want to thank Academy Award® winning writer and producer, Nick Vallelonga, for agreeing to write my Foreword, even though he's never even slightly mentioned in my book. He is one of my greatest friends who has my undying love, respect and admiration. *Green Book* is as close to a perfect movie there is and watching Nick receive a couple of Oscars® and a couple of Golden Globes® for a film that he wrote and produced about an incredible, life changing moment from his own father's life, reminds me how valuable it is to write about and share our stories.

I want to thank Academy Award® winning writer and director Quentin Tarantino for his name and his vast array of powerful and provocative film work. He has always been a force to be reckoned with and watching him grow from young, struggling actor to accolade receiving writer/ director has been an incredible view. Quentin has my deepest respect and appreciation for borrowing his name in the humorous title for my spiritual satire.

I want to thank my first husband, Golden Globe ® nominated actor and professional helicopter pilot, Lorenzo Lamas. Lorenzo is a mainstay in my life and a testimony to how much I've learned about love and forgiveness.

I want to thank the best interviewer in the business, American radio personality, Howard Stern. Without his perennial probing, I don't think I would've been able to find my own voice amidst the obvious chaos surrounding me or the encouragement to share the truth.

A ginormous Thanks to everyone on the M3Publishers Team for their tremendous help and efforts. Special thanks to Ken Levine and Brian Forbes, my publishers, editors and cover art creators. Their enthusiasm, guidance and endless patience were everything. A special thanks to the generous owners and waitstaff at Paty's in Toluca Lake for our red booth office space!

I would also like to thank and acknowledge every family member, friend, teacher, director, co-worker, and random stranger I've ever met who has influenced my life. In ways that you may know or not know, you've helped me survive it all long enough to share some of my most epic fails and ardent saves.

If you find your name in this book, I have two things to say, "You're welcome and I'm sorry."
'You're welcome' if I've written something that you like, and 'I'm sorry' if you don't.
If you don't find your name in this book, I have two things to say, "You're welcome and I'm sorry."
'You're welcome' for leaving you out, and/or 'I'm sorry' that I forgot about you, which might also be considered a 'You're welcome.'

Keep me away from
the wisdom which
does not cry,
the philosophy
which does not
laugh and
the greatness
which does not bow
before children.

~Kahlil Gibran

Table of Contents

Preface 15
Foreword – Nick Vallelonga 17

1. ~ on I should've been nicer to
   Quentin Tarantino 21
2. ~ on acting 27
3. ~ on *Bride of Re-Animator* 35
4. ~ on *Mrs. Sweeney* 45
5. ~ on *Renegade* 55
6. ~ on Lorenzo 69
7. ~ on birth, 79
8. ~ on organs 85
9. ~ on dating 93
10. ~ on valet 105
11. ~ on almost famous 111
12. ~ on yoga 119
13. ~ on poop 125
14. ~ on children 131
15. ~ on parenting 141
16. ~ on laughter 149
17. ~ on death 157
18. ~ on family 167
19. ~ on divorce 177
20. ~ on marriage 183
21. ~ on writing 189
22. ~ on baseball 195
23. ~ on looking up 205
24. ~ on jealousy 211
25. ~ on change 219
26. ~ on aging 225
27. ~ on compassion 233
28. ~ on pets 241
29. ~ on listening 247
30. ~ on hats 253
31. ~ on photography 265
32. ~ on electricity 273

33. ~ on lying, cheating and stealing 279
34. ~ on spirituality 287
35. ~ on Esther 297
36. ~ on kissing 305
37. ~ on reality 311
38. ~ on bullies 319
39. ~ on humor 327
40. ~ on forgiveness 333
41. ~ on repetition 341
42. ~ on entitlement 347
43. ~ on hostage to the outcome 353
44. ~ on players 359
45. ~ on moving 365
46. ~ on education 371
47. ~ on moms 379
48. ~ on dads 387
49. ~ on heroes 395
50. ~ on dance 401
51. ~ on when 409
52. ~ on religion 417
Photo Glossary 429

14

Preface

I wrote this book to share an assortment of my most personal and professional stories with my teenage daughter, who of course, didn't really know what my life was like before she came along.

This body of work is a compilation of my respective challenges and triumphs, woven together to remind myself to let go of what no longer serves me, while simultaneously creating a roadmap for flourishing choices.

This book of life's lessons and hindsight's was written for her, although it has become a love letter of forgiveness and sweet remembrances to me.

I have learned through this experience to trust my unapologetic and fierce truth and in so doing, I found my voice.

Foreword

Nick Vallelonga

I met Kathleen Kinmont when she walked into a casting session for an indy thriller film I was directing, *The Corporate Ladder*. It was like she entered in slow motion, the quintessential tall, beautiful blonde movie star, whose presence and gorgeous smile lit up the room. Remember the scene in *The Godfather* when Michael is in Sicily and sees Apollonia for the first time? Remember the look on his face? They said he got hit by the thunderbolt. *Calpo di fulmine.* Love at first sight. That's what it was like when I first met Kathleen. So of course I cast her for the lead in the film, because luckily for me her acting, personality, intelligence and talent was even more stunning than her beauty. She doesn't know this but there's a scene in the film when her character is applying for an executive assistant job, and when she walks into the office to meet the executive, I filmed her entrance in slow motion, exactly how I remembered it when she walked in to meet me.

We formed a bond and a friendship that lasts to this day. When she asked me to write the foreword to this book, I was humbled and honored. As you will learn after reading, Kathleen has had an amazing life, filled with incredible stories, as well as meeting and mingling with some of the biggest stars in Hollywood. So why she picked me to write this, only she knows. But now with the task at

17

hand, how can I possibly do her and this book justice? I guess, simply, by telling the truth.

The book is skillfully written, captivating, funny, sad, entertaining and endearing. Kathleen is not only a wonderful storyteller, she's a teacher as well. During this personal journey, she opens up about the ups and downs of her life experiences, written in a way so that we can all connect and relate to what she was going through. She walks us through the good times and the bad, and how she learned and personally evolved through it all, then ends each story by giving us life lessons and advice.

Kathleen was blessed by amazing, loving parents, a movie star mother, and a father who was a real life hero that could have had movies written about him. They raised a beautiful family, and Kathleen shined as a loving daughter, and loving sister to her two brothers. She also is a devoted mother to her gorgeous, talented daughter and she is a caring, loving friend to everyone who has been blessed to know her. I am one of the fortunate ones to be included in that group.

So after reading this book, I think you will all understand why, when Quentin Tarantino met Kathleen in an acting class, he wrote a scene for them to act in together, and in the scene, he would kiss her. After meeting her and getting to know her here in these pages, you too will want to kiss her, hug her, lose yourself in her eyes, her smile, her contagious laugh, her personality, her wickedly funny wit, her warmth, her intelligence... well, I can go on and on, but I think you get the point.

You will love her too, as all that have met her do. Love you, Kathleen. Thanks for sharing your beautiful thoughts and life with us in these pages.

CHAPTER 1

~ on *I should've been nicer to Quentin Tarantino*

I was sixteen, on my way to my first acting class in Toluca Lake when I realized, "I'm chewing gum and riding a bike! This acting thing will be a cinch." I had always known I wanted to work in the entertainment business, so my mom said, "James Best has a theatre around the corner. You should check it out if you want to be an actor. Start taking class." My heart was interchangeably pounding with fear and excitement, as I stepped into the theatre and found a room full of adults, many working actors whom I recognized from both television and film. "Oh my God, I'm gonna have to get up there. These are real actors, these aren't kids. They're not teachers who are gonna blow smoke up my ass and say 'Congratulations, you got up on stage and didn't throw up'." Hopeful, I scanned the room for hidden pockets of other teens who also found themselves planted at the bottom floor of this massive ocean of talent and training. There were *two*; my friend, Jackie and some other teenage guy, who seemed even more nervous than me. "Get up there and do it," I firmly whispered to myself. Before long, I got used to blocking out my nerves, and instead learned to allow these sensations to be a part of the experience and charge my work. "Use it, use it, use it!" was drilled into the collective subconscious by our coach, Jack Lucarelli, who seemed equally high on the electric current vibrating from every actor within the four walls of the second story theatre. "If you're having an insane day, use it!" Once mastered, this lesson would serve me well in many more aspects of life.

The eighteen-year-old teenage man/boy would always sit at the back of the class, and always early, probably the first to arrive. He carried a pad and kept a pen in his hand, constantly taking notes, just to look up every once in a while. He was enthusiastic and animated, and to me, his energy felt wildly frenetic. It was clear that he had bigger visions than just the stage and he was entirely *dedicated* to whatever he was plotting down on paper.

One day, the high-spirited teenage dude proposed in passing that he wanted to write a scene for the two of us to work on in class. It involved the characters kissing. "Whaaat?" The room turned into a vacuum as the words played out in slow motion like a silent film in my mind. Never before had I encountered portraying mature, physical intimacy in front of a mostly all adult audience who was already ramped up on the notion of 'everything inevitably boils down to sex'. The idea was terrifying, as I had not yet grown fully comfortable with this in real life. I was still learning. I was still learning how to trust myself and everybody else. I panicked and begged our acting coach to never, ever put me in a scene with this older, teenager. I thought the whole thing was odd and I wasn't comfortable working on material that he was maniacally creating. It was probably a scene from *Reservoir Dogs*. C'est la vie.

And with that, my working relations with Quentin Tarantino got stumped/failed to materialize. Unfortunately, at my age I had no wherewithal on how to navigate a future genius. I have always wondered what the outcome would've been, had I dared to engage with the opportunity. Would we have become friends? What would I have learned from the experience? Would the ebullient energy that initially frightened me have opened me to a new perspective on storytelling? Would the chance to collaborate with a brilliant mind have affected my own approach thereafter?

The age of innocence is a mismatched outfit that is constantly under construction. Until you gain the assurance that a yellow polka dot skirt is best worn without a pair of striped red leggings, you might fumble a bit, unless of course you want to make a statement, then go for it. Self-assurance and a solid footing on how to navigate the external world is also gained through maturing and experience. I've beaten myself up for running for the hills when the unique, creative power of Quentin suggested that we collaborate, but I've learned to forgive the young teenage girl who was still learning to sail open waters with her heart and soul completely exposed.

Enrolling in an acting class is a courageous step. You put your body through heightened emotional transitions and then sit down on a cold chair in front of a mute audience to endure a trusted coach's critique. You undergo several solid rollercoaster rides; emotionally, physically, spiritually, and are left wide open, raw and vulnerable as your protective guard is entirely down. It's an E-Ticket.

There's a reason why actors need space to go deep within themselves and their process. The truth is, I was simply too afraid to get up on stage and kiss anyone in the beginning months of that class. I was still having a hard time just playing someone's messed up teenage daughter. I would have loved to work up to playing Quentin's girlfriend in a kissing scene, but having it come straight out of the gates like that startled me. The good thing was I knew I could say *no* to certain things, and if and when I was ready, I could say *yes*. As an actor, there are so many, many things that are tremendously uncomfortable and I had to develop an understanding of my own boundaries, and how to show up for myself in situations that were uncomfortable to *me*, no matter how innocent they were in actuality.

Before we can fully trust another, we first have to trust ourselves. And if the road there seems to cost you some opportunities, then that is a price worth paying, for nothing is more valuable than the personal freedom of self-reliance. It is not until you master fully trusting yourself that you can fully give what you have to offer. On stage, in film, and in life alike.

I started working professionally at eighteen, yet I maintained my seat in the class to further develop my craft and grow as a person. I was young and I had a lot to learn, and the class provided a safe environment of highly skilled mentors. It was a front row pass to the life I desperately desired to create for myself.

If I have the chance to speak with Quentin Jerome Tarantino again, I'd love to ask him if any of those scenes he wrote in class ever made it into one of his films. From my recollection, I think a few did.

Epic Fail ~ Assuming acting (aka life) is a piece of cake.

Epic Save ~ Live life and eat cake.

Lesson Learned ~ Be kind to everyone no matter how different they may seem. Establish clear, personal boundaries so that one can engage with others from a genuine, curious heart space.

"Everything I learned as an actor, I have basically applied to writing."
　　　~ Quentin Tarantino

CHAPTER 2

~ **on acting**

I started seriously acting around ten or eleven years old. I would practice working up tears on long car trips to Mammoth. I created sad scenarios that would get me to cry quickly so I had a ready case when I needed sympathy during a fight with my older brother, Matt. I never fought with my younger brother, Johnny, so fake tears with him weren't necessary, but with Matt they were my back up ammo, especially if they had "I'm telling mom!" attached to them. I didn't realize that I was working a 'sense memory' part of my brain, which is an acting technique that takes you to a place of real emotion. One of the reasons I love kids is their natural ability to pretend without the need for a paycheck. They do it because it's fun and it flexes their imagination, not because one day they might receive a forty four cent residual check. Btw, that check, assures you that you know for sure, without a shadow of a doubt, that you were once a professional, working actor.

I've studied with many wonderful teachers and bright, young, shiny new actors who I continue to see on television or hear on voice overs and at the movies. I've done plays, showcases, commercials, television, film. I even had a radio show which gave me the courage to do stand-up at the Comedy Store and The Improv. Nothing will tighten the sphincter and get the 'ol heart kicked into gear like the nerves ten minutes before getting up on stage to do stand-up. I didn't know I possessed any low hanging fruit until that point.

I adore actors. I married three of them. If two wrongs don't make a right, what will three make? A trike? I delight in actors and their intense love for all human behavior. An actors' natural ability to get you to believe their truth and their bullshit is a real gift. Acting is the delicate dance between the real and the not so real. Getting to the truth of it is always the quest and it's not always pretty.

I knew that I had crossed over into real 'acting' when I was cast in *The Bride of Re-Animator*. I played an assemblage of several different body parts covered in blood and glue. It was the creation of an exceptional make-up effects team, *KNB FX Group*, the highly skilled make-up artists Quentin Tarantino uses on all of his films. *The Bride* came after *Halloween 4*, which was my first horror film. I have a deep appreciation for the fans of these films, although I'm not a massive fan myself, as I've never been one to steep myself in gore or macabre. It's never been my thing and I don't feel the need to conquer *fear* in that way. I've already embraced *fear* in acting, so to put my mind and body through that emotional ride of being scared shitless as entertainment is not a need nor a desire. It's too traumatic for me, as I'm already pretty hypersensitive. The useless garbage that swirls around in my overactive imagination is something that I've spent years of meditation, long walks and countless hours of yoga and prayer to help put a lid on. I intentionally don't watch a lot of news, especially at night, so that I'm not agitated when I go to bed. Why would I want to get freaked out in my few moments of entertainment? I'd rather watch Bravo, 'Friends' or 'Seinfeld.' Mindless fun and fluff.

I did conquer some pretty deep-seated fear with my love for the film, *The Revenant*. Truly one of the most horrific films I've ever seen. I have a debilitating, paralyzing fear of bears, thanks to my mom and her appreciable acting talents in reading *The Bear Story* ad nauseam when I was a young, impressionable child. This is a short story written by, Robert Louis Stevenson, that would get me buried under the bed sheets trying to find my way back to the womb, where everything was dark and you couldn't understand what the hell was being said out there. If I could, I would've clawed my way back to a place where ignorance really is bliss. I've put myself through that film a few times and each time I become a bit more of a bad ass. Maybe that's why folks really enjoy films like *Saw* because it's not easy to put yourself through that fear and be able to walk away from it unscathed. Another beautiful part about acting, is that it's all pretend, simulated experience, that we only experience emotionally. People have been injured and killed on sets when things go wrong, but it is a safety-first environment, intended to only inflict an emotional cost to the audience.

Through acting, I feel a tremendous bond with fellow actors, especially Leonardo DiCaprio. There is a keen sensitivity in knowing that all those prosthetic pieces that were glued into his face and skull in *The Revenant,* would still be stuck in his hair and ears at the end of every grueling day. The dirt and the blood mixture would be black and sticky all over, especially in places he didn't anticipate. How the day's angst and goop would roll off into the drain in the shower at the end of the workday would be such a relief. Falling into bed knowing that the tattered bits of flesh would be glued back into place with fresh meat, on raw skin, in the frost of the next morning, are all something I've had the joy of experiencing too.

Bride of Re-Animator let me know that I was an honest to God actor. Other than the fake crying in the back seat of the car, I hadn't really done anything remotely close to the monster I played in that film. I do know that the auditioning, rejection and dreams dashed can turn anyone into a monster. I understand pain on a cellular level and the compassion I have for actors across the board will make me a good writer, producer and director. Actors have been lovingly dubbed, 'meat puppets' by the industry. If that's the case, I like mine raw, rare, medium, medium well and well done. I find that acting is one of the toughest career paths out there and the fearlessness it takes to put your whole being on the petri dish for the world to dissect is an extraordinary level of bravery. Especially if you want to make it your career. It's fun if you want to keep it light and stay in the comfort of community theatre but to step into the real world of head shots, agents, managers and auditions, can take the fun away instantly. It gets very real before you know it and the play acting will have to fall by the wayside. The competitive nature of the business and the need to work are excruciating. I would never recommend this job to anyone who didn't have the burning desire to get pretty ugly. It is not a fun or pretty business, even though it's surrounded by fun and beautiful people. A real actor is not on a quest to be beautiful; they are on the hunt to get filthy dirty. We yearn for the moments where we get to dig up the painful bones of our past and put them on display take after take. We want to play anything but ourselves. We bring out our demons for folly and the longer we live, the better the story one has to tell.

I gave acting up for a while to focus on raising my daughter and work behind the camera as a cinematographer, writer, producer and director. There are many facets of the business and as all aging actors begin to realize, there are many ways to be solvent in an industry that is extremely fickle. I also believe that if you really want to be a well-rounded actor, produce something and learn the real value of production, your crew and team work.

I was at a signing convention in Germany and having a light conversation with the lovely actor, Julian Sands, telling him about the different projects I was producing, and he asked bluntly, "What part's did you play?"
"Well, I'm writing, directing and producing, so I haven't given myself an acting part. I'm already wearing so many unfamiliar hats," I humbly responded.
"Oh, god, I hope you haven't given up acting," he scoffed.
"I think I might have," I lamely responded.

31

"Oh Darling, don't quit now. This is when it starts getting *good*," he mused.

Epic Fail ~ Thinking that fake crying would make me a good actor.

Epic Save ~ Real tears come from a place where we can all relate.

Lesson Learned ~ Don't quit, just learn something new while you're waiting.

"To be or not to be, that is the question."
    ~ William Shakespeare

CHAPTER 3

~ On *Bride of Re-Animator*

Cult films are an enigma to the film industry. You don't know you're in one until after it comes out several years later. I did this film over thirty years ago and my fan following continues to grow to this day. I continue to receive fan mail regularly and it literally blows my mind and makes me want to rip my heart out of my own chest all over again and scream, "IS THIS WHAT YOU WAAAANNNNTTTT?"

The Bride of Re-Animator was one of the more grueling auditions I can remember, and the actual shooting of the film is the standard by which I measure all other forms of pain. My call times were 2am and makeup took an average of six to eight hours before I would even step onto the set. I would film for twelve hours and then endure makeup removal for about two to three hours. By the time I got home and scrubbed the rest of the sticky, bloody goo off my body and shampooed the mess out of my back combed, rat teased hair, I had probably been up for well over 30 hours. I looked like Karen *Silkwood* when she stepped out of an acid shower after being scrubbed by a BBQ grill cleaning, iron brush. I was red, raw, and irritable beyond recognition. Thankfully, I was allowed a full twenty-four-hour turnaround to allow my body to heal and my mind to rest. It was just long enough to give me an opportunity to heal the spots that were over-glued and not too long to make me feel like I didn't want to finish the experience.

It was the most of everything you can possibly go through in a character. The "Why am I doing this?" question nagged at me all the way through the film. Especially after I saw the first one. The production gave me a copy of *Re-Animator,* which I decided to watch right before we began filming. Not a good idea, as it had some of the most bizarre, *Caligula*-esque elements I had ever seen. I'm not a big fan of horror, gore or macabre, so this was for me, a spiritual, unicorn rainbow skittle pooping human, not comfortable. Being scared shitless is not on my to do list at any given time, of any given day. I definitely understand how some people are very drawn to constantly overcoming horrific shit. A surging rush of adrenaline from ghastly visuals and terrifying music can most definitely get people to all kinds of mental, emotional and physical climax. However, for me, it disturbs me in my spirit and for that reason I get quickly turned off and don't want to go there. Not even for a minute. So when I auditioned for the role it was more of an acting challenge than an, "Oh God, please give me this part" thing because I can't wait to be in this kind of movie. In fact, the real fear and trauma were in knowing that I had won the role. It was more like an, "Oh crap, what have I signed on to do now?" thing.

The most fabulous and lifesaving part about *The Bride* were my fellow actors, Jeffrey Combs and Bruce Abbott, the stars from *Re-Animator.* Barbara Crampton, also starred in *Re-Animator* and we ended up as besties in the Spring Break comedy romp, *Fraternity Vacation*. Without a doubt *The Bride* would not have been what it was without the ingenious and phenomenal make-up artists, *KNB EFX GROUP*. At that time their team consisted of Robert Kurtzman, Greg Nicotero and Howard Berger. They had some fine and worthy apprentices working alongside them, but these guys were the prosthetics, paint and glue of the intricate character. These geniuses created the look and all the body parts. It was completely my body, no CGI, but after they were finished with me it didn't feel like anything remotely close to me. They took me for a ride in my own vessel that I would've never experienced without their skill set and supervision. Every vein, and exposed piece of flesh was given a tremendous amount of care and thought. These guys are true artists and their expansive careers, resumes, and numerous awards reflect the type of creative individuals they are and as a team there is no one like KNB.

Legendary Academy Award® Winner Special Effects Make-up Artist, Stan Winston was Howard's mentor and I had the great fortune to work with Stan on *T3* with Kristanna Loken. Stan and I spoke quite a bit about Howard Berger and what a great student he became of Stan's and their long history. In turn, I was able to tell him about my conversations with Howard and what a great mentor Stan was to him. A beautiful full-circle moment while creature creating. Quentin loves working with KNB. Maybe one day Quentin will bring me on to one of his films so KNB can put me through some early hours of grisly, gnarly makeup for a scene where I get mauled by a circus bear, only to be put out of my misery with a flame thrower by the Bear Trainer played by Quentin. This would be my greatest nightmare put on film under the watchful eye of consummate professionals. Anyway, these solid KNB guys made working in the most intense experience palpable and I am forever grateful for their professionalism, humor and the talent to always deliver. Plus, they consistently had enough blood in a barrel to make it as goopy and gooey as a mad man could ever want.

It took about two weeks to get ready for *The Bride*. There were several body and face casts to be done at the KNB make-up studio. I had to do a full body cast that they used for making the several body suits that I wore. The Bride was nude, which meant so were my body casts. Cold, wet plaster all over my naked body still makes me shudder to this day. If I'm ever roasting, hot as hell in a menopausal hot flash, all I have to do is think about cold, wet body plaster on my naked boobs and I instantly have the shivers. I froze solid in about thirty seconds and had to endure it for a frigid fifteen minutes. In a word, cryogenic torture chamber. All the casts took fifteen minutes and I did at least twenty of them in one day. Including a full head cast with my eyes squeezed shut, my head yanked back and my mouth wide open, held in a frozen scream while breathing out of straws shoved up my nose. Glamorous, no?

It took about three weeks to complete the filming of *The Bride*. By the last day, I was beyond done. I was well done. I was ripping the prosthetics off my body without the 'Detach all' make-up remover, leaving huge welts on my skin. We were all so exhausted and relieved that this marathon had finally reached the finish line. Everyone was rushing through the final process so we could race home and sleep for a year. On every other day I had three people helping me out of my costume, but this time I only had one spent apprentice and we were dashing through it. That's when it happened. In an unaware frenzied nanosecond, some of the very oily based makeup remover got squirted directly into my ear. My ear canal instantly went weird and I couldn't hear out of it at all. By the next day, my ear was infected, and I was in the doctor's office moaning with pain and cursing the film to no end. I was also thoroughly mad at myself for sprinting through the process that I had no business speeding through. I should have demanded the attention that I had received before. However, that's what happens during a wrap. Everyone is scrambling, blind with sleep deprivation, and focused on packing up their own gear and hurtling to their next job. The lowly actors are left to figure it out on his/her own. This is when being a diva comes in quite handy, unfortunately I hadn't fully acquired that skill set.

It took about three weeks for my ear to stop aching. I couldn't swim for a month and had to keep it away from water during bathing. Have you ever taken a shower and not gotten your ears wet? No, me either. It's impossible. When the movie finally came out, I was pleasantly shocked. It had a ton of assorted weird animatronics and bizarre additions that I never visualized when I read the script but somehow made it into the film. The final product was way more bizarre than I could've ever imagined. I do remember thinking "Wow, is that really me?" Followed quickly by, "Thank God I survived."

It took a few years to realize this was going to be a cult film that would follow me through my life. It took several decades to realize that the fan base would continue to grow as the years went on. The photo still of me ripping my own heart out of my chest from *The Bride* is the fan favorite I sign the most at conventions. Anything from *Halloween 4* is a close second. Although, nothing will ever compare to *The Bride* and the stamina of the experience involved. I had to dig deep on that film, for several reasons.

There was one moment, at the very beginning, when I had all three of the illustrious KNB Team hovering around my crotch, gluing in fake pubic hair. I discovered that I actually had a voice during the process and said, "If anyone in the movie theatre is staring at my crotch to see how delicately you three guys put pubic hair on this creature, then you've all done something wrong." At that point, I grabbed the glue and the fake pubes and glued them on myself. I said something like, "I will not be doing this 'gluing on of the pubes thing' every day, so you better have it figured out for tomorrow." They got the hint. Even the very 'cool Kathleen' had a limit to her game. You have to be such a willing and consistent team player for this sport, but there are boundaries to how far we allow ourselves to get kicked down the field.

I have traveled to many parts of the world and met many people from every walk of life who love this film and the character we brought to life. When going through the process of having to move from La Crescenta back to the Valley for my daughter's new school, I found my new dream location. I instantly contacted the property manager, Bill, who was handling the rental. My time sensitive needs had fueled the urgency to move and when dealing with real estate in LA, you're also dealing with several hundred other applicants also fighting for the same dream location. When I walked in to meet Bill in the garage of what would be my new home, the first thing he said was, "I've been so excited to meet you all day!"

"Oh?" I said smiling, nervously.

"Yes! *Bride of Re-Animator* is one of my all-time favorite movies. EVER." he gushed.

"Really?" I smiled, thanking Jesus all the way to the beginning of my resume. "Mine too!"

Epic Fail ~ Hurrying through anything that requires help at wrap time.

Epic Save ~ Stepping outside of my comfort zone as an artist.

Lesson Learned ~ If it costs you something emotionally and you allow yourself to be vulnerable in the situation, you can trust that it will affect the audience too.

"To share your weakness is to make yourself vulnerable, to make yourself vulnerable is to show your strength."
  ~ Criss Jami

CHAPTER 4

~ on *Mrs. Sweeney*

If *Bride of ReAnimator* was my biggest challenge in front of the camera, then *Mrs. Sweeney* was my birth by fire behind the camera. My mother, Abby Dalton, and I have always had a very close and unique relationship. I am her only daughter and her clone. We look alike, we sound alike, we think alike. I have been gifted with her blonde hair, high cheekbones, buckteeth and every single nuance, down to her wicked sense of humor. We are both actors and athletes, comediennes and equestrians, skiers and outdoor enthusiasts with a love for all things shiny and glamorous. We love our family fiercely and we are both extremely loyal to our friends. The only real difference is that I chose to continue to keep trying new things in the entertainment business, where my mom mostly retired her acting chops after *Falcon Crest* to focus on the golden years ahead with my dad. Along with the help of my brothers, Matt and John, we yanked her back for one more go.

I wrote my first short film, *Mrs. Sweeney*, with my brother, Matt, with the intention of being able to direct. The short was to be part of a *Prank* trilogy that never came to fruition and the script sat on the shelf for a few years. As luck and hard work would have it, a fellow writer, Gerry Cagle, an author whom I assisted in adapting his novel, *Straddle*, to screenplay form, generously decided to finance my short film. We were poised to start filming in January of 2013. Now I had the money to shoot and the crew to film it. I just needed the cast to bring it to life.

My mom was ready to play the title role years before the script was even written. She has always had a penchant for evil characters. When we were very young, she had a recurring chair on *The Hollywood Squares*, the 'storybook edition.' This was an opportunity for celebrities to dress up like their favorite storybook character and answer the hosts engaging questions the way their storybook character would respond. So kitschy. My beautiful mom, mother of three young and impressionable children, wisely chose her favorite storybook character as *The Evil Witch*. I didn't know which evil witch she was, because let's face it, once you've seen one evil witch, you've seen 'em all. My mom has a wicked cackle that can peel paint, and once the mole infested hook nose and creepy black hat were in place, she was unrecognizable. She loved to terrorize her naive offspring with her insane cackle and spooky cliche' references like, "I'm going to get you and eat you for breakfast, my little pretties..." We would scream, run, fart and hide like scalded cats. Ahh, the good old days of growing up in a circus like atmosphere. It was actually a real treat to get her to bring this old bag out of her bag of tricks. My mom, like the rest of us, has many masks that she wears to cope with life, but unlike most, she wears them all ridiculously well. She knows how to get what she wants in any given situation and by God, she gets it.

I knew that Miss Dalton would need to be surrounded by serious actors who knew what they were doing, otherwise she would eat them alive. Not an easy task when the supporting characters are all under the age of sixteen. Although, this is LA, where everyone is practically born on camera, or out here to seriously prove to themself and the family they uprooted, that they really want to do this, so I knew I would be able to find some great talent. My daughter, who has proven to be another clone of my mom, desperately wanted to be part of the casting process. She did not want to be in the film, but she begged me for two solid months to be there for the casting. I relented and brought her with me for our daylong casting session on a Saturday at a Melrose Avenue casting office. Best decision ever. Having a kid behind the desk was an instant way to relax all the kids that walked in to audition. In fact, the young artists that were chosen for the film, each engaged in their own way with my in-house, eight-year-old daughter. It brought out an instant accessibility to each of their personalities that would not have been seen if my own kid hadn't been there. On our way home, through about an hour of traffic on the streets of Hollywood, my back-seat talent scout proved she has a serious eye for brilliance. She single handedly put the young cast together with the headshots from my callback file. Ayden chose Alyssa Brianne Miller, Shannon Kummer, Zachary Haven, Jake Davidson and Caleb Thomas. She was totally on the money, as a year later, all five of my young actors were nominated for LA's Young Artist Awards for their individual performances in *Mrs. Sweeney*. I captured a Best Director award at our first film festival in Florida's *Treasure Coast International Film Festival*. I did not enter a lot of festivals, as it was my first time out and I didn't have a ton of money to enter numerous festivals. I've learned it's really expensive to be a starving artist. I entered in LA and Florida, as that's where my EP (Executive Producer) was located. I only entered festivals I knew I would be able to attend if we were selected.

The actual filming took three weeks, filming only on weekends. We used my home, interior and exterior, and the exterior of my lovely neighbors' homes in La Crescenta. My dear friends, Lisa Marie Wilson and her husband, Mark Teschner, along with Kristanna Loken also offered up their homes in the Valley. We had great winter weather. It only rained one day, but we were inside, so it never affected us. I learned how to produce alongside my brother, Johnny, who was also cast in the film. I also cast my EP's talented daughter, a member of the renowned *Groundling's*, Patric Cagle. I had recently taken a workshop to be seen by various casting directors and found a hot ace actor to play a nondescript Euro lover type, Kyle Templin. Accomplished actor, Bobby Ray Shaffer, who I threw out of a window in *The Corporate Ladder* and who also brought the character, Vance of Vance Refrigeration to life in, *The Office,* rounded out the cast as the Worthless Father to the two derelict kids that lived next door. My favorite makeup and hair artiste, Stacy Rosas, played the cowering maid, Maria. My older brother, Matt, was given the non-speaking role as the Limo Driver and the very hands-on role as Ms. Dalton's wrangler. Esther

Willams's husband, Edward Bell, a fine actor whose talents were used in a photo as Mr. Sweeney. Sadly, his character had already been electrocuted and waiting cremation.

The premise of the film was a modern-day Hansel and Gretel about elder abuse and child abduction. Matt and I wrote the screenplay based on our recollections of a mean, old woman who lived across the street from us on Ledge Avenue in Toluca Lake. As family lore goes, Matt was riding his tricycle when he somehow briefly lost control and rode over a few blades of grass on her lawn. He was three years old and she supposedly chased him off her lawn with a broomstick. There are so many things wrong with this story. First of all, it sounds completely farfetched, but this is how our mom told it, which instantly gave us kids a passport to terrorize the old broad for an entire summer. Along with our trusted hooligan next-door neighbors, Timmy and Wendy, we did all kinds of heinous tricks to that poor woman. During that part of our wayward, *Peter Pan* childhood, the five of us coined ourselves, 'The Secret Five'. We had a mayhem list that was thoughtless and impressive. We put salt on the old bitch's grass to show her how our gang was superior enough to leave a mark. We played ding-dong ditch relentlessly. I was always the one game enough to dress up like a fool, ring her doorbell nonstop, then run away kicking my butt with my heels, screaming like a fool. The final god-awful tricks were placing a hose in the mail slot through her front door and turning it on full blast. Then someone (probably Matt) put a dead squirrel in her alternate mailbox at the end of her driveway. The careless and thoughtless shenanigans quickly came to a halt after those very alarming pranks were reported to our parents and quite possibly the police. The gang was quickly disbanded, and we were not to hang with the neighbor kids for a very long time, possibly ever. That's okay, we had cousins for mayhem, so we weren't too disappointed.

These were all horrible things to do to somebody and I still feel very bad about them. We should've all been seriously reprimanded and served up as stew. Which is exactly how Grimm's Fairy Tales work when kids get their Come to Jesus moment. In a sweeping broom of justice, Mrs. Sweeney gives these brats their comeuppance for all the nasty things they do to her. It really is a feel-good movie. You feel good that an elderly person actually has the balls to fight back, and you feel good about yourself if you've never been mean to someone unsuspecting. It felt good to able to put practically everyone in my circle of family and friends to work on what would be the beginning of my own productions. It also felt good to find new, young talent to create lasting new friendships. But nothing will ever compare to directing my mother in my first 'at the helm' moment and watching her explicitly explain the difference between a *bobby* pin and a *hair* pin to makeup and hair, as we were quickly losing the light.

"This is a *hair* pin. It's long and it's used to *pin* the hair, like this," she lectured, while demonstrating the hair pin use.

Stacy, one of the sweetest people on the planet, gave me the most subtle of side eyes. It was like a 'please help' combined with a 'wtf?'

"This is a *bobby* pin. It's shorter and it's used to *bobby* pin the hair, like this," she continued, while demonstrating her fully polished eighty year old diva.

"Mom, we're losing the light. We need you on set. Please," I begged.

She loved hearing that phrase so much, I could see it wash over her like a morning sun bath. She hadn't been <u>needed</u> on set in such a long time and to see her reaction was everything. The need to feel the desperation of all of us needing her, was a symphony to her ears. It was beautiful and I'll never forget it.

She gently handed all the pins to a very grateful Stacy.

"It's Miss Dalton to you, Miss Kinmont, and don't you forget it," Miss Dalton chimed, as she glided to set.

"You'll always be *Mrs. Sweeney* to me, babe," I lovingly reassured.

Epic Fail ~ Playing mean and nasty pranks on anyone is never a good choice.

Epic Save ~ Making a film focused on the consequences that get served when someone is cruel.

Lesson Learned ~ Payback is a bitch.

"Anonymous blog comments, vapid video pranks and lightweight mash-ups may seem trivial and harmless, but as a whole, this widespread practice of fragmentary, impersonal communication has demeaned personal interaction."
~ Jaron Lanier

CHAPTER 5

~ on *Renegade*

I was hired to play Cheyenne Phillips without ever having to audition. I got fired after four seasons. Lorenzo and I were married for the first season and halfway through the second. We were divorced and working together for two and a half seasons.

They were twenty-two episode seasons and I appeared in eighty-seven episodes. It was the best and the worst time of my life. Working with your partner, friend or spouse can be a wonderful thing and it can also pose some terrific problems. Problems that will affect everyone in the work environment. It can become so noxious; they've even made non-negotiable rules about it that actually get people shit-canned if they date someone in the workplace. Since Lorenzo and I were already married, it was too late to set the tone of nobody dating each other. Besides, that would've wrecked half the fun of being on location for most of the crew.

We began working on the Stephen J. Cannell original series in 1991. It was so exciting to be working with the great Stephen J. as he was a very loving, generous and down to earth Creator. He was so willing to listen to our ideas about character, story line, and script. He was a true collaborator and he made everyone feel at ease with his superpower. He had pretty much done all you could as a writer and show runner, so he decided to write himself an acting part in our show. He really was wonderful as Dutch Dixon and being on set and acting with him was a total joy fest. He wasn't in every episode, but when he did appear, he enthusiastically brought his sly fox, savoir-faire to our all-American show. Besides, who was going to tell him no? I'm pretty sure he didn't have to audition either.

Stephen and Marsha, his wife and love interest since third grade, came to a summer party Lorenzo and I threw at our home in Burbank Rancho. Esther Williams and her husband, Edward Bell, were also there and they shared a table with the Cannell's. As the story was told back to me by Esther, Stephen had offered a part to Lorenzo for a TV show to be filmed in San Diego. Esther thought about that scenario for about two seconds and told Stephen that it would be hard on our young marriage if he didn't somehow include me in the show. So, apparently, Stephen ended up writing the role of Cheyenne with me in mind to keep our marriage intact. Who would imagine Lorenzo and I would split up halfway through the second season? No one, really.

Branscombe Richmond, who played the role of Bobby Sixkiller, my Native American stepbrother, was the one who really had to play both sides of the civil war fence. Talk about an Indian caught in the crossfire. I wonder how many times that happened in the Old West? All I remember repeatedly saying was, "Thank God for Branscombe." That was my mantra every time I stepped into the makeup trailer hearing his big booming voice and litany of silly euphemisms, jokes and endless banter. He made it his call of duty to break the Iceberg B-15 that had formed between Lorenzo and myself. It was hell in paradise. I had a great job on a great show with great people. I was pretty miserable for part of it, but not all of it.

This is how it went down. The first season was bliss. We had nothing but the audience to conquer, which we did quickly. With the 'American Made' everything, which our executive producer Stu Seagull made sure of, we had an instant niche in pop culture. The Harley Davidson motorcycle, the Humvee, the Winnebago, the Native American, the tall blonde, all intertwined with the long hair stud with no helmet. We were instantly embraced in our country and everywhere else. The winning combo theme of an outlaw hunting outlaws, making sure that each week the good guys win, and the bad guys get their ass kicked, was a slam dunk. The impressive guest cast that would show up in San Diego every week was always an exciting treat. We had so many incredible guest stars and wonderful directors on our show. It was a dream job. Until...

Since Lorenzo and I were not love interests on the show, there was a revolving door of 'chick du jour' interests for his character, Reno Raines a.k.a. Vince Black. My character was obviously pining over him, but since we were working together as a team of Bounty Hunters, it was not a good idea to fraternize. Even the characters had better sense. So, the writers had a lot of fun dishing out babes to serve up to Lorenzo's character on a weekly or reoccurring basis. I was pretty used to this as I had dated Lorenzo off and on during his *Falcon Crest* days and had become accustomed to watching him make out and bed down numerous women, as Lance Cumson. I mean, really with that character name? I guess it was in the cards with a name like that. Anyway, I had become somewhat immune to the very odd and unnatural visual of watching the love of my life with someone else. It's the thing we dread more than anything when we fall in love, that we will catch them in bed and/or making out with someone else, which I had already experienced and forgiven.

I knew I had a responsibility in making the female guest actors in particular feel welcome. I had guested on a few shows where the actors were so full of themselves, there was no welcome, or any effort, given to a guest. A special nod to Pamela Anderson. So, when a new female actor would arrive, I would generally go out of my way to greet them and make sure they were happy with wardrobe and had found the healthy side of our craft service table. In other words, I played nice.

One particular pretty actor, who will remain nameless, was a reoccurring guest. I believe she was asked to come back because Lorenzo was crushing on her. What really crushed me was the fact that I was so nice to this bitch. Bitch didn't like her wardrobe, so I asked our costume designer if there was something from my side of the trailer that bitch could wear. Bitch didn't like the food being served, so I gave the bitch an ample supply of power bars from my stash. Bitch didn't like her call time. Too bad bitch, we've all got to get up early. I had to stop waiting on her, as she was digging it, I'm sure. How the hell did this diva end up with a personal assistant played by the female lead? I was beyond dumb trying to please this phony nuisance who didn't like anything. She did like my husband, though. A lot. Enough to continue making out with him after the director yelled, "Cut." I heard about it in the makeup trailer the next morning. God, I love the makeup trailer, it's the bone collector of all gossip and meaning of life. I remember it was the middle of summer and scorching hot outside. When I heard that news, from our lovely make-up artist, and our beautiful hairstylist, my heart broke into a million ice chips, freezing my veins and clouding my eyes with stinging tears. I knew Lorenzo and I really were done in that moment. That he could willingly and publicly display affection for someone else in our workplace was the final straw. It was definitely a moment of truth and all my insecurities instantly rushed to the surface. My only offense was a great defense which was to keep my guard up on this information for quite a while. There are many times as an actor that we become the actor within the actor. In other words, 'use it'. We had a show to do, where our livelihood and everyone else's depended on our performance. I finally threw my wedding ring at him and confronted him, to which he denied everything. Although, after we separated, he and bitch dated for about a minute. It didn't last for more than a few weeks. Lorenzo and I were never together again after that. We did manage to continue working on

Renegade, but they started to cut back on the episodes I would appear in, thoroughly fazing me out.

The minute I got divorced, I thought, "What's going to happen with my job?" That thought basically colored all my choices. I honestly wanted to quit after we completed the second season. I went to Esther's home one night for comfort food and sage advice, and she set me straight on what a good job I had, and how difficult it is to land one in this town. She reminded me that they weren't asking me to leave, which meant they still wanted me there. She told me the work would save me and supply financial security and peace of mind in knowing that I didn't walk away from something difficult. She was right. That which doesn't kill you makes you titanium and I was living proof. I stayed healthy, upbeat and grew as a performer and a person in that third season. Because they were lightening my load in episodes on *Renegade*, I was able to moonlight and guest on other shows during the season. It was a lot of work and I loved it. Esther was right and the work was saving me. She encouraged Stephen to give me the job and now she was encouraging me to keep it. In hindsight, Esther Williams was my manager.

I made my job my 'new marriage' and I did everything I could to keep it alive, including looking the other way on numerous occasions. The only problem with ignoring the drama around me, is that I became numb to the gamut of emotions that were taking place inside me. I went back for the third season, which remains a blur. By the fourth season, Lorenzo and I were getting along in a 'stay in your corner and I'll stay in mine' kind of way. There seemed to be a mutual respect and friendship that was being formed again. Until Shauna Sands arrived. Wow, what an entrance. I had never seen anything quite like her with the lips, the boobs, the shoes. Priceless and shameless. She was a living, breathing trucker mudflap and she made my game look amateur. I had heard that Lorenzo had met someone because Lorenzo himself called to tell me.

"I've met someone, and she needs to get her SAG card, so she will be doing a scene with you tomorrow. I hope that's alright," Lorenzo said.
"Sure, why not," I enthused. I was so worn out with this spectacle; it was not even landing on my tired hide. It just slid off.

Lorenzo knew that I would be kind and easy for her to work with. He knew that I would give her the necessary cheerleading to pull off a three-line office scene with ease. He knew that if I worked with her, somehow it would make everything even more 'nice nice' and there would be no reason to have issue with the newest 'love of his life', which he had just gone into full detail about in an exclusive interview in Playgirl magazine. We did the scene, it was fine. She got her SAG card and an engagement rock the size of her nose. With Lorenzo's help, she also landed the coveted gatefold in Playboy. Because nothing says, "I'm a serious actor!" like Playboy can. There's just so many things wrong with this, it's hard to choose which bit of crazy to choose from. First, if you're nuts about someone, why would you want the world to see their private parts? Second, if you want to be taken as a serious young actor, do a play, or a showcase or put together a reel, don't disrobe for a magazine. There's nothing 'actor' about that, it's just a gimmick to make women feel powerful, when in fact it literally 'strips' us of power when we're spread eagle in our birthday suit. It's like game over, my friend. Now that I've seen you naked, the mystery has vanished. Hence the one-night stand that is not followed up by a call, text or post it. Or being a centerfold that's not followed by a film or TV offer.

"But wait," she breathlessly heaved, "I thought that maybe if I did this, something would come from it." Oh, several came from it, honey, just not a movie or a television deal.

For some bizarre, sensitivity chip missing reason, Lorenzo thought it would be a smashing idea to put up the Polaroids of Miss Thing's thang on the makeup trailer mirror. The makeup trailer is the first place of communal gathering for actors in a henhouse. It is a nonstop bitch fest dedicated to the fine craft of whining, bitching and kvetching. Once a show has been in production for a while, the makeup trailer becomes a respite from the quiet of set and the professionalism that one would think governs all life. It's where you go to let your hair down, just to have it put back in place again. You stumble in crusty and tired and waltz out camera ready. It's the first place you shuffle into at 5am for solace, sanity and face. It's where production directs you and your slippers upon arrival and it's where you generally meet the guest actors excited to get a first glimpse of your production. Well, they definitely received a welcoming sneak peek into a thorough Shauna sighting. There were photos of her newly trimmed privates, which looked like the mustache worn by the guy who invaded Poland. It was so disgusting, embarrassing and beyond poor taste. Her tits and ass were also on display to greet our guest actors who would be joining us for the week. Some of them were innocent kids, but not for long. It seemed everybody needed some hair and makeup those days, as I never saw so many grip, electric, transpo, craft service, caterers, producers and guests of everyone, including their cousins and neighbors, in our fucking makeup trailer. It had all of a sudden become Burning Man in there and everyone wanted a pre-glimpse into Shauna's coveted gatefold. It was beyond gross and would never be tolerated in today's #metoo movement. It was so many forms of sexual harassment, there would be paperwork up the wazoo. What's really unspeakable, is that speaking about it got *me* fired. To this day, the injustice of that moment makes my head spin. I was so focused on being cool and non-responsive to this categorical misuse of power and holding my job, that I sucked it up and said nothing. Unfortunately, I had to blow at some point.

Amidst this fourth season, I had so had it with this endless nonsense. Our beautiful *Renegade* was turning into a shit show on set and I was numb and nonchalant at being totally fazed out. Since I had more time on my hands and had a following with the unflinchingly witty, Howard

Stern, I was given a job working on a radio show in LA called The Bad Girls Club for KLSX, the station that syndicated Howard Stern in New York. My ebullient radio partner, Kimberly Hooper and I, were the only on-air radio personalities that Howard was interested in promoting. Pressed for unearthing dirt on Lorenzo, Howard was relentless on his fascination with all things Lorenzo. Our radio show got about thirty seconds of Howard's interest, while thirty minutes was spent answering honest questions with an honest answer. I was tired, as it was 3am at LA's, *The Monkey Bar*, for live airing in New York. I didn't go on until about 5:30am, LA time, which is when everyone was getting in their car for the drive to set in San Diego. Had I gone on when I was supposed to at 3am, I would have still had my job when I arrived to set that morning. As luck, or fate would have it, I was entertainment for Lorenzo's commute. Unfortunately, he was not at all happy with my performance. I had unleashed the unearthly Kraken and all hell broke loose. I was so honest in my recounting of all things Lorenzo; he was ready to knock my block off when I arrived on set at 10am that morning. He was so fuming, that a massive group of burly dudes from our transportation department were actually waiting for me for protection. Those sweethearts wanted to make sure I didn't get a spinning heel kick to my money maker from our producer, Lorenzo Lamas.

It was a bad day for me and even worse for Branscombe. He had to keep working with Lorenzo and also still be my friend. Branscombe never took sides and to this day is still a great friend to both of us. I have since apologized for all the things I said, true or not, as I know they hurt Lorenzo's feelings. In turn, he also has apologized for the mistakes he made, and like it or not, he was a great love in my life. Lorenzo and I are definitely in deep Telenovela area with our life experience together on this planet. I learned from Lorenzo's tireless work ethic, his kindness and respect to crew and his genuine positive attitude. Fortunately, we share the same sense of humor, which has quelled many problems. We have always been able to laugh at most things in life. I think our humor has saved our friendship and allowed us to continue working together in the most dire of situations.

I am eternally grateful that everything we did on that show is still on the air somewhere and also on a DVD. I can now share this cult show with my daughter and the fans of the world. An outlaw hunting outlaws, a bounty hunter, a Renegade. If we're really lucky, maybe one day there will be a remake, or just a show about the show, *Amid Summer Renegade Knights Dream.*

Epic Fail ~ Being nice to someone who is coveting your husband.

Epic Save ~ Eating crow pie to save your job.

Lesson Learned ~ Don't do the Howard Stern Show when you're tired and resentful. Or do it, Howard will love it!

"One of the things about the whole Harley motorcycle culture is that it's a little bit renegade."
~ John Travolta

CHAPTER 6

~ on Lorenzo

The first thing I would like to say is, I love Lorenzo. I've loved Lorenzo for a very long time, more than most of my life. He has become like a family member to me. The way a person does when you marry them, work with them, divorce them and yet continue to work with them and still continue to care about them. The truth is, even after all we've been through, we still have feelings that are respectful and considerate towards each other. A part of my heart believes that we might have been working something out for centuries and we've almost figured it out. I've learned a lot about myself through my trials and tribulations with Lorenzo and for that I'm truly grateful.

I'm going to go out on a branch and say this time around, I met Lorenzo Lamas when I was fifteen. My first encounter was watching him tell a fascinating story on *The Mike Douglas Show*. I was there at the taping, watching from the sidelines, with my mom, who was also part of the *Falcon Crest* line-up for the show. Lorenzo was born in Santa Monica, California, so naturally, he became a surfer. This helped land him a job on *California Fever,* a short lived 1979 television series that featured a group of LA teens living an awesome life of disco, the beach and romance. The show only lasted for 10 episodes and I had seen every one of them. I instantly became a fan of Lorenzo's character, Rick, the ultimate hot surfer dude. I couldn't believe that he was actually playing my mom's son on a show and that he was now in front of me telling a story about surfing on Mike Douglas's couch. It went something like...

One fine day, when Lorenzo was out in the surf, he noticed an attractive girl on a surfboard. After getting marginally thumped by a wave, he decided to paddle over and strike up a conversation about how totally massive the waves were. When he reached his destination, a.k.a 'hot surfer girl', he casually sat up on his board to nonchalantly show off his surfer prowess to which 'hot surfer girl' immediately started cracking up. Not quite the response he was accustomed to, for sure, I'm totally sure. She shook her head and laughed, as he questioned in a Tom Chisum kind of way, "What am I doing wrong here?" She finally took pity on him and gently gestured toward his face which had a man of war size snot trail smeared across it. This kind of thing usually happens from the 'washing machine' effect of getting 'punched' by a wave. It tends to knock the snot right out of you, only to find its way into your hair or back, or back hair or back onto your face. I couldn't believe he was telling this story on live TV in front of a very silent and perplexed audience. This is not the kind of thing a gorgeous, successful person should be talking about. I could see Mike Douglas and his boner slowly leave the building. I knew at that moment my crush was real and someday I would marry that surfer with snot on his face. I clearly remember stating that to my mom, to which she nodded, "Great choice." She gets it. She always did.

We started dating in my senior year at Our Lady of Corvallis High School in September of 1982. I was seventeen, a few months shy of my eighteenth birthday. He was in his second season of *Falcon Crest* playing the role of Lance Cumson, my mother's son and Jane Wyman's grandson. He was twenty-four, a TV star, and every inch a rock-solid stud. He was a dream boat wrapped in a complete silly goof. On our first date he took me on his managers sailboat on a day cruise to Catalina Island. Herbie Nanas was his personal manager and he was probably hoping to get us out of public view since I was still considered jailbait and Lorenzo already had the unfortunate press of still being married and going through his first divorce. His father, Fernando Lamas, was in the hospital with pancreatic cancer and sadly would never be released to go home. It was a very painful time for Lorenzo but yet here we were, two considerably young people, quietly falling in love on a sailboat in the Pacific Ocean.

It would actually be a bit of a haul of growing up before marriage would ever happen. First, I had to get legal. On my eighteenth birthday I had a party at the Japanese restaurant, *Yamashiro*, in Culver City. This was such a big deal because Lorenzo and I had already made it to the tabloids, which was an exceptionally big deal to my all girl Catholic high school principal, Ms. Trainow. She was not pleased with seeing 'her school' a.k.a Our Precious Lady of Immaculate Valley Virgins of Corvallis, get free press with photos of Lorenzo and myself in The National Enquirer. I tried to explain that that particular rag should only be used to line

71

a parakeet cage but she was livid and thought that I had some kind of control over Hollywood and should stop the press, or stop dating Lorenzo. Neither of which I had any intention or control, until the night of my eighteenth birthday.

My parents were pretty fun that night as they were really turning a blind eye to all the sake that was being ordered and drained. I had about thirty family and friends at the event and as the dinner partied on, I noticed that a couple key guests were missing. One of them was my best girlfriend, who will remain 'nameless', and Lorenzo, soon to be the same. I went to the girls bathroom where I thought I would find my soon to be ex-friend. She was not there. So I shamelessly waltzed into the boys bathroom looking for my soon to be ex-boyfriend, and future ex-husband, who was also not there. I began to head back to the party when I noticed a flight of stairs guarded by a velvet rope. An unattended velvet rope keeps no one out, especially if there's not a bouncer keeping vigilant watch on the forbidden palace. Just like those two distasteful party guests, I hopped the velvet rope and climbed the dark stairs to the dimly lit *closed* portion of the restaurant. As soon as I reached the landing, I could hear the moaning and the kissing and the breaking of my heart. Happy Birthday to me, you fucking jerks. I knew at that moment I was done with both of them and I was now being called back to my party to show the world (or at least my drunk guests) that I was an actress. I took one of the biggest passive aggressive breaths of my life and glided back to the elegant bash and gave a stellar performance of me pretending not to know a bloody thing. Even when Lorenzo and 'nameless' made it back to the table, all sweaty and smiling, I remained stoic and completely in character of Joyful Party Girl #3. In hindsight, I'm mad at myself for ever marrying such a cad, but hey, I was young and dumb and hardwired to love him. He did feel mostly bad, but that's how he was wired at that time too. If I had a nickel for every woman who flung herself at Lorenzo, I'd own a private jet. Anyway, I forgave *him,* eventually, never *her* because she was my friend and I expected more. Pretty lame, I know but I loved *him.* I needed to make someone the bad guy, and this time, it happened to be *her,* whom I read the riot act all night at our very unfortunate sleepover. It was my own remake of Lionel Ritchie's hit, *All Night Long.* That'll teach her. Don't make out with your best friend's boyfriend bitch, especially on her eighteenth birthday because you're gonna hear about it for like, nineteen hours. Just as she was falling asleep, I would spout off some more justifiable angry rants. I wouldn't let her nod off. It was my way of fighting back to something that I had no control over. It was very familiar to the scene from *Trainwreck* when John Cena is trying to fall asleep and Amy Schumer just launches into an inflamed stream of conscious and unconscious thoughts. Like that.

It was a few years, another marriage, and two kids for Lorenzo before we finally got married January 19th, 1989. I was twenty-three and he was thirty when we jumped onto a plane with his two young children, A.J. who was five and Shane, three. It reminded me of the Immigration sign of the fleeing family, the way we all took off for Vegas to elope. I guess I wasn't as pissed at him by then. They say the hardest part of forgiving is forgetting. Lorenzo's good looks and charm obviously brought out some premature dementia. Plus, I've been crazy about him since day one. We had another marriage ceremony a year and a day later (Lorenzo's actual birthday) at Lakeside Golf Club, where Lorenzo and I departed from the reception in a helicopter off the first tee. We were married for about 5 years and I loved being his wife and stepmom to his two children. Unfortunately, I was never given the opportunity to meet his youngest daughter, Paton, and sadly the absence of her would cause many concerns.

Lorenzo and I worked together on six independent films, four years of a television series and numerous celebrity charity events and fundraisers. We did just about everything together, worked, played, worked out and enjoyed many rides on his Harley escaping to far off, glamorous destinations such as Barstow, The Rock Store and my favorite, Lake Isabella. We experienced similar childhoods, given we were both raised in the entertainment industry. We both became actors, sharing the spotlight with famous parents. We were working towards the same goals. He spoke up for himself. I spoke up for myself. We respected each other and we did have a lot of fun. We honestly had a pretty good run at it for a while. We loved the same things and had a beautiful life together that consisted of God, family and career. All the right mixings for a solid future, except there was something missing. I don't think it's fair to say that it was him, or me, or solely anyone's fault when two people grow apart. He was always my choice and I take full responsibility for my actions, as they are mine and mine alone.

At some point, I remember I stopped being an adoring fan and began to develop my own perspective. I was confused by some of his decisions and was left to figure things out on my own. Nothing wreaks havoc on a relationship like your point of view of someone shifting. It didn't mean I stopped loving or caring about Lorenzo but my outlook of who he was changed. I'm sure his point of view about me shifted as well. The moment I started questioning his character, was the instant our partnership and marriage began to dissolve. A few recent 'friendly encounters' have taken us back to where we started, however, when I gaze at our big picture, this story has definitely played out its sequels. We are different people and have grown in different ways. We still occasionally work together in celebrity appearances and we have chosen to remain friends. His family, especially his incredible younger sister, Carole, remain a part of my life and I value all the vast and rich relationship's I continue to foster. My formative years were encapsulated by Lorenzo and to deny anything other than appreciation for our incredible experience would be a great disservice to the love that was once there.

Epic Fail ~ There is no epic fail with love, only epic growth.

Epic Save ~ When the marriage tanks, be willing to go back and dive for the pot of gold friendship that brought you there.

Lesson Learned ~ Forgiveness takes a while, but it will happen if you're willing to let go.

"Nothing is inevitable with relationships."
        ~ Lorenzo Lamas

CHAPTER 7

~ on birth

My beautiful, successful and sporty picket white fence parents, Jack Smith and Abby Dalton, already had a two year old son, Matt, when I arrived into production in 1965. I use the word production because CBS was literally waiting on me to finish up with my incubation process (they rarely used the word pregnancy back then, too vulgar) for arrival on their season closer of the hit sitcom, *The Joey Bishop Show.*

I was a month late and my mom was receiving daily calls, sometimes twice a day, from the show. It was at the end of their third season and my stunning mom had already played out this coochy-coo story line with my older brother in the first season. They were probably never planning on having a sitcom revolve around toddlers with sarcasm-on-steroids comedian Joey Bishop at the helm. Although, he did truly master the look of complete and total exasperation, probably due to my mother's impending overdue due date. Which was way too much 'due due' for the network. They were already planning to call the ball and cancel the show, just as soon I dropped. I had nothing to do with the cancellation but I had everything to do with getting their final shot and bring back a crew that had been put on hold and hiatus for a show that would never see the light of day again.

I was finally born on Joey's birthday, February 3rd. I was a whopping and unforgivable 8 pounds, 14 ounces and 22 inches long. I had long hair and fingernails and fully developed vocal cords. The look my mother gives me every time she recounts the story lets me know that it was not in any way a fun delivery. It was nothing like the 6 minutes it took my parents to conceive me during a bathroom break in an itinerary laden personal appearance as the Azalea Queen at a festival in North Carolina ten months prior. I did mention they were quite athletic.

"Welcome to the world, kid, you've just been cancelled," was my baby announcement. No wonder I didn't want to arrive, I was already being shut down. I got my SAG and Unemployment Card the same day. Oh well, back to the drawing board. Fortunately, I was an infant and had no idea what a drawing board was, or failure or rejection. Back then it was just eat, sleep and change my diaper, something we all aspire to for the golden years.

Joey Bishop was named my baptismal godfather. Since we shared the same birthday and I got his show scrubbed, they decided to give him something else he didn't want - me, in an overly starched white linen baptismal gown. Imagine putting a newborn with sensitive, rash prone skin in a dress with the consistency of sandpaper for a one-hour baptism ceremony? Wtf people? Are we losing the lightbulb on this idea or what? Thank God for the flash of camera's and chronic colic to distract me.

"Screamed bloody murder through the whole thing," is the recollection of surviving family members. I occasionally stopped screaming to vomit. I don't think Joey ever visited me again after that holy day. That was fine by me, as I later received new, hipper godparents, Victoria and Stan Cutler. Victoria, an artist and model who escaped from Hungary and Stan, a comedy writer from New Jersey, never had kids, but they've always had cats, so they were totally used to screaming and vomit.

I recently screened the pilot of *The Joey Bishop Show* with my mom. She loves watching herself in her movies and shows and gets a big kick out of what she used to look and sound like. Her commentary on herself is priceless. Watching her being entertained by herself is magic. It's like she's enjoying an old friend who never ages or has a bad day. She really was intensely beautiful and truly funny. She had already honed her skills playing Jackie Cooper's wife, Nurse Martha Gale, on *Hennessey,* the show that coined the phrase, 'dramedy'. It was also the show she was on when she met my dad, Jack, giving her a solid pair of Jack's for husbands. Jackie Cooper directed several episodes of *Hennessey* and Miss Dalton was already a seasoned pro when she was brought on to play Joey Bishop's wife, Ellie.

Ellie was given the most fabulous introduction to the show from Joey, who brings her onstage to join him as his wife and sexy sidekick to his comical life within his comedy show. This was the big thing in the 60's to have a show within the show. Nothing is quite as entertaining to people outside the business, as the people in the

81

entertainment business, so why not make a show of it? Desi and Lucy did it. Dick and Mary did it. Everyone was doing it, so why not? Turns out Shakespeare knew what he was doing. After seeing my daughter's middle school play of *A Midsummer's Night Dream*, I finally understood the meaning of the play within the play, which is basically everybody is in love with someone else. Aah, such is life.

My life began on a sitcom and now looking back, it became one. My birth didn't cancel *The Joey Bishop Show,* the network did. My mom was essentially grateful because "Joey was a real pain in the ass" and it freed her up to play Jonathan Winters wife on *The Jonathan Winters Show.* She has always thanked me *and* God for that.

Epic Fail ~ Being born into a show that had already exhausted the cute baby thing.

Epic Save ~ Being born into a show that had already done the cute baby thing. You're welcome, mom.

Lesson Learned ~ When one show closes, another one opens.

"A child is a gift from God."
    ~ Lailah Gifty Akita

CHAPTER 8

~ on organs

My mom has always been a fan of a silent auction. She would say, "It's a great way to score a prize without the hassle of having to raise your hand." She enjoyed the freedom of waltzing around the endless tables of items and quietly debunking someone's fantasy of a Mexican getaway with a five-dollar increase. While in my freshman year at Providence High School in Burbank, my mom graciously attended their annual 'give more money to the private school' shindig. They don't serve vodka at these events, so she would naturally get pleasantly warmed up before departure. At this particular event she must've scored a bottle of wine from one of the gift baskets because she was burnt toast by the time she came home. Upon entering the front door, she announced that she didn't buy anything, but thinks she might have donated one of her organs at the event. I was horrified. Why would my mom do such a thing? Doesn't she know she's too old to donate her parts? She's like fifty or something, nobody can use that old stuff. It's faulty! The warranty is worn out and/or expired. How could she have done this to me at my brand-new high school? Hadn't I suffered enough? I'll be the laughingstock! My mom donating her organs to my school? What the hell?! What is wrong with her and how desperate is this school? I better transfer, just in case.

As I was planning my escape route from furthering my education to a quiet life with the circus, the doorbell rang. It was an organ delivery for my mom. Already? They really must've liked what they saw of her blonde hair, tits and teeth. They were ready for the innards and they wanted them now. I told the guy at the door that she was still alive and not quite ready to give up her liver or her kidneys. Besides, she was still sleeping off her hangover and when that was done, she was going to need to have some breakfast and a bloody Mary, so her day was already full. I further explained that she had a lot to do the following week, she had acting work, manicure appointments and taking care of three teenagers. Mom's hands were full. So, thanks anyway, Mr. Nondescript Delivery Looking Guy but she would not be able to participate in any kind of organ donation right now. Besides, you're sick! Wait 'till she's stopped breathing, you vultures!

He looked at me like I was way too young to be on crack and said, "I'm here to deliver an organ, not take one."
"Ohhh. Well, that's different. You can leave it on the porch," I retorted.
"It's too big to leave on the porch."
"EWW!! Gross! What is it? An elephant heart? What in God's name did she buy?"

In that moment, I knew what it must feel like to be on the spectrum.
"I'm going to need an adult to sign for this. Can you go get your mom?" Delivery Guy over annunciated.

Waking up my mom from a party night was not the most sought-after mission. She would usually still be a bit wasted, so the verbal filter was most likely still on pause. She liked to sleep in something skimpy or nothing at all, so getting her to the door in a half state of dress, tired and buzz worthy, was not something I wanted to sign up for. Her ability to launch into a verbal assault at any given moment was something to marvel. She has such an ability with words and their pairing, she can turn a simple phrase into a weapon in nanoseconds. I was so weirded out by this dilemma; I had no choice but to go wake her. Gently.

"Mom?" I gingerly tread.
"What?" she groggily requested.
"Good morning mom."
"Is it?" she groaned.
Four lines in, we're not looking good soldier. Abort the mission! You heard me, I said abort, abort!
"Time's it?" she inquired.
I glanced at the glow of the blue numbers on the digital clock.
"Almost noon," I quietly cooed.
Most parents have already donated several parts and organs I'm sure at this hour, so she should be feeling pretty good that hers have still been resting and continuing to process the alcohol from last night's gala.
"Mom, there's a delivery man at the door that needs you to sign for the organ."
"An organ?"
"Yeah, I know. Gross, right?"
"They don't want mine. Trust me."

87

"I bet."

"What?"

"Nothing. Just, can you get out of bed and sign for it? The front door is open."

'The front door is open' always got her up, as we were robbed once and the horror of that event has never left her.

"Get me my robe. Let's find out what this jackass wants."

"Okay, mommy."

That's right, get ready jackass. My super mom is on the way for you and your organ.

Blech.

We got to the door and mom was tucked into a robe and looking just like Marilyn Monroe, if she had made it to 50. The delivery guy had already unloaded the massive organ, which was now perched on the front porch.

"What the hell is **that**?!" my mother shrieked.

"Get some popcorn, this one's gonna be good," I said to no one.

"You just need to sign right here, please ma'am," the pitiful delivery guy pleaded.

"What exactly am I signing for?" she retorted with a death stare.

"An organ," he trembled.

"And where am I supposed to *put* the organ?" she coyly purred, as she slowly took the pen from the delivery guy who was getting ready to sport some wood.

This pathetic delivery guy was so love/hating his job right now. I'm sure nothing has quite compared to a bedraggled blonde arguing in her robe about where to put his organ.

"In the living room!!" I blurted, getting ready to have another brain seizure.

Thankfully, I was mostly well for this exchange and was able to maneuver out of another mortifying moment with mom. I led the delivery guy and his organ into the first open spot. He and his men rolled this great big, colorful, multi-dialed, massive tone creating church organ complete with foot pedals and a very loud amp into the living room. My mom curiously followed. By the way, side note, no one in the family played piano, keyboard or organ. My brother Matt plays guitar and my brother Johnny plays the bass. I'm more of a back-up singer with a tambourine part of the band, so obviously this church organ had been delivered to the wrong Partridge Family. Fortunately, Delivery Guy found the perfect resting spot for our brand new, never to be used, dust collecting organ.

"Aah, perfect," mom said. "I'm going back to bed."

Epic Fail ~ Not realizing that there might be several meanings for one particular word.

Epic Save ~ Realizing that there might be several meanings for one particular word.

Lesson Learned ~ Don't buy an organ, just donate one.

"I think you should automatically donate your organs because that would turn the balance of organ donation in a huge way. I would donate whatever anybody would take, and I'd probably do the cremation bit."
~ George Clooney

CHAPTER 9

~ on dating

When you are used to being in a relationship, which I've spent most of my adult life in relationships, dating can be painful. I've been fiercely independent for quite some time, and had my fair share of dates, to which actually led to dating a few. It's still a bit of a hit and miss, and I'm still up and standing for the challenging journey. I believe three marriages has placed me at 'expert' status in the field of marriage. I'm currently working towards receiving the same laurels in the wonderful world of dating.

The fun part about dating is getting to know someone by going out and doing things. It's the artistic dance of having something fun to do while allowing personalities and core values to organically shine during whatever activity has been chosen for the date. For example, you can learn a ton about a person playing mini golf. Do they cheat? Are they able to communicate during the activity or are they overly focused on the game? Do they have to win? You can learn a great deal from a date at a movie. Do they talk through it, hog the popcorn or endlessly make a move on you in a dark setting? You can learn a fair amount about someone on a hike. Are they in shape, ramble on about a rotten ex or are they over complimentary in an attempt to make out with you in poison oak? To a great extent you can discover a possible suitor at a meal. Do they chew with their mouth open?

Are they abusive to the wait staff? Are they a pain in the ass with their order or talk about themselves the entire freaking time? If the goal is "I want to marry my best friend" then becoming friends first is vital. Becoming lovers is easy, it's the emotional investment which takes time and consideration, and it is actually a whole lot of fun when you're doing it with someone who respects you and above all, someone you can **trust**.

Personally, I have a real problem with the current concept of dating. I feel like it's been ramped up in an effort to quickly cut to the end game, meaning sex. Is there really any way that you can know if you are emotionally, spiritually and intimately safe and compatible after just one or two dates? Are you actually considered <u>friends</u> by then? No.

I need to be specific about today's definition of the word *dating,* which is what happens before a *relationship* is announced. Both words can imply that you're sleeping with someone, but *dating* is definitely not a *relationship* in today's world. *Going out* means that you are meeting up with someone to go *do* something and it's not considered a *date*. *Hooking up* is considered a *booty call* in millennial slang. So, for me, a *relationship* girl, it is hard to be casual about the whole *dating* experience. Once I put the word *dating* into effect, i.e. casually sleeping with someone, it is already a quasi-commitment to each other. Unfortunately, it is not always that way by today's measure.

We live in a society of instant gratification. Look at the spinning 'loading wheel' on your phone for 33 seconds and you're frustrated. We are becoming conditioned to getting everything we want, right away. With just a 'click' we can instantaneously pay bills, purchase plane tickets, select one out of thirty six options of toothbrushes (of varying features) on Amazon - all delivered straight to our door, or electronic mailbox, without having to suit up and endure the wait of long lines. Everything is faster than it has ever been and there are endless choices. This also spills into relationships; it is a natural evolution of society. Dating apps like Tinder are the Amazon of reaching potential mating options. Endless choices, instantly. You can save interesting profiles for a later time when you've worn out the idea for the first one. "I'll contact him/her later," increases the odds of meeting the right person, or the right hookup. It's an easy marketplace for casual sex. "What the hell? Why not, it's a free world! We're consenting adults! I'm not hurting anyone."

Except, we are. We are hurting *ourselves*. The price of this type of instant gratification is **high**: disconnection, self-loathing, insecurity, loneliness. Pretty counterintuitive at best. We subscribe to connect but end up feeling lonelier than most are aware of. We thrive in community; we are not wired to be alone. In fact, a sense of social connection is one of our most fundamental human needs. "Disconnected dating leads to an endless cycle of loneliness, hunting for the next fix to feel better, leaving still disconnected and empty and ending up with a deeper sense of loneliness."
~Dr. Brene` Brown PhD LMSW

The options are so overwhelming, some shut off completely and refuse to wander the well chartered territory of superficial friendliness. For me, it's mostly impossible to date more than one person at a time. I've known people that can date several people simultaneously. I've been impressed with their physical and mental stamina of keeping names straight in that kind of marathon. I could never do that since I naturally fall in love way too easily. Once I've been with someone physically, I have the great hopeful expectation that now the other person is also feeling the same and wants to stick around and have a committed relationship. Or that intimate part has played out in a way that becomes a turn off and it's quickly time to move on. Also, when you don't want to be with someone, but continue to have sex with them out of convenience, it sends a confusing message to the other person who might be emotionally invested. Truth is, once bodies have entwined, so have spirits, and to jump from one body and spirit to the next can leave the heart and self-esteem tragically confused.

I think the reality is people, i.e. a lot of guys, want sex before they want love. Or they don't want the responsibility of a relationship, but they want the sex that comes with it. Me, I want love and then I want what naturally develops from that kind of intimacy. I went on a spontaneous hiking date with a young guy, who immediately after the hike texted me that he was in love. I thought, wow, one walk up the hill, he's already in love and I'm finding out through a text. I'm pretty sure <u>when you're professing your love for the very first time, it should be done in person</u>. Note to self.

One unfortunate date experience ended in a pussy grabbing sexual assault. This very tall and somewhat attractive man and I had been on a couple of dates, and even though I was attracted to him, I was still on the fence about *dating* him and becoming intimate. I'm moving like a tortoise in the desert of dating and want to carve out the necessary time that it takes to really get to know someone and feel secure. I was doing my best to guide this person into the concept of *courting* while realizing most men aren't very patient when they've been drinking. He walked me to my car, opened the door and I gave him a hug goodnight. Before I knew it, his hand was down my skirt, and into my panties. It all happened so quickly; I wasn't even quite sure *how* it happened. It was like a magic trick of repulsive, arrogant, entitlement. I jerked away from the fucking jerk and quickly quipped, "Smooth move, Trump."

The grinning fool took that as a compliment and blurted, "Thanks!"

I couldn't speak as I fumbled for my keys and got into my car. As I drove away in frozen shock, all I could think was, "How the hell did I not know he supported Trump?!" Ew.

When I called him on it the next day, he replied, "I was just being playful."

I honestly don't even know how to address this situation, other than to write about it and tell him to lose my number. Thank you, next.

Today's habit of instant gratification arguably also plays a large role on our increasing breakup/divorce rates. We are already being programmed to expect getting whatever we want *right now.* When a partner does not comply or see things differently, rarely does a dose of new-called patience and a working through the uncomfortable mentality drop out of a cloud free sky.

"Can you wait 'till I'm ready?" she asked.
"Sure," he said, as he swiped his phone and thought, 'I get everything else I want, instantly. The next one will probably deliver.'
She shuddered at being able to read his thoughts and his cell phone in his hands.

What I believe to be true is that if you are looking for love and a lasting relationship, dating should be the part that lasts the longest. I think the longer two people date, they have a greater chance cresting the wave into forever land. Some couples believe that you should just keep dating and skip marriage, as it certainly has wrecked quite a few seemingly good relationships. However, once you are married, you have to remember to continue going on dates, as long at it's with your spouse.

It is not until we start taking responsibility for ourselves and our own needs that our dating habits will evolve into a more harmonic process that is closer to our true nature of nurture, connection, support and love.

I think we put a lot of stock in the fact that someone else is in charge of bringing joy into our life. There is a universal thought that has been hammered into all of us which goes like this, 'If I was with someone, then I would no longer feel loneliness and pain. If I had someone to share all this pain and loneliness with, they would naturally take it away.' The truth is, I've been very lonely in relationships. I've actually experienced tremendous pain because of relationships. Today I am in charge of my own joy and my own self-worth. I'm currently dating myself and one day I will take myself to Paris and fall in love with me.

This concept of happily ever after is right here, right now. I'm already in my ever after and I take care of myself and I treat me right, right now. I think it's a tremendous disservice to females to make us feel like someday some dude is going to have to rescue our lame ass. That *anyone* is not complete until we have met our better half is a steaming pile of malarkey.

I will never rule out finding another partner to enjoy life with and I realize that to attract the type of person *I* would want to be with, *I* will have to exude the same qualities. In other words, what I am looking for in someone else, are the things I need to practice within myself. Since I'm now a practicing Ball Room Dancer I have created ~
My Dating Profile for Patti Stranger :-)
Hi, I'm Kathleen and I'm looking for A Ball Room Dance Partner who also happens to be:
Kind - Every moment is an opportunity to practice kindness.
Tall - I got that.
Attractive - Take loving care of mental, physical, and spiritual Self to feel one's personal best.
Athletic - Do something physical on a regular basis.
Smart - Flex the mind with fresh and creative material with a willingness to learn.

Funny - Embrace the lighter side of life and laugh regularly without hurting others.

Loves their job and is great at it - Choose to put energy towards work that one truly enjoys and relish the time spent doing it.

Generous - Give! It is the major component of receiving.

Trustworthy - Be accountable, honest and admit wrongs.

Has long-standing friendships - Be aware of and choose with care the inner circle, and nourish these relationships like flowering gardens. Nothing says more about someone than the company they keep and the friends that remain close.

Loves children - Admire the imagination of children and their playful nature. Don't trust anyone who doesn't love children.

Loves animals - Embrace the unconditional love and friendship of a pet. Don't trust anyone who doesn't love animals.

Considerate to old people - Respect and appreciate our elders' stories, wisdom and history. Run for the hills from anyone who is inconsiderate to the elderly.

Respectful - Respect myself, and others.

Compassionate - Increase emotional intelligence and maintain a peaceful atmosphere. Caring about others pain is a most vital human quality.

Spiritual - Nourish daily with prayer, meditation and gratitude.

Strong faith - Discover the pathway to finding solutions which quell stress, anxiety and fear. With God as my witness, we are never alone.

Stylish - Take a moment to think an outfit through before going out.

Likes to party but not to excess - Practice moderation. Having fun also has a barometer of when to end the party. Sobriety is also a beautiful gift to the receiver.

Loves to plan ahead - Take the time to set goals in life and future destinations. Having intentions and events to look forward to keeps one motivated.

Spontaneous - Be organized enough in life to be able to pick up and go at a moment's notice.

Responsible - Pay bills on time, stay current on taxes, take care of responsibilities. Having one's act together is a massive turn on.

Clean - Maintain clean hair, skin, teeth, gums, house, car, clothes and soul. This is all very attractive.

Loves family - Being a loving and caring family member makes life more beautiful. This can be a tricky one, since not all families get along, but it's more about how we can still care about a family member, even if we don't agree with them. Abusive family members need healthy boundaries.

Loves to travel - Continue traveling; keep exploring different cultures, art and history. It is delicious.

Loves to be home - Create a sanctuary that is safe, comfortable and welcoming where one looks forward to coming home.

Committed - Stay dedicated to core values.

Polite - Treat people with respect and kindness. Never underestimate the power of 'please', 'thank you' and 'you're welcome'.

Gentleman - Exercise integrity, self-respect and grace. "A lady is a woman who makes it easy for a man to be a gentleman," said my dad.

Courteous - Apply the Golden Rule ~ "Do unto others as you would have them do unto you," said God.

Emotionally available - Be willing and able to say what one's heart is feeling.

Great kisser - Be accessible to someone else and their touch. A great kiss happens when two people are in sync. If kissing is a language, a good kisser is someone who says very clearly, "I like you."

Bottom line, at the end of the day, I would like to be with someone who truly cares about me and my day. Someone who is willing to share past, present and future dreams, and has an enlightened sense of self. Shouldn't be too hard to find.

Now, in all fairness and honesty, I have had some pretty amazing 'dates' where there was not a lot of discussion about any of this stuff, or anything else for that matter, and still the night was, well, let's say 'memorable.' Those were a bit more rowdy times for me and given where I am currently in my personal growth, I wonder where is that person now?

Exactly.

Epic Fail ~ Thinking you need someone to complete you, when you're already complete.

Epic Save ~ Take responsibility of who you choose to be in life and the universe will answer.

Lesson Learned ~ Know your self-worth and that you are worthy of love and respect.

"Never let a fool kiss you, or a kiss fool you."
    ~ Joey Adams

CHAPTER 10

~ on valet

There's nothing quite as fun as getting dressed up, going out on the town and meeting up with friends on a Saturday night. The freedom of having your own car, some money in your pocket and the night sprawled out before you like a colorful unicorn piñata, just waiting to be smashed to bits and shared with your pals. The joy of not having to find a parking space and splurging on valet parking like a big shot, knowing you'll safely get your car out front when you're good and ready to leave. I've had a few nights like that, dancing the night away, meeting up with old friends and occasionally making some new ones. I always love the serenity of getting in my car and driving home with all the new memories and business cards at the end of a wild and crazy night. It really is simply way too much fun.

One particular night, I decided to push the limits of my personal freedom and joie de vivre by leaving the bar with some friends to go up to their house in the hills and drink for free. I knew my car would be safe because it was with the valet in front of the club. I'm so smart.

At around 3am, I decided it was time for me to go, so I called for a cab with my new gal pal, Nadine, and I assured her I would give her a ride back to her place, which was close to the club where I, the genius, had left my car with valet. We pulled up to the valet station, which no longer had any people and was actually no longer a valet station. It was just an empty sidewalk on Hollywood and Vine with some stained chewing gum and broken dreams. Where were 'the guys?' Where was the stand with all the key fobs and unreadable ticket stubs? Where was my freakin' car, dude!? I had a sizable freak out and then Nadine said, "Don't worry about it, you can spend the night at my house, and we'll find your car in the morning." I assured her that we were already in the morning and that it was still a very good idea and I graciously accepted. Stay positive, even when you don't have a clue.

Thankfully, I still had my valet ticket with print only a leprechaun could read and not a phone number in sight. But at least it was my ticket and it was something. Of course, I couldn't sleep because I was stressed to the gills, so my new bestie, Nadine and I played cards and watched the sun come up. I began the day in another cab trying to locate the 'pop up valet' that had stored my car somewhere in Hollywood. Now the area was a farmers market and I'm walking around fresh fruit and veggies, and parents with strollers, in my club clothes at 8am on a Sunday morning. Brutal.

I remember mumbling to myself, "I'll never do this again. Black tights, tap shorts and black boots on a Sunday morn at the Farmers Market makes me want to sing some Kris Kristofferson *Sunday Morning Sidewalk.*" I saw the same outfit on someone else a few weeks later and wondered if he had lost his car the night before too.

I was really only at the beginning of my stress and Nadine, the champ that she was, was fully over it. She didn't have a car, lucky girl, so she couldn't help me find mine. My taxi rides had already proven fruitless, so I had to call for back up. I had just finished directing my pilot, *Fame Game*, so I called my executive producer, Payam Pedram, who still thought I was pretty cool, until this moment. He generously drove me around town for what was probably the longest hour of my life. He was mostly upbeat in the first half hour, driving from one underground parking to the next. I had no jokes, no sleeves and my ability to be clueless had kicked into full gear. The second half hour we were both despondent. He started to think out loud, "Maybe your car has been towed somewhere near LAX." I was quietly imploding in the passenger seat until we reached the last parking lot in the area. It wasn't in the last place we looked; it was in the last place that it could possibly be. Thank you 8 pound, 6 ounce baby Jesus! My car, a divine miracle to behold and it only cost eighty dollars to get it out of valet jail! There are no signs posted or anything on the ticket that says how much it will cost to get your car out of a sleepover, but man was I happy with finding my sweet red Momzda. She was as cute as the night before I abandoned her.

Epic Fail ~ Leaving anyplace without my own personal car that brought me there.

Epic Save ~ Meeting a kind friend to shelter me and calling a kind friend to rescue me.

Lesson Learned ~ One word for party nights, Uber baby.

"Dude, where's my car?"
    ~ Ashton Kutcher
      in *Dude, Where's My Car?*

CHAPTER 11

~ **on almost famous**

Nothing will keep you more inspired, driven and hanging on to the dream like being almost famous. It's like playing the lottery and always winning ten bucks. You won a little, so therefore you keep playing. I believe real fame happens in your twenties, and then it continues to shine, as does the star the fame was bequeathed. Some diminish under that kind of constant spotlight of attention. Others flourish and burn brighter from the adoration and continual flow of offers and swag bags. The opportunity for real fame is mostly over by the time you hit thirty, so if you're looking to make it big, big like the bigs, you have to hit it hard in your twenties and pick and choose some great material. Most people in their twenties wouldn't recognize good material if it sat on their face. In my twenties, I was just looking for work. I said yes to several things that I should've probably passed on, but I was thinking work begets work. In the entertainment business you're only as good as your last job and pay quote. So for me, it was one step forward, three steps back on several occasions.

It is fun to be recognized, I won't lie. It's not fun to be recognized when you're not looking great or if you just took a huge bite out of a Rueben sandwich or if you're in the hospital getting a boil lanced off your ass. All of which have happened to me. I had the unfortunate luck of having a pimple on my butt turn into something worse, a boil. It was right on the fold of where my leg and butt cheek connect, so every time I took a step and every time I took a seat, I was more than highly aware of the throbbing agony. It was torment and beyond embarrassing. It made me feel dirty and depressed. It grew quickly and needed immediate attention, so I drove my own pulsating ass to the ER. It felt like I had been shot, the pain and the heat were so intense. I was officially *Forrest Gump*.

I checked in, gave my insurance card and waited my turn for someone to check out my butt. Of course, I got the tall, good looking emergency room *male* nurse, who gave up his career in modeling to do something worthwhile in his life. Thanks God, you crushed it. As he was listening intently to me dancing around the fact that I have a great big sore on my heiney, he said, "Wait a minute, weren't you Cheyenne from *Renegade*?" Official *FML*. (Fuck My Life)

Really? Now is my turn to get recognized as I'm getting ready to drop my pants and have the hottest male nurse ever to walk the planet lance a boil off my ass? *Renegade* has not been on in decades and now? Really? I wanted to say no, I'm not that actor, but ego and the hopes of possibly getting better treatment kept me honest.

"Yes, that's me. (Yay.) Did you like the show?" I inquired, hopeful that he would begin administering anything to knock me out of this conversation and this moment in its entirety.

Preferably Demerol or Propofol or something comparable.

"Like it? I loved it! I grew up watching that show. I had such a crush on you," he cheerfully contributed to my pain.

"Oh wow, thank you. That's great. It was a fun show to work on," I added lamely.

"Take me now, God," was all I could think out loud. I was ready to walk the plank and drop into the abyss. 'If I grab the scalpel and slit my wrists, I'm still in the emergency room and they will foil my effort in record time. So, note to self, this is not the time or the place for suicide.' It would be a quick lesson in futility to even attempt such a daft maneuver, plus my poor butt was pounding from the rush of stress. I was so screwed, chewed and barbecued behind the green curtain. I had nowhere to run.

"So, let's take a look at your bum," he quipped.

"Yes, let's, because I was really hoping this experience could get worse," I snidely chirped.

I dropped my leggings, laid face down and waited for some professional bedside manner to kick into high gear. Not a chance.

"Oh wow, that's a real doozy you got there... And the boil is alarming too."

Not quite sure if there was a compliment in there, but as long as he sees the boil on my butt, we're in business.

"So, what are you gonna do about it? Call the fire department? Because it feels like my ass is on fire."

I'm not too willing to give many people the last

laugh while watching my dignity and self-esteem line up and file out the door.

"Well, I'm going to have to give you a shot, which might sting a little, then I will lance that sucker right off you," he said with alarming authority.

I shivered at the whole concept. Then I started to sweat. I was definitely going into an acute state of shock, totally different from a cute state of shock, which is like being proposed to in a public place or having someone throw you a surprise party, which is adorable. This was horrific.

He pulled back the curtain and I must have passed out, because he was back before I knew it with a syringe and a fresh tray of medieval slicers and dicers.

"There might be... some *slight* discomfort," he calmly instructed. Hospital dialogue inter-pretation ~ "Brace yourself, honey. This is going to be alarming."

If it wasn't agony before, the slicing pain of that shot into the boil was excruciating. I let out some god-awful string of expletives that would have inspired Andrew Dice Clay. It was a streaming mosh pit of vulgarity rushing out of my screaming mouth. Sometimes the only thing we have left is the F, S, C and MF words to let loose the terror in an uncontrollable situation. It was either that or grabbing the gonads of my newly acquired fan and twisting them until he puked. It wasn't his fault. He was trying to help me by numbing the throbbing volcano on my rear, before he had to lance it and dig out all the hot lava. My superhero, who I wanted to kick in the teeth.

It took about a minute or two for the numbing agent to work its magic. Enough time for a few of the other emergency room staff to check in on the foul-mouthed female sailor/truck driver.

"Nice word combo," I heard one staffer remark. Points for creativity in the emergency room, works for me. Before I knew it, Nurse McDreamy, worked his magic and brought the Matterhorn on my butt down to a small bunker. I now had a hole in my butt the size of a pea. Another one. :-)

It took a while for the wound to heal, which gave me a lot of time to ponder if anybody else on the planet ever went through anything quite as disturbing. I'm sure not, as this was a plethora of pain, embarrassment and mortification, given the 'almost famous' moment. I guess it did get my bad seat a good seat in the house. Thank you *Renegade*.

Epic Fail ~ Boils are always an epic fail, enough said.

Epic Save ~ Even though it sucks, go to the doctor and get help.

Lesson Learned ~ If someone recognizes you, acknowledge it, it might help you get better treatment.

"Stardom isn't a profession, it's an accident."
~Lauren Bacall

CHAPTER 12

~ **on yoga**

My mother was a yoga enthusiast who attended Bikram Choudry's yoga class in Beverly Hills back in the 70's. This was the decade of super funky clothing and *Dolphin* shorts, a special kind of see through nylon with nothing to strap you in. My brother Johnny and I were in the middle of our summer break when mom carted us to our first yoga class. I don't know that we were especially eager to go, but she was. We were at that midline age of too young to leave at home unattended, yet old enough to know what's what.

We got to the class, which was quickly filling up, and we were immediately assigned by Bikram to enjoy the class from the back of the room. I'll never forget the bright illumination of florescent bulbs, the smell of dank carpet, the pinkish walls of the studio and the guy in front of us.

Bikram Yoga is hot, not in a sexy way, but hot in a 'I need some water and a ceiling fan' kind of way. It's so uncomfortably warm that most people opt to wear as little as possible. Bikram was wearing a diaper for God's sake, that just tells you how hot it is. He was pretty impressive sitting there in his pull-ups, barking out asana's (poses) from his little baby perch. He was weird. He seemed too mean to be a spiritual guide, but everybody seemed to respect this little baby man and they followed his demands to twist and turn their bodies into pretzel like forms while stoically sweating away. I think the trick to yoga is not looking like you're uncomfortable. The longer you can maintain a 'I can't feel a thing' type of expression on your face the better you are at yoga. Bikram was the most expressionless human being I ever saw, and this was before Botox.

Johnny and I were doing pretty good for first timers. We were athletic kids, but nothing prepared us for this class. As we moved from one uncomfortable posture to the next, we were noticing that every once in a while someone would cut the cheese during class. We would look at each other, knowing it came from somewhere else in the room and just do our own personal best to not lose it. There is no music played during Bikram's class, so there's very little to mask the sounds of heavy breathing, grunting and passing of wind. His squeaky, whiny and difficult to decipher Indian accent was the second thing breaking the silence. He was thoroughly enjoying watching us suffer in the back and did nothing as far as adjustment or encouragement. He secretly knew this would be 'one and done' for us both. I knew he was not a kid enthusiast as I saw his eyes roll upon introduction, yet we were giving it our all for this sage like dictator a.k.a. pompous prick.

I'm guessing we were about halfway through the class when we gracefully moved into the 'standing bow' position. This position requires you to stand on one leg with one arm forward while hoisting the other leg up with the other arm. You then lean forward like you're reaching for an imaginary friend to catch you, who doesn't. The trick is to not fall flat on your face. When tall people do this pose it's very beautiful as it just reeks of poise, strength and giraffe like wonder. The guy wearing the *Dolphin* shorts in front of us was demonstrating how truly flexible he was and as he leaned forward with one leg swinging up in the air, both of his nuts came swinging out of his poor excuse for shorts. I had a full prepubescent view of his sweaty, purple nad sack as he let it all hang loose while sucking air. I looked at Johnny like my eyes had just seen the forbidden truth of grossness and that was it. Johnny and I hit the floor in uncontrollable heaving laughter. I don't know if it was the heat or the endless farts or that we had just been enlightened by all the bowel twisting and heavy breathing, but we were in a euphoric state of hyena bliss. Bikram's diaper must have been full because he was not a happy baby man. He escorted us out into the changing area, or lobby or whatever the holding pin penalty box was for his studio. We were still rolling out there for another 45 minutes until the class was over. Our mom apologized profusely for her very normal children while Bikram looked at her like she must be 'nuts' for having brought her spawn to his elitist class. He told her to never bring her rancid kids back to his studio space again. Hooray!! Who would want to go? It smells like an extremely nervous *U-Wash Doggie* plus you're going to get nards thrown in your face at any given moment. It's an assault on all the senses. When we told her what happened in the car she wanted to turn around and go back and tell that man in his saggy diaper that he should be ashamed of himself for putting us in such a scandalous situation. We convinced her that it wasn't necessary, and I was sure he would be hit up for something like that in his future, which he was, numerous times.

I didn't take another yoga class until I was thirty-three, while on vacation on Martha's Vineyard. While biking around the island one day, I noticed a sign for a yoga class held in a very small non-denominational Christian church with gorgeous stained-glass windows. I ventured in and never left. I became a yoga instructor around five years later and I have practiced ever since. It's a way of life that I feel everybody yearns for. We were made to twist and turn and breathe. It helps athletes to stay flexible and every non athlete to stay in shape. It increases metabolism, improves sleep, stabilizes posture, lowers blood pressure and helps you poop. There is every good benefit from something that doesn't include any kind of apparatus. However, I suggest investing in a jock strap if you're thinking about breaking out the 'ol *Dolphin* shorts.

Epic Fail ~ Taking a young kid to an elitist yoga class with a younger sibling.

Epic Save ~ Finding a gentle yoga class for beginners in a welcoming environment.

Lesson Learned ~ Always sit at the front of the class if you're not interested in watching private parts accidentally drop from someone's shorts.

"Yoga is the art work of awareness on the canvas of body, mind and soul."
         ~ Amit Ray

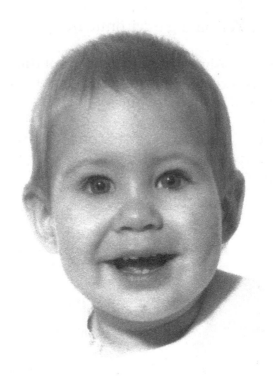

CHAPTER 13

~ **on poop**

I attended several schools in the Valley before ending up at the school of life for college. My first charge was Laurel Hall in North Hollywood. I started at pre-school across the street, then moved to the main campus for kindergarten. The school seemed huge with its large field and the grownup kids that seemed like high school students that were actually only 8th graders. They had a homecoming dance and king and queen of the court and bonfire rally's. It was straight out of *Grease*. In second grade I had developed an overwhelming crush on what was probably a 6th grader, a surfer stud with blonde hair and a devil may care attitude. He was way too cool for school and he literally didn't know I existed. Literally.

During one fine school day, my stomach was acting especially weird. I usually vomited over most things, but this particular afternoon it was a thunder from down under and I knew it was going to be a mad dash to the potty. With my Partridge Family lunchbox in tow, I sprinted for the girl's restroom. As soon as my fingertips touched the bathroom stall, I was too late. It was an explosion of mass proportions and not the way I wanted to end the day. My mom had just bought me brand new underwear and I was at a total loss for how I was supposed to handle this particular crappy situation. Thank God I had my lunchbox, as I was able to deftly wrap my soiled undies in toilet paper and safely store them inside my now defunct Partridge Family 'dump truck.'

I cleaned myself up and noticed that there must have been a Guardian Angel with me, because nobody entered the bathroom during that time. I was able to have some semblance of privacy during one of the most painfully embarrassing moments in my life, up to this point. Actually, this was the most horrible because I had to walk to the nurse's office without wearing any underwear at a time when miniskirts were the norm. In fact, skirts were so short that if you were writing on the chalkboard and lifted your arm up, you exposed your underwear. That was a walk I'll never forget as I did my best to make myself look completely normal while trekking the length of the campus to get fresh panties from the nurse. This experience would later trigger a multitude of nightmares of wandering around school to eventually notice that I wasn't wearing any clothes. From there, the nightmare would turn into an espionage suspense thriller of how I would be able to score some clothing.

Once I made it safely to the nurse's office, I opened the door only to find my hot surfer dude crush sitting on a cot with a thermometer hanging out of his mouth like a cigarette. He was definitely channeling James Dean nonchalance when he blurted, "What the hell is that smell?" The thermometer never left his mouth as he jumped off the cot and strutted over to me and my foul-smelling lunchbox.

"Oh my God, it's coming from your lunchbox!" That was it. I knew instantly what dying a hundred deaths felt like.

"Jimmy, go sit back on the cot,... the cot, ...the cot... the cot..." the Nurse echoed.

She gently took me by the shoulder, brought me back to life and led me to her back office where she rummaged through a bag of clean, gently used underpants. Apparently, I wasn't the first to have a shitty day at school. She was kind enough to not ask me what happened, as it was a fairly obvious story to surmise. I was so emotionally charged and ready to blast it out, just like my bowels had done ten minutes prior, "I pooped my pants, what the hell do you think happened?!" But fortunately, she was sympathetic and she certainly saw my look of horror when 'Jimmy' added insult to injury. The good thing was now I knew his name and whenever I heard it down the hall, I could run the other way.

When I came out of her private office after putting on my clean, ill fitting, gently used, 'new' underwear, I only saw the thermometer on the cot. Jimmy had split. He was either fully grossed out, or he was miraculously feeling better, or he couldn't wait to get to his friends and tell them about the kid who came into the nurse's office with a Partridge Family lunchbox full of poop. Keith Partridge instantly became less than cool. My life in that moment shifted. I inherently knew that if I could survive this, I could survive anything. It became my *Titanic*. I was cold, lonely, scared, love struck and sinking. The nurse gently assured me that I could stay in her office until school ended. I took that lifeline, as sometimes we need some recovery time after a round of shock treatment. She wrapped my soiled panties like someone smuggling hashish from Turkey and placed them back in my stupid lunchbox. Those nasty ass panties were triple taped by that diligent RN. I never used that lunchbox again. I brown bagged it until I got a Scooby Doo lunchbox the following year. It was my own personal joke at the new school I would be attending in the fall.

I've helped quite a few kids, including my own, with the retelling of this story during painfully mortifying moments. One talented kid, Alyssa, a 12-year-old actor I cast in my short film, *Mrs. Sweeney*, went up on her lines one day. She ran off the set and I found her around the corner, quietly crying in the rain. She is an excellent actor and always knew her lines and everyone else's, so when she went up on her own lines, she was particularly hard on herself. I had just seen the film *Lincoln* and was moved by his tireless story telling in making his point. I quickly pulled out the poop story, which had her giggling pretty quickly. I pulled out a pencil and demonstrated Jimmy talking with the thermometer in his mouth. I hadn't even gotten to the ill-fitting underwear part before she was pulling out her mini sides and took a glance and said, "Let's get back in there and do this."

It's always good to bring it back to when we were all kids and doing our best and falling short and giving it another try.

128

Epic Fail ~ Wrapping up soiled poop pants to take home. (Just toss 'em in the trash. Preferably outside.)

Epic Save ~ Being able to walk around without any underwear and knowing where to quickly find some.

Lesson Learned ~ Life is not about how many times you get knocked down; it's about how quickly you get up.

"It happens."
　　　~ Tom Hanks in *Forrest Gump*

CHAPTER 14

~ on children

I love kids. Ever since I was a kid, I've always enjoyed being around them.
"Puh-lease, sit me at the kids table. I want fun!" I always secretly shout to myself.
How often do we get stuck with the adults, at the drunk table, who tirelessly burden us with all of their adult drama? I'm so sick of it, I could barf in my shoe. In fact, that's what I'll be demonstrating over at the kids table.

Children are born pure with generous love and joy in their hearts eagerly waiting to share it with anyone who will hold them, love them and take care of them. As children, we are influenced by those who care for us the moment we arrive, and this begins our first world view. Based on how quickly our needs are met, sets us up for how we respond. Babies let you know clearly by screaming bloody murder that they have needs. Our job as a parent or caregiver is to do our best to figure out what the heck they need this time, until the next time. It's a relentless cycle of giving.

I remember the exact moment when my daughter was about a year and a half and she woke up in the middle of the night screaming. I was exhausted from moving into a new home with all the joys of moving with a one year old. I was stressed and got up with a mighty, passive aggressive, "UGHHH, what now?" Truly, one of the more natural sounds moms and dads make while parent rearing, especially in the middle of the night. I realized right then that this was not the habit I wanted to assume as a drained mom. I remembered that this might be one of those 'new environment night terrors' that toddlers encounter and decided that instead of being put-out with an angry tone, I would instead walk in with compassion and kindness and offer my service with love and patience. I do my best to bring this same face to every need she has and I have to say it serves me well.

The things I love about children are: They say what they mean. They are not concerned about people pleasing. They are honest. (minus the little 'baby lies')*
They dress for comfort. They travel light. (toothbrush, hairbrush, princess dress, bow and arrow) They let you know how they're feeling, right away. They are vulnerable. They want to learn stuff and they like to know why. They have a wide-open imagination that will take them anywhere they want to go and get them out of any bit of loneliness while igniting the fire that burns inside all of us that anything is possible.

My brothers and I were always encouraged to use our imaginations and would get a lot of laughs from our parents and their friends by performing skits. I would don a fur coat and massive sunglasses in preparation to play Miss Dalton and my brothers would take turns as our dad, Jack, and Mary, our Yorkshire Nanny. This was our first foray into improvisational sketch comedy, deftly

132

playing the intricate characters who had the greatest impact on our lives. We knew these characters inside and out and calling them out on their own ridiculous character traits was pee worthy. They were pretty much always game for giving us the spotlight and allowing themselves to be ridiculed and roasted.

JACK
Has anyone seen my glasses?

Abby is hard of hearing and likes to deflect by constantly using absurd word arrangements for laughs.

ABBY
What?! Your asses? You have more than one?

Mary feigns embarrassment.

MARY
(British accent)
Aw, core blimey. Anyone for a spot of tea?

This lunacy would go on for a good ten to twenty minutes. Meaningless banter and crazy imitations of the ones who loved us most. It was an awesome release of making fun without hurting anyone's feelings. The same way my daughter and I would play "Dollies" with her soft fabric Disney Princess dolls. I don't know how it started but Cinderella became an entitled little so and so and my young daughter and I decided to take out all of our pent up aggressions for the week and toss that doll across the room, up into the ceiling fan and officially uninvited her to all our tea parties. She deserved it. Cinderella was a brat and was mean to the horses. When she was finally allowed to ride, she would get bucked off and tossed into the moat. We spent countless hours throughout Ayden's childhood playing Dollies and giving ourselves permission to act silly, laugh and giggle our faces off.

I think this is why I fell in love with acting. Observing and taking in a character that you identify with and creating a picture of someone where before there was just an idea of someone. I love bringing someone to life that was once on a page and nothing but dialogue and a description. Breathing that character into a human form is profoundly imaginative to me. Plus, the table where the actors sit is usually always going to be the kids table.

Fueling this imaginative process and allowing it to grow opens up the limitless well of possibilities that life has to offer. As children, we are all actors on the stage of our own life, taking each other in and acting and reacting to our own personal comedies and drama's. It's not until children get older and become more influenced by the environment around us, do we have more opportunity to lose the play and become critics of ourselves and critical of others. Little kids don't know judgement until it's been instilled.

I always feel a natural connection to children and am aware to the impact of childhood. I'm hypersensitive to the way people treat their kids, even strangers. Thank Hedy Lamarr for cell phones and the ability to be able to pull them on each other like a Psycho Cyber Safety Patrol. The cell phone is a video camera that can carry a terrific amount of evidence to people who are bullies. All bullies need to remember that. We should also remember that trying to take a kid away from their parent might do more irreparable damage. I believe we just need to encourage each other to be the best parents we can possibly be.

I recently saw a woman, with a very little boy who had the most amazing head of hair. The morning sun caught his magnificent curls in a way that said, 'All is right with the world'. As I sat in traffic, I saw him begin to wander away from the watchful eye of his intense, muscular mom. Without a word of warning she grabbed him by the top of his scalp and pulled him back to her side. He screamed and burst into raging tears as he was lifted off his feet. It was shocking and horrible and before I knew it, my passenger window was rolled down and I was screaming at the top of my lungs, "BE NICE, MOMMY!!!"

I was shaking as she looked over at me like Bigfoot and dropped him from her grasp and began to storm over to my car. She honestly dropped her screaming kid onto the concrete to come over and kick my ass.

"Ohhh, sh-shit," I cringed to myself, "another nut-job I want nothing to do with," as I quickly rolled up the window, locked the doors and floored it. I burnt rubber out of there before she had a chance to scalp me too. Fortunately, there were some bike police up the road I yelled to while passing, "There's a crazy lady in the street back there who's abusing her kid!" I saw her in my rearview mirror, screaming with all the extra body language that says, "Pick me, I'm the lunatic!" Thank you for letting the cops know where you're at, bad mom. Poor kid. Next time I'll just quietly videotape, while pretending to take another selfie.

Having been a stepparent three different times to six different kids, I learned that the most difficult part of a marriage with kids that don't belong to you, is you should say as little as possible. Be there for the children and their needs at all times but commenting on their behavior is appreciated in very small doses, or at best none at all. Parents are quite egocentric when it comes to their offspring. Anything other than lots of positive reinforcement, should only be tempered with various degrees of, "Oh, my."

Kids love praise, it's good to give it to them. It's a calorie free energy. Praise encourages them to do something else to get it again. Love is a drug, they're not joking. Emotions actually create a chemical change in the brain and send out multitudes of stimuli to the body. Mean words create stress stimuli, nice words create uplifting stimuli. Stimulating, right?

John Fulgum wrote the most awesome book, *Everything I Need to Know I Learned in Kindergarten.* The list in his book should be the new *Pledge of Allegiance,* since it looks like we're not saying the old one anymore. It should go something like, "I pledge to play fair and share. I'm not going to hit anybody, and I will put things back where I found them. I won't take things that aren't mine and I'm going to clean up my own mess. I will say sorry when I've hurt someone. I will be aware of wonder and when we go out into the world, we will hold hands and stick together. Amen."

* *My daughter, Ayden, used to tell me what I would refer to as 'baby lies' when she was very little and learning to talk. She would test the boundaries of what her imagination was telling her and what was real, which was only completely validated by how willing I was to go along with it. She would spin the darnedest of tales, until she would get stumped on how to continue with her 'baby lie' because her improv skills weren't fully developed. I hold 'baby lies' as accountable as Santa Clause, The Tooth Fairy and Easter Bunny. All of which I was doing my best to convince her of their reality, knowing full well it's a full-blown made-up story (lie) told only in an effort to have some fun. Sorry whatever youngster might be reading this for the spoiler alert. **

Epic Fail ~ Destroying anyone's playful imagination.

Epic Save ~ Sticking up for anyone who is being abused in any way, shape or form.

Lesson Learned ~ Be kind, patient and loving to your child, again and again and again, no matter what the hour or how exhausted you are.

"There really are places in the heart you don't even know exist until you love a child."
    ~ Anne LaMott

CHAPTER 15

~ on parenting

One of my favorite references for raising children comes from Kahlil Gibran's, *The Prophet*. He says that God is the archer, the parents are the bow and the children are the arrows. The parents' bow should be strong and flexible, so that God can aim for great places to shoot your kid out into the world. It is such a great image and so very true. The stronger and more flexible I become in my daughter's growth, the more she thrives.

When I was growing up, my brothers and I were occasionally waaaay out of control. I'm sure our parents were often overwhelmed by three young kids. My older brother, Matt, always had a penchant for mischief. He was a definite 'push the envelope' kind of guy. Me and our younger brother, Johnny, did our best to keep up.

One fine weekend, close to Thanksgiving, we went up to the duck hunting club where my mom's dad, Papa Ray, was a member. It was a huge ranch up in Hemet where guys and gals could get together and shoot some unsuspecting ducks. They had a cabin with two bunk rooms, which looked like barracks, one for the men and one for the women folk. It was a great place to gather with our favorite cousins, The Hecks. Our older cousin, Dean, would jump on the Honda minibike and we wouldn't see him again until they packed up the car to leave.

Our other cousin, Gary, who is only two weeks older than I am, was the perfect foursome to our terrible threesome. If me and my brothers were fire, Gary was the gas. If my brother Matt was the Mastermind, Gary was the Chosen One to start the engine. There was a time when it was an actual vision quest on how to behave badly.

Our parents were busy getting drunk on noon martinis when the children decided to go explore near the hay baling truck, just a few hundred yards away. They could see us *playing* near the truck, but they had no idea what we were *doing* to the truck. It started off as a simple game of, 'Who could throw the rock closest to the truck?' Sounds fun, in theory. Then crash, a window got broke. Funny how nobody remembers who threw that first rock. It's quite spooky how dementia runs in our family. The next thing I remember is we became like chimps hopped up on sugar and meth who just escaped from the zoo. We went ape shit crazy on this poor defenseless hay baling truck. It actually wasn't too defenseless, the thing had zip line cables that could literally rip your arm off. Gary and Johnny almost discovered that traumatic note when they released something that made them both see their lives flash before them. I remember somebody saying, "Whoa, that was close." And then we got bored or called to dinner or both. It's pretty much a blur when you're busy being a hoodlum. You get caught up in the mayhem of knowing full well that you're doing something you shouldn't, and you're on a high of not getting caught. Until you do, and then the world crashes on you like some kind of horrific hippopotami weight of the world. You're like, "Wait, I didn't mean to get everyone on the planet upset from my stupidity. It should only affect me."

I remember the next morning a ranch hand came to the house to talk to Papa. He walked him out to the hay baling truck, which Matt, Gary, Johnny and me could witness from over our bowls of Cheerio's. There was seriously *nothing* cheery about that moment. I was already blaming our superior nanny, Mary, for not being there on the trip to keep us kids in line while our parents got blind drunk on vodka and vacation. I was really liking my excuse for getting in trouble, it was lock solid. Plus, there was Matt who got blamed for mostly everything and then add Gary, the cousin factor. I was gearing up to blame the world when Papa came back. He didn't even glance at any of us very guilty children, he just got Uncle Ron and my dad to come out to the hay baling truck. Now the four of us were starting to whimper and genuinely freak out. We knew we were so busted, and we were feeling that squeamish angst of the walk to the guillotine. The parents were hungover and very quiet. Painfully quiet.

When Uncle Ron and dad came back, they both said the same thing. "It's time to pack up." Apparently, we had totaled the truck. We broke every window, slashed the tires, pulled the engine to pieces and zip lined the cable into a tangled mess. It was a very expensive weekend. It cost us the rest of our stay, and the coming Christmas. Our parents were so devastated at our hard to fathom behavior, they cancelled Christmas for that year. It was the punishment to end all punishments. When I look back on the damnation, it was fitting.

Johnny got meningitis that holiday season and was in the Intensive Care in an oxygen tent for a couple of weeks. He sure showed them who held the emotional cards. This was my first indicator that stress really does wreak havoc on the body. My parents were a wreck. It was more than traumatic on everyone. We weren't allowed to give a present or receive one, so I was pretty upset when Johnny came home from Children's Hospital with a barf tray filled with goodies like, gauze, band aids and a shower cap.
"It wasn't fair!" I whined. I remember my mom giving me stink eye to last a lifetime on that complaint.

We were pretty good for a while after that. Maybe good for a whole year. There was just one more incident of defacing property with some stain berries down at the Marina, when the moms, my mom and Aunt Shirl, made another attempt of bringing the hooligan cousins together on a trip to San Diego. We were staying at some ridiculously swanky hotel surrounded by beautiful yachts and sailboats. Spring was in full bloom and the berries on the bushes were not edible, but they sure sailed through the air with ease. When the berries hit a boat, they left the most perfect, exploding stain. It looked like a paint ball splash. It was like we were all temporarily inhabited by famed artist Jackson Pollack, splashing paint all over a canvas. Except it was someone's pricey watercraft that we were destroying. We were like raccoons in a Disney film.

The kind of old movie where the burly old mountain man, after gathering all the things he will need to survive the long winter from the endless haul to the mercantile, leaves his immaculate and organized cabin for another long day of bear hunting. He lumbers in to find a destroyed cabin covered in honey, flour and raccoon prints. Kind of adorable but really not nice. That's what our mentality was like back then, obnoxious rascals.

It wasn't too long after that my older brother, Matt, ended up in a boarding school in Arizona for a year. That gave us a pretty clear window to regroup and grow out of the destructive stage.

So, in the case of the parents as the bow, children are the arrow and God is the archer, my parents were pretty strong and flexible in their decision to only launch one arrow out of state at a time. We got the point.

Epic Fail ~ Allowing rambunctious kids to play without supervision will lead to raccoon results.

Epic Save ~ Johnny and Gary not losing an arm or digit on the trucks zip line.

Lesson Learned ~ Some punishments can last a lifetime.

"Punishment is what you do to someone; discipline is what you do for someone."
       ~ Zig Ziglar

CHAPTER 16

~ on laughter

My mom is professionally funny. She is a master of the obvious and throws her material at the wall like a machine gun. My dad is surprisingly funny. He sits back and launches something out of left field that lands and becomes a memorable one liner forever. My older brother, Matt, is acerbically funny. He is a lot like our mom and his well of material is intense with unusual perspectives. My younger brother, Johnny, is enjoyably funny. He is a lot like our dad and will wait his turn for the floor to deliver a sweet joke dessert. Our family has had decades of repartee and inside jokes that go deep into the 70's beginning with the many indecorous moments in Mel Brooks cult classic, *Blazing Saddles.* This film was the blueprint of our humor and we screened it a ridiculous amount of times. Too many to count. We memorized the dialogue and sang "He Rode a Blazing Saddle" like it was an anthem. This film would be in so many violations of appropriate humor today that it would never get made. It's truly one of those films made to offend simply everyone on the planet. Even the Universe probably got offended. Mission accomplished and hats off to Mel Brooks and Warn your Bros for hitting the bar.

Who doesn't love a good laugh? It's heart opening and comparable to being in love, it's that powerful. It relaxes the belly, swirls the oxygen in our lungs and allows our face to make the most beautiful, carefree expression. Laughter is unique to everyone and it is vital. Except when it's at your own expense. I've been told that most comedy comes from making fun of someone or something they do. But how can something that gives the soul so much joy and heightens the wellbeing of a body, also bring so much pain along with it?

Being laughed at sucks so hard that you'll do just about anything to make it stop, including making fun of yourself before anyone else has a chance. I've been bullied. Who hasn't? None of us are immune to being picked on by parents, siblings, childhood and school friends, co-workers, society, the population at large. Get in your car and get 'the finger,' that seems to be the LA high five. My go-to response has been to smile and give the 'peace sign.' However, you never know who the 'victory' sign or a simple smile is going to piss off today. So it's really not a good idea, because just like a text, the gesture can lose its tone. Just keep your eyes forward, watch the road and do your best to ignore the butthole giving you the finger in the car next to you.

I love the noteworthy dialogue Matthew McConaughey brought to the Emmy's ® one year in reference to Woody Harrelson's response to how he deals with things that are bugging him.
After several thoughtful moments Woody's response was, "I just forget about it."
The audience roared from this great advice.

I used to laugh at everything in an attempt to be supportive or in an effort to just go along with the laugh. Now I find myself taking a moment to actually see if it really *is* funny or am I just trying to fill the awkward space of someone's lame attempt at humor with a fake, country club ha-ha? We learn to develop phony, nervous noises that sound like uncomfortable breathing, mostly inhales. We put on a phony, dead eye smile and grin and bear it. I hate it and it reeks of guilty response. I know that I am generally an enthusiastic audience member and I always enjoy a good laugh. I believe having a healthy sense of humor about yourself is vital, but there's also a limit to how many times someone throws you under the bus for laughs. So be aware when people use laughter as a form of putting you or someone else down. Simple solution - if it's not funny, don't laugh.

Having been the butt of several jokes, I've never enjoyed mean spirited humor. There have been a few people in my life who have tried to break me down with their humor. I had to learn that words are like birds, and when released, can just fly away. And if mean words are being used in an attempt to be funny, be like the bird and fly away. Mean things written or said are hurled to cause stress and it's a personal practice to not let mean stuff written or said leave you feeling worthless. Just pay attention and stand up for yourself and others when you can. When you get the urge to make fun of somebody else for a laugh, remember how it hurt when someone did that to you.

Laughter at the expense of others will also land somewhere on the person making the joke. I went to a healer one day and told her about a person that I wanted to focus on who I had some pretty bad moments with in the past. I told her, "I really hope I can get to a better spiritual place with this person because I'm tired of wishing he/she gets hit by a bus."

She looked at me for a long, noteworthy moment and said, "I hope you don't get hit by a bus."

I said, "Wow. Thanks. Me too." How much was I paying for this advice?

She continued, "When we wish something or say something bad to someone else, we essentially bring it upon ourselves to happen in our own existence." I definitely wasn't paying her enough for that piece of stay with me forever 'peace' of advice.

There are so many wonderful ways to be funny without hurting someone. I believe Ellen Degeneres has the blueprint and we all know that the positive components of laughter are ridiculously huge. My dear friend, Lisa Marie Wilson, author and cancer survivor, was advised to watch comedies while going through her treatment. She watched comedy after comedy and she discovered it for herself; the more she was laughing, the better she felt physically. A study done in 2005 by the University of Maryland Medical Center showed a link between laughter and healthier blood vessel and blood flow. It raises good cholesterol and lowers inflammation in our heart. It helps us boost our mood and appreciate life more. Laughter helps minimize mental, physical, and emotional pain by looking at a situation from a lighter side.

One excruciatingly painful day on the set of *Renegade* had me in massive tears and an emotional train wreck. Lorenzo had invited our publicist, Joe Sutton, to the set to make a public statement that we were separating. I was completely caught off guard in the middle of a day, in the middle of the show and in the middle of our second season. I burst into hysterical sobbing and was immediately needed on the set. "Good freaking luck!" I sobbed, "I need to speak to Stu!" Stu Segall was our executive producer and a big bear of a man who could be kind and a hard ass all at the same time, the way executive producers are trained to be. He was summoned and I instantly heard a knock on my trailer. Actresses freaking out and refusing to come to set spreads like wildfire over the walkie channels and since I was never a problem, Stu was quick to respond. I had my adorable tan Miniature Pinscher, Macho, with me in my trailer. Macho had become the *Renegade* mascot and was also quite fond of Stu. He jumped up and down when he saw Stu enter and I collapsed and sobbed on Stu's shoulder, while my dog humped Stu's leg for a good six minutes of balling. When I looked up and saw that Macho was having a honeymoon moment on Stu's shin, I burst into the most uncontrollable laughing through my own tears I've ever encountered. Stu really took one for the team that day, as I was able to go dry my face and get back in the makeup chair for a massive touch up. The thought of my little freaky dog, front paws clenched around Stu's shinbone, feverishly smiling like a chupacabra will always bring me to an outright lol.

My daughter recently had a birthday party sleepover with six of her friends. Seven teenagers is a breeding ground for a whole lotta laughs and high jinx so as a single mom, I called in for backup from my dear friend, Carmen Moreno, a very skilled and funny actor. There was one point, about halfway through the popcorn, candy and festivity fueled evening, where we could hear the girls downstairs laughing at something so full throttle, we just had to eavesdrop. We sat in the stairwell, listening to the girls roar with laughter. Naturally, as actors do, we pulled out our miming skills, as we already had paper face masks on. We began imitating the giddy teenagers, pretending to paint each other's nails while being super overly dramatic. In one swift moment, with our face masks and pajamas on, we were swept up by a tsunami of hilarity. I was honestly crippled with laughter, a complete and total hot mess of a mom on the stairwell, tears streaming from my eyes, choking on the laughs and instantly thrown back to the future of being a carefree kid at a slumber party. Which is exactly what I was, all through the surrender of un-controllable laughter. These are the moments we remember and the greatest healers of our body and soul.

Epic Fail ~ Laughing when it's not funny.

Epic Save ~ Learning how to laugh at yourself and stare down a "not funny" remark.

Lesson Learned ~ Nothing works as well as walking away from someone endlessly laughing at you.

"It is cheerful to God when you rejoice or laugh from the bottom of your heart."
~ Martin Luther King Jr.

CHAPTER 17

~ **on death**

One of life's greatest lessons is death. It's something we spend a lot of time pondering, dreading and dodging. Nobody is wired to die; we are wired to live. Survival is our inert radar and we are created with one instinctual fact; we are born with the inertia to want to live. Fight or flight is what we share with the animal kingdom. It keeps us going.

I was introduced to death when I was four years old. My grandfather, Burt Smith, my dad's dad, had a massive heart attack and suddenly passed away. He was a great dad, loyal husband, excellent businessman and a kind and generous volunteer pastor. He was a tremendous influence in my dad's life. The only memory I have of my Papa Burt is sitting on his lap, along with both of my brothers in my first home on Ledge Avenue in Toluca Lake. It's a memory that is also a photograph, so it's a wonderful thing to remember that time and have a photo that reflects the experience. I don't remember how my dad coped with the loss of his beloved father, but I do remember there was a respite trip to Del Coronado to help ease the pain.

Del Coronado is an impressive hotel near San Diego, located on the Pacific Coast of Southern California. The hotel has been around for quite a while and is considered a pretty swanky stay. When we arrived at the grand valet my three-year-old brother, Johnny, dropped trow and decided to pee in the fountain. He really had to go and yes, 'hello, we've arrived'. From there, it just went downhill for me, as I was already carsick and throwing up in the car, bushes and concrete. Nobody has good aim at that age.

At this particular stage in my life I had a hypersensitivity with texture. I didn't like anything scratchy, itchy or abrasive. Specifically, sand. Sand was the bane of my existence and I hated it with a screaming passion. I think this was the first time anyone knew how much I hated sand. I don't think they brought me there to torment me, they just didn't know. I didn't even know. I was four and discovering all the things I liked and all the things I despised.

I'm sure the week-long trip to Coronado was looking like a hostage situation for my poor parents who were grieving and looking for a moniker of intermission. Thankfully for them and for us kids, we had the most incredible four foot eleven, British nanny, Mary Rogers. She was the mini-me version of *Mrs. Doubtfire.* She was the most chipper, wonderful Brit from West Yorkshire, who would repeatedly save the day throughout my young life. After about two days of me screaming my flipping head off over the sand on my hands while the rest of the family attempted to enjoy a day at the beach, my parents decided to send my adorable ass home on a train with Mary. So much for vacation time with the family, now I get to go on a train with Mary and have a whole new adventure on a train! Did I mention the train? Pure joy! No more gritty sand in-between my toes, or in my nails or in my bathing suit. What a relief. This is what I remember about the passing of my Papa Burt.

It wasn't until I was nine years old that I was really hit with the magnitude of death. My best friend in third grade, Carol, tragically drowned in the Jacuzzi at her home. We used to play this game where we would go under water and breathe the air bubbles releasing from the Jacuzzi seats. Jacuzzi's were a bit different back then with a grate at the bottom that had a suction system for filtering. The seats had little holes that would release air bubbles, and that's what we used for our underwater breathing. It was safe, however, on this particular day, the grate at the bottom of the Jacuzzi was missing. Her parents were present, but thought that Carol was just doing what we used to do: breathe off the bubbles... The suction at the bottom pulled her down, while her parents were unaware that she was drowning. It was a tragedy that still haunts me to this day.

When I arrived at school that following day, one very strung out kid ran up to me and yelled in my face, "Carol died!" He was young and had not been practiced in sharing tragic news, as none of us were. We lived charmed lives in a war free zone. We weren't used to serious tragedy, so this was a new raw emotion. Stupid kid. I felt instant nausea and knew I needed immediate help. I wanted to run home and be safe in my mother's arms. I was lost, devastated, confused, scared. I couldn't talk. I was hyperventilating and in shock. Once again, I ran blindly to the nurse's office. I cried and screamed for my mom. They called her, but she was not home yet from dropping us off at school. I had to wait until she was able to return to school to pick me up. I remember going back to class for a moment and seeing the tear stained face of our other best friend Sabrina. Sabrina and I ended up graduating high school together at Our Lady of Corvallis. We were pretty inseparable the three of us. Only death could have robbed us of that special friendship.

There wasn't any grief counseling back then. I simply went to the funeral with Mary, my great hand holder. It is my first memory of a funeral. I remember the wave of pain hitting me when I saw that small, white casket. Mary and I gasped as we both broke down, grieving together, holding onto each other for dear life. Because that's what it is, dear. Life. It will never be more precious than when you're experiencing death. We reach out to one another in death like our life depends on it. It's profound the pain that we experience once the other person is no longer feeling any discomfort at all. It's almost like we have to experience the pain and agony of someone else's death, so that we can get to the other side of our own life.

I realized that I had never really dealt with the loss of Carol until I had my own child. All of a sudden waves of terror and sadness would wash over me. I remember when my daughter was just a baby sleeping in her car seat, I had a vision of Carol and her young life ending so early. I had to pull over and sob at the loss her parents and siblings had to endure. It's horrible to imagine enduring life with that kind of pain. I realized in that moment, what every parent feels is the need to protect and watch over our children, loved ones and pets to the best of our sane ability. The truth is that we won't always be able to be there and save them. There are times, when at no fault of anyone else, something might happen. When we sign up for life, we also sign up for death. Every cute little puppy will age into an old dog that will eventually pass. It's inevitable and we need to honor the passing of life with as much love, support and dignity as possible. As we live in perilous times, filled with random senseless threats, where anything can happen at any given moment, we need to meditate and pray for the good. We need to focus on a good life and treat each other with kindness and compassion. There's never a good day to die but there is always a good day to live. Fortunately, we will only die once but every day we are given the opportunity to *live*. We should strive to bring our A game and fill it with empathy and kindness.

We all arrive with an expiration date. A day that we will no longer have a voice. As an adult, if we haven't taken the time to create some guidelines for when we depart, then family, friends and the government will be left to figure it all out. Death in the family can change relationships and some family members and/or friends can get bent way out of shape when entitlement and greed are part of the picture. My mom always says, "Where there's a will, there's a relative." If you are elderly, middle aged or Type A like me, you can gift your special loved ones a great favor by going through some 'talking points' before the great inevitable divide.

My dad helped me create a list of what to do before, during and after our imminent transition. It could save a life. Literally.

TALKING POINTS
<u>What to do before, during and after death</u>

PROPERTY
Real Property:
Does the Trust hold title to the home?
Is the mortgage paid off?
Personal property:
Is there a list or written document that sets forth wishes re: personal property?
Possibility of *videotaping to state wishes?
Information re: value?
Insurance on any of the personal property?

MONEY/FINANCES
List of all bank accounts:
Savings
Checking
List of all sources of Income and Details:
Benefit payments (Social Security, Veteran Benefits, Residuals)
Investments
List of all assets i.e. home, furnishings, jewelry, art
List of all creditors
List of all debtors
Safe deposit box

SAFETY
List of everyone who has a key to the house
Is it necessary to change locks?
List of all medications

List of all treating doctors
Health Insurance information

INSURANCE
List of all insurance policies
House
Medical
Life
Location of policies
Anything that needs to be transferred from one person to another or to the Trust?

MEMORIAL REQUESTS
Location of Service
Who would you like to Speak on your behalf
Favorite Music
Favorite Flower
Favorite Scripture or Poem
Favorite Joke

* Videotaping home furnishings such as furniture, art, jewelry, etc. is non contestable. It's as simple as holding up a current newspaper, stating your name and date and documenting items to whom you'd like the item to go to. Make a copy for yourself, Trustee, Beneficiary and Lawyer.
Remember ~ This is all sensitive information that must be held confidential by the Trustees and Beneficiaries.

I will never forget when I was married to Lorenzo and I thought something horrible had happened to him. I thought he had been hurt or killed on his motorcycle because he had been gone so long on a motorcycle ride with my brother Matt, who on another occasion I had also thought died. I was beyond upset and beside myself with grief, imagining the worst when he got home. He took me in his arms and held my sobbing body and said, "You have nothing to fear but fear itself."

"Oh, please with the annoying cliché!" I screamed, "I just don't want anything to happen to you!"

"I know," he assured, "but you can't worry yourself to death. Just put your trust in God and let your heart rest."

It's good advice and I do my best to practice that concept every day with prayer and meditation. If we are too focused on death and losing someone, we miss the opportunity to love them while they are right here.

Epic Fail ~ Living like we have an endless supply of time to get it right tomorrow.

Epic Save ~ Living like there's no tomorrow.

Lesson Learned ~ Trust is a practice, not just something earned.

"Death is not the greatest loss in life. The greatest loss is what dies inside us while we live."
~ Norman Cousins

CHAPTER 18

~ on family

My family heritage is Swedish, Norwegian, Scottish, Irish and Welsh. I think of myself as an Irish Viking. I envision my ancestors, covered in pelts, all sitting at a pub laughing and telling stories and trying on each other's Spangenhelm helmets. Horses and langskips patiently waiting outside.

My mom's heritage is from the Scandinavian side with several of our early pioneers landing in Utah and embracing the Mormon faith and all its spoils. Her parents, Gladys, is of mystery ancestry from Tennessee, and Ray, of Norwegian descent, were both from hearty salt of the earth families of their own. My dad's heritage is from the British Isles of Scotland, Ireland and Wales. These people were all born in the late 1800's which made them all pretty solid, scrappy souls. They never had running water or electricity as children. They endured the Great Depression, World Wars and knew a different set of tough times. Our families, including all of our ancestors who survived multiple plagues and ran from dinosaurs, were from 'survivor stock'. All of which makes me just want to step into a warm pub and get out of the damp cold.

My mom and dad and I share the same family line-up, three middle children of three children. My dad had an older sister, Evelyn, and a younger brother, Don. My mom had an older brother, Sam, and a younger sister, Shirl. I never knew my cousins from my dad's side as they were much older and never made an effort to reach out. My Uncle Sam had three kids, Perry, Lee and Lauren. They were older than me and my brothers, so our childhoods never lined up but I've gotten to know Lauren in our adult years and she is a blessing. My Aunt Shirl and Uncle Ron's two sons, Dean and Gary, are more like my two 'other brothers' and our close relationship is compiled of many, many memories and an enduring effort to constantly create more. My cousin Dean married a gorgeous neurologist, Christi, and their striking daughters, Kate and Grace, are more like nieces than second cousins. My fine nephew's, Mac and Jack, my brother Johnny's sons, are proving to be fine represents of carrying on The Smith Family name. All the stunning cousins from my mom's side are numerous and amazing, as the genetic gene pool is so intense, no other DNA stands a chance. I didn't know that the ancestry of Amazon women and men originated in Utah, but looking at my clan of tall, athletic blondes, you'd beg to differ.

We choose our friends. Family is chosen for us upon arrival. If we're lucky, we will inherit more family through marriage. If we're lucky again, divorce will divide family and friends into separate camps. If you trifecta in luck, you might end up with a great relationship with someone else's parent, kid, or ex, even though you might never be 'family' with that person again. I continue to have great friendships with many of my brother's ex-wives and girlfriends. Sometimes those people brought into your life are meant to have an independent relationship without the one that brought them to the party. It is a mature human, practiced in letting go, who can encourage another relationship to flourish, even when you are not a part of the picture.

I have been very lucky with stepchildren. Each set has proven to be a true gift in my heart. Stepchildren are the lovely little pawns in life who dutifully follow the happiness of their parents' current love. In my case, I fell in love six times with three marriages. Lorenzo's two children, A.J. and Shayne, precious and adorable, were only five and three when I became their stepmom. Paton, Lorenzo's baby with his ex-girlfriend, remained with her mother, so I never had an opportunity to welcome her into our family. My second marriage brought three more beautiful stepchildren into my life, Gillian, Jake and Luke. They arrived as teenagers full of life, schedules and soccer practice. These five very unique and different stepchildren will always remain in my deep, lasting memories. My third marriage brought one forever, brilliant being into my family, Aubrey Swander. She is the one I refuse to relinquish. She has become like a sister to my own daughter and quite possibly the sole representation of all the steps I've known and loved before. I think the most difficult part of becoming tremendously close to a family member is when they leave us. That's when we know the true depth of love and attachment, through loss. In other words, if you really want to know how much you love someone, just see how you feel when you're missing them. Aubrey was already an adult when her father and I divorced, so fortunately she was able to clearly communicate her own independent relationship with Ayden and myself. Besides, her dad, Doug, is a good guy who gets it.

Film sets always turn into a family. The director and producers are the parents, and the actors and crew are the children who quickly become first cousins. It's ridiculously incestuous and always a bit sad to say goodbye. Just like a regular family, it's difficult to leave once you've been brought into the fold. Like any environment where everyone is living, working and creating under the same roof, family should feel safe and comforting. It is the one thing we will truly fight for to protect. As a mother, there's nothing I wouldn't do for my child. As a daughter, sister, niece, aunt and cousin, my family will always be a priority. I am very lucky to be in a family that I would have chosen, if it hadn't already been chosen for me. I don't know that I believe we have the ability to choose our parents, as I don't have any recollection of that experience, although, if I did, I stuck the landing. I do know that I have the ability to choose my behavior, as I've been thrown into a few family mixers that I didn't anticipate.

When Lorenzo and I started dating in my senior year of high school, his father Fernando passed away from colon cancer. It took him very quickly, in a matter of weeks. It seemed he was diagnosed and before I had an opportunity to meet him, he was gone. Lorenzo did have a chance to tell him that he was dating Abby Dalton's daughter before he passed. Fernando had directed several episodes of *Falcon Crest*, so he knew my mom well. He smiled at Lorenzo and said, "Good stock." I figured he thought I came from a good family or that I'd become an excellent brood mare. Either way, I took it as a compliment, since I'm an avid horse lover and I do come from a wonderful family. Lorenzo was someone new in my life and I never really knew him without the loss of his father coloring his spirit. I think because I have been so personally colored and defined by death, it was a familiar place for me to comfort him and do my best to lift his spirits. My dear friend and Corvallis sister, Colleen, had just lost her father to the same type of cancer. Her dad was not just her entire world, he was also our beloved volleyball coach, so he was a mentor of mine too. His passing was tremendously painful for my friend, our class and our school, so I clearly knew what Lorenzo was experiencing.

Lorenzo asked me to accompany him to his dad's funeral. It was the first funeral I attended for someone I had never met. Funerals are not just a celebration of life for the lost loved one, they are a step toward closure for the living left behind. They are specifically for supporting the surviving family members and friends of the dearly departed. When you don't know what to say to someone who has lost someone close, just attend the funeral, it speaks volumes. It is not an easy task, but neither is grieving. Compassion is a universal emotion that says, "I feel for you, therefore I am here for you and I will be there for you in your time of need." This is really only shown by showing up. It's that simple and it involves effort. When I have stepped into someone else's pain and held their hand and given comfort, I have found great emotional rewards and formed lasting bonds. I do it daily with my own daughter and our relationship is amazing. Through my compassion she now shows me her compassion with our aging family members. She is not afraid to be a part of the circle of life. She realizes that our world isn't always unicorns and rainbows, although I do my best to keep the magic and beauty alive and well. There are tough times and there are even tougher times we have to navigate. If we don't have the love and support of family, blood related and adopted, the tough times can be unbearable. We might find ourselves so lonely and filled with despair that we could do something irreversibly tragic to ourselves, causing a horrific ripple effect with family and friends left behind.

I met Lorenzo's stepmom, Esther Williams, for the first time at Fernando's service. Esther and Fernando were married for twenty-two years and Lorenzo loved 'Essie' (the nickname he gave her as a child) very much. I could see why, as she was chock full of life, love and understanding. She was so gentle to him in this darkest hour of his life. Lorenzo worshipped his dad and he was lost without him. I was just seventeen and Lorenzo twenty-four, but we both instantly matured that day, as we became 'family' in the spirit world. Esther took me under her wing and she never let me go. Lorenzo and I would marry eight years later and divorce five years after that, but on that day, I felt a closeness that I still feel with him today. I felt his pain and I was there to comfort him through a tremendous loss. No matter what we ever went through after our marriage was over, our spiritual selves will never forget how we carried each other through loss.

For me, family is not just about the craziness of the holidays, although that's always a ton of fun. It's not just the birthdays, anniversaries, and weddings. Family truly kicks into high gear in pain, loss and suffering. It's the not-so-pretty ugly times that show us who we really are and what we're made of. That's when family matters the most. When we look around the room, through our tears, to see the brave hearts who showed up to help us through this. Granted, not everyone can always make it to a funeral due to something or other, but if you're in the locale and able, show up. Just be a generous family member in general. Be there for each other, unless of course it's a toxic situation that calls for personal boundaries.

Epic Fail ~ Missing a moment to give someone strength in their time of need.

Epic Save ~ Be there for someone when they are grieving, even if you never knew the departed.

Lesson Learned ~ Family is a gift that arrives in many packages.

"The most important thing in the world is family and love."
~ John Wooden

CHAPTER 19

~ **on divorce**

Thank God for it. It's sad and a total bummer but nothing is worse than staying in a relationship that compromises your safety and peace of mind. It's painful and much like a death but it's not death. Everyone gets to reassemble and move on, hopefully peacefully. Kids recover and have the chance to live with a more tranquil parent, who should be happier now that they're away from the parent with whom they are no longer commingling. It's most definitely a loss and I know about it very well, and I also know that people can move on and will recover if they do the necessary steps. Civility and harmony should be the motive. It was already bad enough, don't continue to resent and hate the person as, "Resentment is like drinking poison and waiting for the other person to die." Thank you, Carrie Fisher, for that pearl of wisdom. She knew about divorce too.

My parents split up when I was in first grade. They were apart for four years. My dad dated a different chick every month. My brothers and I lovingly remember that time as, 'Bitch of the Month Club.' My mom was in a few 'relationships' with newfound 'family members.' We all of a sudden had a new 'Uncle' John and then a new 'Uncle' Jack. Why are you sleeping with an uncle, mom? Seems weird.

There was one poor dude that she brought up to Mammoth with me and my brothers for the weekend. We had just sat down in the very crowded cafeteria in the main lodge, where my mom was deflecting questions about my dad from the locals. I was feeling the altitude and the weirdness of being up in Mammoth without my 'ski patrol dad' and desperately trying to ignore my mom who was all goo-goo eyes with lover boy. It made me want to hurl, which I did, all over 'Uncle Cliff's' scrambled eggs, bacon and toast. Some even jumped into his coffee. Who wants to go skiing?

That's what divorce feels like. It's like barfing in public. Everyone feels so sorry for you and they give you that sad, "Oh, no..." combined with a back the fuck up face. Nobody who was ever really in love and honestly walked down the aisle and committed their heart to somebody, ever wants to see that dream die, but sometimes it does, and a part of you dies with it. It's awful. Don't let it kill you though, especially if you have kids. They need you to keep your act together.

My parents were a great example of a great divorce. Their divorce was so spot on, they ended up getting back together after four years of being kind to each other. I'm pretty sure they were still enjoying the occasional conjugal visit and they never poisoned the well by saying horrible stuff about each other to us kids. The point is, they remained involved in life and kept their revenge body in shape, and their personal swords of resentment sheathed. Granted they looked like Jon Hamm and January Jones from *Mad Men,* thirty something, successful and extraordinarily good looking. Thankfully, they had the emotional clarity to not be wicked with each other or use us children as pawns.

Once my dad started getting somewhat kinda maybe serious with a woman named *'Jan-ice'* (that's how my mom said it) my mom decided to stop sleeping with 'family members' and locked horns with dad again. They never actually signed their divorce papers, so they continue to count those missing years as part of their anniversary total. They call it, 'time-off for bad behavior'. They got back together and never looked back. They don't talk about those years or bring them up as firearms in arguments. It's just been forward momentum ever since they reunited. It was so long ago, it's almost like it never happened. I believe they needed that breakup to realize how important they are to each other. They are a very rare breed. My dad says the hardest part of forgiving is forgetting. So when I ask him what the hardest parts were to forget, he always says, "I can't remember." That guy... he's something else.

I know that if I had allowed my first marriage to break me, I wouldn't have had an open heart for love to come around the second and third time. I'm honestly cracking up at how crazy that sounds, but love does keep coming around. Think of it this way, if you were brave enough to do it once, why wouldn't you be brave enough to do it again? Love is like jumping off a cliff, but it's not really jumping off a cliff. It's an emotional risk that the body can recover from as long as you put loving, good things in its wake when it's slipping away, dead and gone. Like throw a party for God's sakes. You're going to be rid of that person, so let peace begin. This is a good time for the sound of trumpets and fanfare.

We have memorial services for our dearly departed. I believe it gives us a chance to reconnect with relationships that bring us back to the person we lost. Billions are spent annually worldwide on marriage ceremonies to celebrate love. Why is there not a ceremony or a service, other than court, to dissolve a marriage? A 'Dissolve the Knot' ceremony. I am hereby declaring a new Hallmark Holiday - Divorce Day! I'm thinking that it should be on the Throwback Thursday before Valentine's Day. Throw back as in, 'catch and release'. It's a day to celebrate releasing your partner with love and good riddance! Have a gathering of your old wedding party and celebrate the wonderful age-old question of, "Who are you going to side with?" Have a day to toast your 'significant other' right out the door. Have one good hooray for the good 'ol days. Then every Divorce Day after that you can send your ex a card letting them know you're fine with, "Don't worry about me, I'm still so glad we're apart!" and "I really don't miss you at all." Think of how good it will feel to keep sending and receiving a note of "Still not loving you anymore, and I'm still okay with it!" with sparkles and butterflies. I really hope Hallmark is getting all this. I think if you're planning to have a pre-nup, there should also be money set aside for a Dissolve the Knot shindig. I think a clam bake at the beach would be perfect. It's fun, it's outside and you never know, you just might meet someone. And whatever you do, stay positive, it's the most attractive quality a person can have.

Epic Fail ~ Thinking you'll never find love again. We are already love.

Epic Save ~ Pick yourself up, dust yourself off and continue to put one foot in front of the other.

Lesson Learned ~ If there's a window for a way out and you're not feeling loved, respected or safe, use it. Save yourself, no one else will.

"Some people think that it's holding on that makes one strong; sometimes it's letting go.
      ~ Unknown

CHAPTER 20

~ **on marriage**

I've done it three times. Once should've been enough, but there's no quit in me. I still consider myself mostly lucky in love, since I've had more than my fair share. I do believe in marriage, even though my three attempts ended up in divorce, I still thoroughly believe in the concept of making a commitment to someone and seeing that through. I've been witness to several good marriages that continue to thrive. Even my own parents who were happily married for ten years, split for four years, only to reconcile and are still together celebrating fifty-nine years of wedded bliss. They are still so in love with each other, it's a marvel to encounter.

One of my favorite lines about marriage comes from a Ricky Gervais film, *The Invention of Lying*. This movie is brilliant in its concept where everyone in the film is brutally honest due to the fact that lying has not yet been invented. The moment of truth about marriage takes place between Rob Lowe and Jennifer Garner at the altar. The priest gently inquires, "Do you promise to love, honor, and respect each other as long as you both feel like it?" They look lovingly at each other, smile and shrug, "I guess." Now that's an honest answer in which we all can relate. As long as I feel like it and you don't do something horribly dastardly to me, I'll stick by you. *Unless* you cheat on me or become a drunk or a drug addict or you have such a full blown midlife crisis that you end up pushing me out of your life, sure I'd love to stay with you. We can definitely have a happily ever after, as long as it's not at the expense of my own personal sanity, safety and core values.

When my third marriage rolled around to Doug Swander, I was absolutely freaked by having to write my own vows. I sat on having to complete that task for so long, I put the pro in procrastination. When I finally drank enough wine the night before, I grabbed a pen and cut loose with, "What can I say that I haven't said before?" And I really meant it. I was at such a loss of how to rephrase the notion of, "I will love you. And only you. Forever." It felt so unrealistic and farfetched. I went for it anyway and decided that, "Yes I can love one person at a time" and "No, I don't need to drag the last marriage, or two, into this one."

Here's the truth, people change. We are constantly changing from the moment we are born to the end of our demise. We learn, we live, we fail, we get back up again. The seasons and the weather are constantly changing, and we are right there with them. We evolve like the planet and it's just a mere blip of time we're allowed to enjoy this place. We can't expect someone to stay the same or feel the same forever. It's humanly and evolutionary impossible. We are not allowed to not change. Father time marches heavily across all of our faces and every experience leaves an imprint. We can pretend to be the same person day after day, but we're not. I can carry the same attributes but even though I'm a mostly somewhat positive person, I'm not the same fool hearty kid I was at eighteen, nor do I look like her. I've already experienced enough disappointment and hard knocks to bring my level of awareness up and what I've learned is, marriage is a major responsibility. The toughest part is finding someone who grows with you at a similar rate who simultaneously doesn't bug the shit out of you. I've done my futile best in the picking department and so far, fallen short. Does that make me a failure at marriage or just someone who keeps their heart open to love and experience? I'd say the latter because I don't want to speak badly about myself.

My dad is a collector of quotes and he displays them under a plastic sheet that covers the cherry wood on his desk. He keeps photos and uplifting messages under this piece of plastic to remind him of how much he loves his life and family, as he's writing out checks to pay for everything. Out of all of his cherished quotes, this one's my favorite, "Good judgment comes from experience. Experience comes from bad judgment." Is that the best or what? It just puts everything into an open, positive perspective. The good, the bad and the ugly are simply a whitewash of steppingstones into something to repeat or not repeat.

I truly admire my dad and how he can take any situation and shed a life force light on it. He truly finds God and levity to any given moment. He is a one of a kind guy and I pray to God and Saint Anthony to find that special someone who can be just as fun, funny, athletic, successful and loyal as he is. He has great faith in knowing, "Things work out best, when you make the best of the way things work out." As long you stay open to finding a solution, you will. He has another killer quote under that plastic liner that reads, "I know there's a solution to my problem, the problem is, I haven't found it yet." The good news is, there's a solution to every problem, so simply vow to keep looking. Marriages that stay together are those who have that kind of mindset. Finding solutions together and growing is a wonderful thing and yet, sometimes the solution to the problem is to not stay married and that is survivable too.

Epic Fail ~ Expecting someone to never change.

Epic Save ~ Embracing growth, regardless of growing pains.

Lesson Learned ~ We either change and grow together or we change and grow apart.

"A successful marriage requires falling in love many times, always with the same person."
     ~ Mignon McLaughlin

CHAPTER 21

~ **on writing**

Being able to sit down and write without getting distracted is a luxury. It usually happens in the early morning, before the distractions have had a chance to wake up. Yesterday, I vocalized my commitment to writing and that I will stay on track to artistic and creative endeavors, regardless of how many stresses and distractions in my life, for I will not let them win. Well, sometimes they win, like yesterday.

I had my computer set up, which is basically an invitation to all my social sites and email. By the way, back in the Hemingway days, writers didn't have that problem or temptation with typewriters. They sat down and they typed. Simply pulled out a sheet of paper, lifted the bar, rolled it in and had some proof at the end of their session that they wrote something to be marked up with a pencil to be retyped by lamplight at midnight. Aah, the good old days, that I don't remember, or was a part of. Today is more of a hyper focus. Turn off your phone, including the vibrator part and just do it. You know, just lock yourself away from the world, so you can write about the world.

If I'm lucky, and I've stayed on budget, I have my lovely housekeeper, Sandra, show up once a month to help me clean. Sometimes she brings her very shy and super sweet little girl, Karla, who at five had never said a word to me. I was never sure if she spoke English or Spanish or if she was just too terrified to speak at all. I always said 'hello' and 'so nice to see you' type dialogue and out of politeness she would nod, like most people do who are too afraid to speak. Sandra and Karla were both at my house on 'The day I was going to write'. I immediately set up Karla with a video in the den to keep her busy, as I quickly got on the phone to talk about how I was going to write to my dear friend, Miranda Frederick, who I speak to a cool dozen or so times a day about all the things we do every day that keep us from writing.

I joyfully announced, "Today I am going to write."

"Awesome! You go girl!" Miranda cheer leaded.

We have been besties for longer than most and our ability to continually lift each other up through the years is a beautiful habit.

"So, I'll call ya later," I reassured as I hung up, went into the house and announced to Sandra and the rest of the Universe, "I will be in my studio. Writing."

At that moment, from behind me, I heard this teeny, tiny little voice, a dead ringer for Cindy LooWho from Who-ville say, "Can I come?" I looked around and nearly fell over. Did that adorable little mute angel child just say something?

"You want to go out in the studio with me? And write?" I asked, with the hopes of her not really wanting to.

She nodded.

"I guess there's lots of toys out there for you to play with," I said with the hopes of her having imagination skills that would keep her occupied with little or no help from my improv skills.

190

She nodded like a bobble-head, joyfully displaying her effervescent five-year-old gap-toothed grin. "O-kaaayyy," heavy sigh, while spinning out a professional actor smile, "let's go then." She took me by the hand and there went my writing session.

The next two hours were spent pushing her on the horse swing. Setting up the hammock and swinging her in that for a blissful five minutes. Playing with all of my daughter's two hundred and thirty-one horse toys. Cutting up watermelon. Loading up their car with furniture my daughter has outgrown, starting with Ayden's old desk that Karla was going to use for writing. During this fabulous free time in life, while my house was being lovingly cleaned by her mom, Karla told me many stories about her very full, young life. She told me all about the beautiful new headband and new shoes her mommy recently bought for her on a trip to Mexico. She told me about falling out of a hammock when she was two and it was the first time she tasted "blood." I noticed every time she said the word 'blood', her little tinkly voice would drop to a lowering boom. The word 'blood' actually changed the pitch of her voice. We talked about doggies, rabbits, butterflies and shooting stars. We ate watermelon in the shade and took some photos with her new furniture. She wanted my daughter to see how happy she was to be receiving these worthy items. We did everything but write. It was glorious.

By the end of the visit, she took me by the hand and said with the tiniest voice that could

mimic the first drops of gentle rain on a tin roof, "It would be okay if you wanted to baby-sit me sometime because you talk to me. And my mommy could call you and you could tell her that I'm okay and having a good time."
Someone please hand me a tissue.

The beauty of announcing your plans is that it gives God a chance to say, "Yeah, sure. Riiiight." As a righter of wrongs and writer of life, I know that I need to be available to the whims and winds in the willows. I'm so grateful my emotional door was open that day to a poetic two hours of this precious being who finally opened up to me, right when I was ready to shut the studio door. Karla speaks perfect English and unlike me, also speaks perfect Spanish. I do believe, like me, she will remember the day she received her first desk. Who knows, maybe she will be a writer one day too.

Epic Fail ~ Announcing, "I'm headed off to write!" Just do it, don't say anything.

Epic Save ~ Staying flexible to life and open to priceless moments.

Lesson Learned ~ Life is what happens when you're busy making plans.

"Start writing no matter what. The water does not flow until the faucet is turned on."
~ Louis L'Amour

CHAPTER 22

~ **on baseball**

I am a diehard Dodger fan and I love baseball. There are several times throughout any given day, I wonder, "What are the Dodgers doing? Are they training, getting a massage or taking a shower?" I dream in Dodger blue and I watch Dodger Access about every day. I love the players, coaches, announcers and the entire organization. There's no better place to cast your cares aside than Dodger Stadium, the second happiest place on earth. (A polite nod to Mammoth Mountain and Disneyland)

I've been lucky enough to attend Dodger games since I was a kid. My dad had season tickets and they are some of the best memories I have with my brothers and my dad, learning about the intricacies of the game and the revolving door of players. I am now aware of the power of the game and its ability to take you out of your own personal drama. There is something about baseball that lifts me to a place of joy that I wouldn't have ex-perienced if I had skipped the game. It truly is my most favorite pastime. In the off-season I watch and study old games, just like the players and coaches. I couldn't possibly be more invested in a team. They are *my* Dodgers and I bleed Pantone 294.

Luck seems to follow me around Dodger Stadium. I have met several famous actors, artists, musicians but there is nothing more astonishing to me than an athlete in their prime. I have had the great pleasure of meeting a few of them and I'm always in awe. The kind of discipline and talent it takes to make it into the Major Leagues is phenomenal. They make it look easy, but I know that it's one of the most difficult on the planet. There are so many factors involved, it's amazing anyone gets in. It's like trying to make a movie in Hollywood. The difficulty is mind-boggling and then once it's done, trying to get everyone to see it is immense. Perseverance, hard work and timing are huge components but even then, you have to stay healthy, inspired and enthusiastic during the longest playing season of any other sport. Baseball season is a marathon for the players and the fans. It's a grueling give-all-you-got experience, then wake up and do it again the next day. It's a team sport that relies heavily on individual skill and camaraderie. I love that. Everyone has a special talent for a specific spot, and they all depend on each other as a working machine. Every single player is a necessity to the finished product. I guess it reminds me of a film set where you depend on every person to help create the finished product. You can't be an actor without a crew. Even if you're doing a one-person show, you still need someone to work lights and sound. Baseball is not a solo act and players that don't get that fact usually get traded.

My dad had reserved seats in the first level, along the first base line. I remember them to this day: Aisle 20, Row R, seats 1, 2, 3, 4. With the emerald green grass before us and the wafting scent of hot dogs, salted peanuts, and beer, the scene was perfectly set for our beloved, Vin Scully, to enthusiastically announce from his perch, "It's time - for Dodger - baseball!" No matter what happened in your week or month or year, in that moment you belonged to the club, to the view and to our boys in blue. I learned to love baseball in those seats. I especially loved being able to look up to the left to see Vin Scully, joyfully commentating away. When we weren't at the game, we would faithfully tune him in on the radio. Like many, I've been listening to his brilliant play-by-play, stats and stories all my life. I've never heard him run out of something to say with his captivating, spirited delivery. His consistent voice has thoroughly deepened my love for the game and **our** team, The Los Angeles Dodgers.

I've been pretty lucky in my life, but one particular Dodger game against the Colorado Rockies made all else pale. On September 15, 2015, my ab-fab friend, Miranda, invited me and two of our other fabulous friends, Kristanna and Lisa, to her extraordinarily excellent seats along the third base line: front row, just to the left of the Dodger dugout. These seats are compliments of Miranda's life partner Paul, and his brother Craig. If I thought the seats growing up were good, Miranda's seats are rock star. We tend to get a lot of action in those seats, including the occasional tossed ball from a player or coach. I know that every potential at bat could be a probable screamer into someone's skull, so I was keenly adamant about all of us paying close attention to every pitch. Especially the lefties.

During our pre-game pow-wow, we discussed that if a pop-up foul came close, we really wanted Justin Turner to catch it. None of us were looking to be that random, stupid idiot on National TV that disrupts a potential out for our guys. We agreed that we would exhibit good sportsmanship and catch a player, not the ball. Unless, of course, the ball happened to come right for us, and for that, I would have my mitt, which I promptly left in the car. I was pretty upset about that because I had promised my younger brother, Johnny, that if I caught a ball, it would be his. Pretty ballsy, I know, but I've had a few thrown my way. I attempted to leave the stadium to get my mitt, but once you're in, there's no leaving and coming back. Miranda comforted me by cooing, "Just catch it in your hat, buddy, you've done it before." She always knows what to say.

We/I like to get to our seats early so we can watch our Dodgers warm up and possibly get a ball signed. Another amazing perk of Miranda's seats is the chance to see the athlete's up close. More often than not, a Dodger or two will sign for a brief moment before the game. This particular lucky day, Corey Seager signed our balls. Dodger McDreamy extraordinaire. What an incredible player and ridiculously gorgeous young man. Wow. Way to go God, high five and thank you Universe, Corey signed my ball that day. I gave that ball to my older brother, Matt, for Christmas. Major killer sister points. As Corey signed the ball, I was able to tell him how happy we were to have him on the Dodgers and congratulated him on his recent first solo home run. And you know what he said? "Thank you." Swoon. Talent and class. I was pretty much floating for the next 4 innings.

Somewhere in there a foul ball came dangerously close to us and Justin Turner almost landed in our lap. Swoon again, and oh yeah, Justin for President!! I'm with Hunny on that. Shortly after, another foul ball was hit, and Antonio Sabato Jr. caught it. Triple swoon. Antonio is friends with Kristanna and they had already said hello, so we waved and that was also very cool. And then it started to rain, and I mean a weird downpour, in LA, at Dodger Stadium. Really, it did. Everyone was like, "Whaaaat the fuuu...?" A large part of the crowd instantly ran up the steps for shelter. Typical LA moment. "No way! It's raining! What do we do? Run!! Run for your lives!" And I was all, "If the guys are on the field and they're still playing, then us girls are still in these seats." We were drenched, it was awesome! We were lovin' it. And then it happened...

Brett Anderson was pitching. Carlos Gonzalez was at bat. I'll let Vin Scully take it from here. "... and he flares one off third. 0 and 1 the count. And a nice catch down there, aah, the old hat trick. Haha, that's great. Yes indeed, you deserve a curtain call."

So yes, I caught a ball, in my hat, in front of my gal pals at Dodger Stadium, with the one and only Vin Scully commentating over one of my greatest dreams come true. After reviewing the footage, a few thousand times, I've noticed that I'm instantly stunned that I caught the ball and I immediately look to Justin to make sure I hadn't messed up a play. JT gave me a cool thumbs up, to which I casually nodded and then naturally, I looked up to the right to Vinny, hoping he saw that, which apparently, he did. The fantasy of catching a foul ball and having Vin Scully commentating over it is a Dodger fan dream moment I'm absolutely sure many people have had. The thrill of it actually happening is something I absolutely love to share. Vinny's pure joy in watching me enjoy the moment is what I believe makes us all fall in love with him over and over again. He's infinitely in the moment and as welcoming as rain on a hot, end of summer night.

The best part of having a 'Vin Scully Moment' is that I've been able to hear about other Vin Scully Moments from family and friends. My dad has a terrific Lakeside Golf story involving Vin and Dick Whittinghill, another one of the great radio personalties of all time. They were playing a round of golf and my dad, like most golfers, is in a constant state of improving his game. That day he was carrying a "Golf Tips from Ken Venturi" that he routinely took out of his Ken Venturi shirt pocket as they approached the sixteenth green.
"What do you keep pulling out of your pocket, Jack?" Vin queried.
"Golf tips from Ken Venturi," my dad confidently answered.

Well that's all it took to get a three to four minute monologue of Vin's most professional golf commentating performances of all time.

"Here he comes, ladies and gentlemen, Jack Smith, at the eighteenth green, at the U.S. Open. This is it folks, this is for all the money. He's lining up his putt. He's lining it up... but wait, what's that there, that he's pulling out of his pocket? Is it, wait, I can't quite see it, maybe we can a get a little closer... Aah, yes, the old shirt pocket trick. Golf Tips from Ken Venturi. Good thinking, Jack!"

My dad was laughing so hard, he could barely blurt out, "It came with the shirt!"

Golf is not necessarily a team sport but it sure is fun when you have an engaged audience.

My mom has a great story about Vin Scully that starts with her screaming to my dad, "Pull off the road, I need some Cracker Jack!" She was pregnant with me and experiencing a massive Cracker Jack craving while listening to Vinny commentating on the radio. Maybe that's where it all started.

I even had the great opportunity to share my foul ball catch to former Dodger catcher, Rick Dempsey. Rick caught the final ball, on the final game, of our last World Series win in 1988. My foul ball footage has been a fantastic ice breaker. My own catch sparked Rick into telling me how he willed himself onto the Dodger team back in the day. Truly an amazing story about vocalizing your vision. I hope he writes a book about it one day.

I've shown my foul ball catch to so many people, not only because of the fun catch but because one of my heroes is doing the voice over. As a Dodger fan, who truly loves the game, this has been a great thrill of my life. I'm writing this story as a humble thank you to Vin Scully, for all that you do, all that you've done and your continued legacy to one of the greatest teams on the planet, our Los Angeles Dodgers. WE love you Vinny. YOU deserve a curtain call. Btw, that September 15, 2015 game was timeless. It went on for 16 innings. Vin commentated the whole thing. Talk about a hat trick.

Epic Fail ~ Leaving my mitt in the car.

Epic Save ~ Catching a ball in my hat.

Lesson Learned ~ Never take your eye off the ball.

"Love is the most important thing in the world, but baseball is pretty good too."
        ~ Yogi Berra

CHAPTER 23

~ on looking up

When we are children we spend so much time looking up, mostly because we are little and largely because of the wonder of the world. The magnitude of the sky, the stars, the trees and life around us makes discovery immense. We look up to see birds, planes, possibly a man in a cape or more likely a drone. The planet is teaming with life and things dancing around us, way more than the eye can see or the brain can fathom. It's no wonder someone wanted to make sure that we could have the whole world in our hands, just like God.

I remember the wonderful conversations of yore when great debates were held and laughs were shared over who were the stars of The Magnificent Seven, or can you name The Seven Dwarfs or The Seven Wonders of the World. Aah, the days when nobody had the answer. It was fun. Now everyone with a smart phone is a theorist, authority and conversation killer because they got the answer to the random conversation starter first, only to kill the inspiration to communicate with the fast answer. The phone might help you get to your destination and allow you to take a photo or video, but for the love of God, put your phone away the minute you arrive to your destination with someone. It is so rude to constantly check your phone or text while spending time with someone, especially your kids. They need your attention and your face looking at theirs. Your eyes looking into their eyes. It's an imprint of connection that will be lost forever once they are launched into the world. Unless they already have their own phone, which should be encouraged to be put away as often as possible.

We have a responsibility to engage and be interested in people that we love and care for. We also have a responsibility to be safe while driving, flying and basic street walking. There is a huge sudden rise in pedestrian deaths. It's a simple theory, when you're looking down, you are not seeing what's going on around you. People are walking into fountains, street poles and cars making sharp turns while texting with earbuds in and head down.

The neck was made to support the head, which is the heaviest part of the human anatomy, besides your ass. The head can weigh up to fifteen or twenty pounds. I am a springboard diver and I learned that by just turning my head a certain way in midair, my body will follow into a flip or turn or inverted spiral spin, just from my head movement. So, I've been consciously using my head for a while now and in my consciousness, I am looking up more often. I know how my neck and shoulders ache from too much work at my computer or looking down at my phone. I'm not fond of the numbness and headache that follow, so I take breaks and look up. We can't fight the tsunami of technology; it's already here like an invading alien on the planet. Its tentacles have clearly gotten ahold of everyone. We do have the power and control to set it down and make an effort to look up when we're walking, talking and meeting someone for breakfast, lunch or dinner.

One day, while driving on Wilshire Boulevard through Beverly Hills, I noticed a nicely dressed guy in a suit walking briskly on the sidewalk. He had the usual flare of a pedestrian with earbuds in, cell phone in hand and head down while texting. A Type A personality, totally and completely unaware to the world around him, lost in his bubble of self-important bliss.

"That tool is going to walk right into the alley, without looking up and get creamed by a truck," I said out loud to no one.

Sure enough, he stepped right into a blind alley driveway while a large, white, laundry truck slammed on its tired brakes.

It was a flash of a moment while I screamed, "Mother of God!"

The guy in the suit kept walking, head down, still texting, oblivious. The two employees in the truck looked at each other like they just soiled themselves. Hopefully, they might have some clean shorts in the back of their 'Fresh Linen' laundry truck.

I'm purposely doing my best to keep the phone away every time I'm out with my daughter. I make the effort to keep the conversation lively and engaged. I ask questions, we share stories, discuss ideas and plans. I think it's important to look like you are having the time of your life, because we are, and before we know it, even without checking who just texted, our time could be gone. I'm doing my part to bring conversation back to the table and keep the phones under it. An occasional selfie is fine if the timing and light are right, otherwise just keep a lookout for Superman.

Epic Fail ~ Missing the moment of truth by searching for answers on a phone.

Epic Save ~ Placing electronics firmly down for earth and face time.

Lesson Learned ~ Look both ways before crossing the street and no texting while walking, driving or sharing a meal.

"It's easy to be ignorant but it's very intricate to be aware."
　　　　~Shahrukh Khan

CHAPTER 24

~ **on jealousy**

I believe jealousy is born from insecurity. When we are thoroughly comfortable in our skin and feel we have accomplished a substantial amount and want others to succeed as well, it's virtually impossible to feel jealous of someone else. Unfortunately, there will always be those who have not found their life's fulfillment, so they find ways to find fault with those who have. There might be times when you think you've conquered the world, only to find out that your best friend might be conquering the world a bit better or on a bigger scale and making more money and getting the job you wish was yours. How do you support them? Or do you find a way to bring in some insecurity to mess with their game? I've experienced both sides of the fence on this issue. I've been the source of other people's jealousy and I've been jealous. It's the worst feeling and very hard to shake.

I was thirty-seven and feeling the loss of my second marriage, the cold shoulder of the business and living in a small apartment. I had given up my home in Burbank Rancho with two horses in the backyard and two cars in the garage. I went from having a lot, to having a lot less. My life felt like it was in a storage space and I was in a holding pattern. It was a ton of fall out after another huge war that was waged on my heart and my plans for the future were once again annihilated. I couldn't fathom that I was alone again and the family that I had loved and cared for was ripped out of my life, never to be together again. I was numb, until my dear friend, Kristanna Loken, my doppelgänger minus fifteen years, was going up for the role of a lifetime to play the female cyborg in *Terminator 3*.

I met Kristanna in Orlando, Florida when I was cast to play her mentor in the TV series, *Mortal Combat*. I was there for two weeks for the two-part finale of their first and only season. I was instantly impressed with Kristanna's friendliness and her work ethic. She was nineteen at the time and I was thirty-four, yet we shared so much in common, a love of family, acting and horses. We became instant friends. When we hugged each other for the first time, it was like hugging myself. We are almost the same height and weight; she might have half an inch on me. We have the same interests and the same sunny outlook. She is so naturally beautiful and one of the most photogenic people I've ever met. Above all, she is a very hard worker and when she commits to something, she truly gives her best efforts. I have deep respect and admiration for people who have tremendous discipline. Like an athlete, a performer needs to train and condition themselves for the long haul and Kristanna is a consummate professional when it comes to the pacing of a performance. After *Mortal Combat* wrapped, Kristanna moved to Studio City and we went on a great Hawaiian horseback adventure where we rode every day in the rain and the sun, swapping stories and creating a bond that would last for life. I knew that I would never be jealous of her because a. she was much younger than me and we would never be up for the same parts and b. she had become like the little sister I had always yearned for and I felt instantly protective. Until she was cast in the role that would change her career.

The auditioning process for *T3* was like the Marathon at the Olympics. Kristanna went back so many times, it was almost cruel. They saw everyone in town for the role, except me, and it went beyond the room to breakfast meetings and phone calls and just when she thought she could endure the fact that it might not happen, she got the part. She got the phone call when we were out on the trail, riding in Griffith Park. She was riding our friend Annie's horse, Sassy, and I was on my horse, Calamity Jane. It was an ecstatic moment on a cell phone, and I could feel the little seed of jealousy form. It was wonderful and awful at the same time. Here was my dear friend who I had been rooting on and cheerleading and now she won the game, and my pompoms were beginning to drop. Thank God I was on my own horse to give me strength. It was a surge of joy for her and a surge of, 'What's happening to my life?' for me. She was on the phone fielding calls of congratulations for the rest of the ride. I was watching her existence instantly change and drift away on a cloud to Never-Never Land while I was stuck in reality on Survivor Island. What a beach.

I remember the knot in my stomach was growing and I felt horrible for having the feeling. I would wake up and wonder what kind of wonderful things were being planned for her and how she would be treated now by everyone. She would be a movie star diminishing all the other little TV performers like myself. She would be traveling more and getting more roles. I knew the process very well; I just didn't know I would have such a front row center seat to someone else's fame. It was a shock and even though I was thoroughly ecstatic for her, it was too close to home on the kind of scenario I had envisioned for myself one day. I didn't know that a life-changing role could land so close and not be happening to me. On top of it, we were paying the same amount on rent, except she had a two-bedroom house with a yard and a dog. I had substantially less space with no yard, no dog and no amazing job to go to every day. The jealousy was alive and kicking in my belly and I had to get it out. It was pretty bad, and I was ashamed to be having this daily emotion. It was a new view and I hated it. My beautiful friend was getting ready to embark on the biggest challenge of her life and I wanted to be there for her emotionally and spiritually. It had become the biggest challenge of my life as well, but I couldn't share it with anyone, except God, to whom I prayed for a calling.

I had just gotten out of the shower and was looking at my dripping wet naked form in the mirror thinking, "Why didn't I get a callback for that Viagra spot?" And then the phone rang. It was Kristanna. Yay. She was obviously excited about something else that was 'amazing' and couldn't wait to share it with the one person who knew what she was going through and could lend an ear and validate how terrific everything was for her. Yippee. She asked me how I was doing, and I said I was just admiring myself in the mirror and thinking how similar we are. It was true but it was more like

'I'm still in great shape, why am I not getting called?'

Kristanna replied, "That's why I'm calling you. They're casting my stand-in and I immediately thought of you."

Talk about a huge helping of humble pie right in the kisser. Wow. So, this is what God in action looks like? Thank you, thank you very much.

"Would you do it?" she asked, ripping to bits the silence that was consuming me.

It was the moment of truth unlike anything else I've experienced in my career.

"For you, yes, I would do anything," I said as the knot in my stomach instantly went away. It was like giving birth; once the baby is in your arms, you have no memory of the pain or any interest in reliving it. You now have the joy in your arms, and nothing can touch that feeling.

"Awesome buddy!! You're going to have to audition but I'll be with you all the way," she cheerfully said. "Can you come down today?"

"I'm on my way," I chirped, all of a sudden light as a feather.

Hey, where did the bag of jealousy go that I've been carrying for a month? It had instantly vanished and now I was on my way to fight for my spot on the squad. I knew it was not going to be easy playing 'second team' as I had always been the actor on set, never a crew member or a stand-in, but it was going to be a hell of a lot easier than not being on set and wondering what my friend was experiencing every long ass day of the six month shoot.

I got the job and we worked side by side again for one of the greatest memories of our lives. We shared her joyful experience together and I shared my gratitude for bringing me on board. It was a great film and she did a tremendous job. Her life changed and so did mine. I learned a lot from every angle of that set and it was rich with every opportunity to learn from the best of the best.

I declined a credit on the film, as the credit was Kristanna's, and I was more than happy to help. If there was an award for Best Stand-In, I'm sure I would have received a nomination and no surprise, my speech is prepared.

Epic Fail ~ Thinking that I'm above being jealous.

Epic Save ~ Reaching out to help someone who seems to have it all.

Lesson Learned ~ Acknowledging a feeling by facing it head on.

"He that is jealous, is not in love."
　　　～ Saint Augustine

CHAPTER 25

~ on change

Anyone who says 'some things never change' is absolutely right. The sun will continue to rise and time marches on. There will be nothing changing about that. However, because time is the only thing nobody can control, we are in constant change because of that simple fact. Every day we are closer to the end. Even though we have plans and ideas and things in the works, anything can happen to change those intentions. There have been wonderful times where I've chased the dragon of time and tried to recreate a moment, only to wind up short from my attempt. You can't repeat what has been done before, it's near impossible, as it will be a different moment. The day, weather, mood, and the person you're with, has had some growth, minute or magnificent, that has changed everything to be different. Embrace it, as that concept is something that will not change.

I remember the most common phrase at the end of every school year in my yearbook signing was, "Have a great summer and don't ever change." That is just pure lame advice. Number one, I always grew at least two inches every summer since I was swimming and out in the sun and growing like a weed on Chernobyl. I would come back to school in the fall a good foot taller than all the boys, every year. So I'm sorry, but I've changed, and I still had a remarkably great summer.

The biggest summer of change was when I grew boobs. That was like having a brand-new bike every day for a year. All of a sudden I held a new super power, like Thor's hammer. When the braces came off and my Dorothy Hamill cut grew out, I was all of a sudden a tall blonde with lots of attention from a very sudden change. The awkward tween had been shed and the new blossoming into a young rosebud was super weird and exciting. I was mostly a tomboy with two brothers who I tried to keep up with and the thought of their friends ever finding me attractive was new territory. My breasts got so big for my frame that I eventually decided to change that when I was twenty-three and got a breast reduction. God did his best, but the heaviness and constant attention drawn to my chest felt like an even bigger weight than the magnitude of fun pillows that was resting there. I am a big supporter of changing something that you don't enjoy about yourself. It takes courage and a good support system, so be sure to welcome both.

The seasons change and we change with them. Our wardrobe, our skin, our hair color, all goes a little paler and dormant in the winter. It lightens and brightens in the Spring, when we visit the hairdresser and buy a fresh pair of sandals. It's a substantial cleanse to depart with all the tired, pilled and moth-eaten sweaters and clothes we've grown out of or are just plain sick of wearing. We get rid of the old and bring in the new. Just like a snake shedding its skin, we do the same. There is no way on earth that we ever stay the same. There is a famous author, Marie Kondo, who is a major mogul on organizing. She says the best way to release anything in your life is to ask yourself one simple question, "Does this bring me Joy?" If yes, you keep, if no, you give away. Genius. No wonder she's a millionaire.

We move to new homes, states, countries. We meet new friends, release some old ones and we change. We change our ideas, our loyalties, our politics, religion - even gender for some very courageous people. Sure, some things haven't changed, because we don't have the capacity to cure all disease or fix every frustrating political problem, yet. However, the way we care for and treat each other definitely changes.

I have one character trait that I'm pretty sure will stay with me for life: compassion. I believe compassion to be my true essence that motivates me to do many things. Compassion is the great emotional quality that helps me realize that I'm not helpless, as long as I care. Caring to the point of compassion will give me the impetuous to say or do the right thing to help someone in need, including myself. Compassion can be a gentle smile to someone who looks lonely, or being helpful to someone who has fallen down.

I don't think I will ever change the way I feel when I see a parent being mean to their kid. That is something I wish I could change but I can't. I can call the cops or videotape and get involved, but it's not always a good idea. I wish I could change terrorists and the lack of value for human life from vexed and crazy people who carry century old resentments that drive them to do horrific things to innocent people. I wish I could change the fact that my parents are getting older and in pain from tired joints, achy backs and memory loss. But who am I to stop change? The only thing I can change about things that are defeating, is myself. I can take a break and turn off the news, pray, meditate and do my best to help the ones I love and get involved with something that lightens the load of being powerless.

I can also move my location, which is a lot of work, but worth it if the change brings peace and a better outlook. We are born, we live, we learn, we grow, we change and then we're gone. It's what we choose to put in-between the space of all that time that is going to make a difference to ourselves, and those around us. The one thing we can change daily, besides our underwear, is our perception. I believe there is always time for a change. In this brief moment, a change has already occurred.

Epic Fail ~ Wishing that everything stays the same.

Epic Save ~ Growing with ourselves and encouraging our changes.

Lesson Learned ~ Sometimes we have to be very brave to make a change and have impenetrable faith that it will be better on the other side if we take that leap.

"If you don't like something, change it, if you can't change it, change your attitude."
    ~ Maya Angelou

CHAPTER 26

~ **on aging**

If there's nothing more interesting than watching an actor's mind at work, there's nothing more fascinating than watching time march across an actors face. We become so accustomed to seeing someone in their prime, or when they began their career, it's a shock when we see that they are no longer what they used to be. Athletes, actors, artists, musicians and basically all humans, are mostly looking and feeling their best in their early twenties and thirties, sometimes forties, (fifties if you're JLO) after that it becomes a who's who of what's dat? The old ageism industry reference of, 'That one didn't age well' is tired and old and needs to be laid to rest. If we learn anything through aging, it's to treat people with respect.

I'm an older mom. I had my daughter at thirty-nine. Most of my high school friends with kids have already sent their kids to college, some have already become grandparents. I am so grateful not to be a grandparent yet. I'm stretching out this experience for all it's worth. I'll let my daughter know when I'm ready to be a grandparent. I think that's fair. Somewhere in my seventies will be nice.

Aah, the 70"s, the decade that was fun for almost everyone. They were a rainbow blast with bell bottoms. Everyone was singing about Coke or doing it. It was a lot of bead wearing and hand holding and perfect harmony. It seemed like a park setting was the perfect location for everything. I was ten in 1975 and those were my wonder years. Wondering how my mom could get into pants that tight and why was she wearing a turban if she's an American. Simple stuff like that. You just wonder and marvel at the world during that bright young age of discovery. There are so many things you want to ask a question about but you're still too afraid to get the answer. You just know you're not ready for it.

The 80's were pretty bizarre. It definitely took decadence to another level. It seemed like the bigger the hair, the bigger the shoulder pads. Pantsuits and bushy eyebrows were all the rage. Drugs and alcohol were such the norm, that normal was considered a permanent buzz. Thanks to photographs and foggy recollections of piecemeal stories by friends and family, I have some way to recount the 80's, but for now I'll just reference old tabloids for facts.

I worked a lot in the 90's, my most photogenic prime, which means no wrinkles yet. I remember waking up not too long ago and looking in the mirror and realizing... "Those aren't fucking sheet scars?!" Age happens, to almost everyone who doesn't live in Beverly Hills. We age, we get older, we slow down, we knit. In the entertainment business for a woman, that happens around thirty-five, as opposed to men who live to be one hundred and five and still get to make out with the ingenue. Can I just say I'm puking a bit? Thankfully in today's new regime of 'Time's up!' we can speak up about the injustices out there. I'm definitely disgusted by all the power abusers and truly despicable people out there but we still need to be better than what our gender and age is all about. I'm aware that on film, your shelf life has a lot to do with how you look, but more than anything, life is about how you feel. If you feel love, you show love. If you feel anger, you show anger. If you feel fear, we see it. If you feel strength, we see and feel that too. If you feel kindness, compassion and gratitude throughout your day, we want to be around you like moths to a flame. Don't let age define you on how you should feel, just keep learning and getting better at something imaginative. Nothing keeps you young like a new beginning. Even if it's just a new pair of walking shoes. Keep getting out there and get some fresh air. We have to roll with aging, otherwise we just rollover.

I became a mom in '04. This was when my life was no longer just *my life*. Hopefully, when parenting arrives, so does a transformation of priorities. I now have a very special purpose that requires a lot of gear, finances and rest. It also demands a lot of compassion, patience and the occasional glass of chardonnay. It becomes quickly apparent how much a schedule becomes your lifeline. A child will hopefully reflect those traits and have less chance of falling off the rails into the turmoils of a lost society. I think the 'happy parents' are the ones who are organized, look deep into the calendar to make plans and have the discipline to be prompt and prepared. I'm not perfect and I fail quite often on this. My plans get occasionally confused and the occasional job can throw a wrench into well intentioned schedules. It's the biggest challenge thus far, to organize and follow through with two very full and structured lives. I don't know that I'm getting any better with age, but I am putting more information into several devices, so at least I'm learning a little more technology. Hooray! Gratefully, I've been blessed with a daughter who is highly motivated and loves life. The greatest gift is to raise someone who is interested in the world around them and looking for a place to contribute their own gift to the planet. I'm pretty sure that's the point in life, to love and be loved. To question everything and enjoy the discovery of age-old answers.

My daughter loves to play with my weenis, especially when I'm driving. She'll just reach over and start tugging on it. It is so f-ing freaky! It drives me nuts and cracks me up at the same time. It is the quintessential most wonderful part of our relationship. I love it and hate it more than I can share. First of all, I didn't even know it was called that freaky ass word until she told me. So, my daughter, the scholar, already knows more than I ever will. I stopped being even close to capable with helping her with her math homework in the fourth grade. So disturbing. I've always enjoyed writing, so we're good in language arts. (I've noticed that parents just love to take credit on kids report cards, if they're doing great.) I love to read, so there's that, but damn the rest of it. So thankfully, she already is, and will continue to be, one of my great teachers in life, except for the math. I'm honestly looking forward to all the ages that accompanies her growth and mine. Especially the photos.

It's the long, saggy weenis thing that I'm not too fond of. And for those wondering, the weenis is the wrinkled-up skin behind your elbow that looks like a troll with no eyes. Ew. I just saw an ad for a TV show, *Hollywood Darlings*, where one of the actresses says, "I love being in my thirties. I'm finally comfortable in my own skin." To which another actress replies, "Why, because it's more loose?"

There are so many wonderful things about life, why would we quit? People are living so much longer now; they're outliving their resources. What happens when old people run out of money? I'll tell you; they move in with you or they become homeless. If you don't want your parents moving back in with you, or on the street, keep giving the old people a job. There's got to be some more ideas out there to keep our elderly interested and important. That's why it's really important to continue hiring the folks with their AARP Card. We still have a lot to bring to the party. Wisdom and experience are at the top of the list. Just keep your hands off my weenis and everything will be fine.

Epic Fail ~ Aging with anger and resentment about the things you can no longer do.

Epic Save ~ Living a long and happy life, with kindness and forgiveness towards yourself and others.

Lesson Learned ~ We still have so much to learn.

"To laugh often and much; to win the respect of intelligent people and the affection of children; to earn the appreciation of honest critics and endure the betrayal of false friends; to appreciate beauty, to find the best in others; to leave the world a bit better, whether by a healthy child, a garden patch or a redeemed social condition, to know even one life has breathed easier because you have lived. This is to have succeeded."
    ~ Ralph Waldo Emerson

CHAPTER 27

~ on compassion

One of my favorite acting classes that I had the privilege attending, was a cold reading class with Sandy Marshall. I loved the actors in that class, as they were all seriously talented and mostly working actors. It was a tremendous group and I looked forward to every class as a therapeutic lifeline. It was three hours of angst relief and it naturally fed my need to be creative and active in my craft. I was in love with Sandy's personal style of, "Like it or don't like it?" approach to every acting scenario. She broke things down with an innate sense of ease and she didn't mince words or pussy foot around feelings. As an actor, you are creating 'moments' around heightened senses, allowing everything to affect you personally. Above all, your point of view needs to be as sharp as a Wilkinson blade. When you have something deeply personal happening in your own life, you can either leave it at the door, or if you can't shake it, you bring it with you to class and use it. One particular class, I was about seven months pregnant, and had no choice but to bring my baby belly with me. I had been doing a play throughout my pregnancy, so I was more than comfortable being on stage pregnant. Although, on this particular day of my gestation, I discovered that not everyone is comfortable being around someone 'with child.'

We would always start the class with a series of Repetition. Repetition is an acting exercise designed by Master Teacher, Sanford Meisner. In Meisner's view, "Great acting depends on the actor's impulsive response to what's happening around him." His key exercise, spontaneous repetition, is designed for the actor to develop that dormant capacity. Meisner's approach trains the actor, "To live truthfully under imaginary circumstances, to discover or create personally meaningful points of view with respect to the (written or improvised) word, and to express spontaneous human reactions and authentic emotion with the utmost sense of truth." ~ Borrowed from an acting class brochure on the Meisner Method.

So in a nutshell, this stuff really works for nutty actors who are all stuck up in their head with an 'idea' of how they want a scene to be played. This eliminates that notion and gets the actor in the present moment 'to be' instead of 'to act'. Simple right? It's not rocket science but there is definitely a formula for great acting, like any other thing that takes exceptional skill, it takes time and practice. We aren't born with the notion of being great at something and even for those who are a 'natural' trust me, they still have to practice and hone that gift. This is why we have practice, rehearsal and mock scenario's to get ready for the real thing.

So, what does this all have to do with compassion? I was brought on stage by Sandy to do some Repetition with another fellow student. He was a great looking guy, but my brain won't allow me to remember his name, so I'll call him Dude. Dude was almost always the angry actor guy. He found his mojo in a scene by finding disdain with others. He embraced his cocky, superior attitude and did his best to make everyone around him feel like lowly commoners. He was basically a really good-looking bully.

In Repetition, the first moments are used to take in the other person you're working with. You observe clothing, hair, make-up, the whole person, and ultimately acknowledge the behavior of the other person and how your observational words are landing on them. A simple beginning to a Repetition could start with recognizing what the other actor is wearing like, "Blue shirt." That phrase gets repeated until an authentic emotion is triggered from repeating 'blue shirt'. This sounds easy, and definitely weird, but it's not easy, it's naturally awkward. The instant when suddenly someone becomes real and present, have been some of the most amazing moments I can remember. The significance of split seconds surrounding this exercise, and where it can take an actor, are truly mind blowing and mesmerizing.

So, cut to - me, my belly and Dude are on stage. I'm supremely pregnant and thoroughly hormonal, and we are looking at each other for about six seconds before Sandy tells Dude to start. Dude launches in with, "I don't get it."
I am instantly thrown off guard but dutifully repeat, "You don't get it."

In Repetition, you change the personal pronoun to keep things landing on you in a personal fashion. It's quick and thoroughly effective.

"I don't get it," Dude repeated, while unleashing his favorite acting tool, disdain.

"You don't get it," I replied, while hurling one of my favorite utensils from the 'I couldn't care less' category.

"I. Don't. Get. It." He pointed to my belly. The stage went silent. It was like a vacuum had sucked all the sound out of it. I immediately started to swirl and felt a rush of heat to my face as my belly kicked and moved. I had to repeat.

"You. Don't. Get. It." I said as I looked down at my swollen belly holding the sweetest mystery of life. Then a tear fell. Instant pain came from this onslaught from Dude. I was in shock at how quickly someone hurt me and my unborn baby. In that moment, Dude was a murderer to me. He was someone who I couldn't trust for a nanosecond and his vile attempt to humiliate me and make me feel I had done something wrong to the planet by being here in my state of mother-to-be made me feel instantly worthless and scared for myself and my baby. I wanted off the stage more than any time I can ever remember. It was powerful.

"Crying," Dude said with contempt, noticing my tear and shaken state.

"Crying," I repeated, with as much 'duh you dumbass, this is what happens when you're mean to a pregnant woman, you asshole.'

Subtext is the most interesting part of an acting moment, and when you can get as much in there as possible, you're really cooking with grease and the emotions are splattering all over the place.

"Crying," he repeated like it was his biggest pet peeve. I could hear him rolling his eyes.

"Fuck you," I responded. It was all I had left.

"Fuck me," he eagerly responded like it was a victory cry. We had now landed into his favorite territory of anger and self-loathing. Not a good combo for someone who I've already labeled a murderer.

"Okay, great work," Sandy heroically interjected, saving me from a serious demise with Dude. I was shaken and Sandy could see it, so she saved me by pulling Dude off the stage and replacing him with a compassionate and gifted actor, Garret Dillahunt. I had recently become a fan of his work on *Deadwood*, not even aware that he had been cast as two different characters on the same series. That's how much range this incredible actor possesses.

"Pregnant," Garret smiled, as my heart started to beat normally again.

"Pregnant," I whispered, as a relief of joy surged through my body.

"Pregnant," he beamed, embracing my nirvana.

"Pregnant," I nodded, silently thanking him for being the reluctant hero.

"Okay, great. Now Kathleen, I want you to do Repetition with your baby," Sandy instructed.

Garret gently stood off to the side as I moved to center stage and stood there with my hands gently touching my baby bump, repeating words back and forth from me to her and her to me.

"I love you."

"You love me."

"I will take care of you."

"You will take care of me."

"I will teach you things."

"You will teach me things."

"I am happy to have you."

"You are happy to have me."

"I can't wait to know you."

"You can't wait to know me."

"You are the best thing that's ever happened to me."

"I am the best thing that's ever happened to you."

"I respect you."

"You respect me."

The class was silent, except for a few sniffles. I looked over at Garret, supportive in his stalwart stillness. Sandy broke the silence with, "What do you think will be the one thing you want your daughter to learn from most in life?"

Without the slightest hesitation I responded, "Compassion."

Sandy smiled, "Good choice. Come on down, let's get to cold readings. Who's up first?"

Epic Fail ~ Assuming that anyone who sees a pregnant woman is happy for her choice.

Epic Save ~ Not letting someone's disgust destroy you.

Lesson Learned ~ Let a bad moment pass so that something and someone better can step in.

"Mama was my greatest teacher, a teacher of compassion, love and fearlessness. If love is sweet as a flower, then my mother is that sweet flower of love."
~ Stevie Wonder

CHAPTER 28

~ **on pets**

I love animals, especially the ones you can cuddle or ride. I have been the owner of many animals including cats, dogs, horses, bunnies, hamsters, fish, birds and snakes. I never had a monkey, but I did have a child, so I will include her to my menagerie. I've looked after enough pets to know that they are as much of a responsibility as a child or any other kind of relationship in which you feel accountable. They depend on us for food, water, shelter, love and vaccinations for the duration of their life span. Unlike a child, they never grow up and learn how to take care of themselves. They are forever hostage to our schedule and whatever food we have in the pantry or barn. They are dependents, but unlike a child, we unfortunately can't claim them on our taxes.

The love and companionship a pet can bring are sometimes greater than the human touch. They ask for nothing but food, water and a safe place to call home. They respond to gentle sounds, gentle touch and consistency. They love a schedule that they can count on and they thrive when that schedule is honored. Anyone who says that animals are not emotional creatures has not spent enough time with an animal who loves them. They are one of God's greatest creations and they enrich our experience on earth. Thank you, God, for every animal, even bears and sharks, which I will never own.

One of my first pets was a bunny that my dad brought home for Easter. We had never had a bunny before and at four years old, it was about the greatest thing my dad ever did. I loved that bunny more than anything and the first thing I wanted to do was give my bunny a bath. I don't know where my parents disappeared to when I was uncoiling the hose and getting ready to give Sweet Bunny Bun Cakes her first trip to the beauty parlor, but I was briefly on my own. I was going to get my bunny so clean and fluffy, she would be so happy with her soft shiny coat, she will be so... I didn't know that rabbits hate water. They are so frightened of it that she scratched me real good, so I squirted her in the face for just a second with the hose. That was all it took to fill her tiny little lungs before she drowned right in front of me. I don't know whether it was the water, or I had simply scared her to death, but my bunny was dead in one day. I was beyond devastated. I was inconsolable. I had never cried so hard in my four-year-old life. It was thoroughly shocking and dramatically traumatic. I never had another bunny after that. My daughter wants a rabbit and I just can't do it. I'm permanently scarred from that tragic day and there's really nothing I can do about it. When I saw Fatal Attraction I got to relive the horror all over again. Thank you Glenn Close, you boiled it.

I don't know where our sexy white cat, Snowball, came from but she arrived at our house pregnant. She was the Toluca Lake hot pants and had kittens every six months like clockwork. The first few batches were adorable, and we were able to find homes for them pretty easily. We were those scruffy kids with a box of "Free Kittens" outside our local grocery market. Those were the days before PETA stepped in and wrecked the Norman Rockwell glow of animals reproducing all over the place. I don't know why my mom never attempted to get Snowball fixed. I guess she thought it was our precious 'pet' project that kept us out of the house in desperate search of another 'mark' who didn't have an offspring of our very fertile and horny cat. We had run out of casual friends and neighbors who didn't already have one of our kitty's spawn, so we would sneak kittens into unsuspecting friends' homes and pretty much leave them there. A lot like the fire department, no questions asked, given the fact that you can't ask questions from someone who drops something off like a reverse porch pirate. One of our good family friends growing up were The Avalon's. They had eight children, so it was pretty easy to give a kitten to one of the gullible younger kids, as there were just too many of them to keep track of. Although, Mrs. Avalon, Kay, was pretty damn sharp, and you'd have to be a certified Ninja to get something by her. Fortunately, my brother Matt and his bestie, Frankie, Mrs. Avalon's oldest, were Ninja's in training and like Danielson from *Karate Kid*, they had stealth in their répertoire. Their mission was to find a home for the last three kittens Snowball had pushed out into the world. Snowball had become acquainted to the fact that we were taking her kittens away from her and like any mother who wants to keep her children, she started hiding them in the Christmas boxes in the garage. Their hungry crying always gave them away and we were able to easily locate them at the bottom of a box buried under a glittery wreath. It was not an easy chore and my feelings were always mixed about the situation. It would have been so much easier to drop Snowball off at the vet for a little snip, snip. Had I known that was an option, I would've opted for it, but this was still back in the day when cigarettes were a good choice for dieting, so we were still pretty much on the *Mad Men*/Neanderthal spectrum.

Matt and his trusty sidekick, Frankie, nabbed the final three kittens and put them in a box and placed them in the basket on my bike and rode away. I was sad and Snowball was pissed. I remember she kept crying and hissing and looking for her kittens. It was pretty tragic this stupid cycle of life we were all on. However, nothing compared to the wrath of Kay Avalon who pulled up in her station wagon with about five and a half kids in the back. She slammed on her brakes so hard in front of our house, I think four of those kids ended up in the front seat, maybe one in the glove compartment. One terrified little Avalon got out and placed the box of mewing kittens on our yard. The little tyke barely had a chance to get back in the car before Mrs. Avalon laid rubber and peeled out. It was my first drive-by and it was intense. Snowball was ecstatic and my mom was worn out. I never thought kittens could piss someone off like that. I guess that's what happens when you have eight kids, there's just simply no more room for another mouth to feed or someone to clean up after. You're already chock full o' nuts.

My mom finally got Snowball fixed and the sweet little cat passed away pretty quickly after that. I think she felt her contribution to the planet had served its purpose and she was tired. We did get to keep her three ne'er-do-well kittens that I named Shadrach, Meshach and Abednego. Biblical names for our little gifts from God and Mrs. Avalon.

Horses and dogs have since been a mainstay in my life. They don't get knocked up as easy and the companionship and deep connection is unbearably indescribable. I simply love them and I can't imagine my life without one or the other.

Epic Fail ~ Not being a responsible pet owner and neglecting to neuter your animal.

Epic Save ~ Keeping the babies from your beloved pet and giving them Bible names.

Lesson Learned ~ Don't ever give a bunny a bath and every pet deserves a good home with someone who loves and cares for them.

"Until one has loved an animal, a part of one's soul remains unawakened."
~ Anatole France

CHAPTER 29

~ **on listening**

Some of life's most epic fails are when things get lost in translation. "I didn't mean it that way" or "You must have heard it wrong" or "Can't you take a joke?'" These are just a few damage control phrases used when things aren't heard correctly. This is why the Repetition exercise is so valuable. Repeating what someone has just said to you is an excellent way of establishing what's been said and how it's been said. It's a definitive way to communicate, the same way they do it in an air traffic control room. Copy? Copy that.

I was fifteen and had just returned from a water polo tournament at Pepperdine University. My cousin, Dean, an incredible water polo athlete, played for UCLA, and my childhood best friend, Josie, accompanied me to the game to watch Dean and the rest of his teammates swim around in their mostly naked, wet with bulging muscles, teeny tiny speedos. It was a long day in the sun hunk gazing, and when we finally returned back to my parents' house, we found my Uncle Ron and my dad watching the basketball game. My mom was in the kitchen.

"Hi Mom!" I said, while she was standing beside the refrigerator, filling a glass of water from the built-in water dispenser on the fridge. The water stopped and she quietly said to me, "Honey, Matt's dead."

"Fuck you!" It blurted out of me like a braying sheep before slaughter.

"Oh sweetheart," she soothed, "try not to take it too hard."

This was my brother she was talking about! Try not to take it too hard?! I was tumbling down a very dark and dank rabbit hole. My mind was colliding and imploding upon itself. All the thoughts of my brother and how we struggled to get along were smashing into each other. He was supposed to come home tomorrow from his long vacation trip to Bermuda with Josie's cousin, Frankie Jr. and his family. He had been gone for a month, just long enough for me to start to miss him.

"How...?" I was able to form the word, but not finish the sentence.

"He was hit by a car," my mom gently responded, "but it happened quickly. He didn't suffer."

My tears and hysteria quickly followed this last, very dry, statement. I couldn't believe how calm my mom was reacting.

"She must be in shock," she said as matter of factly as 'hold the onions.'

I could barely see or breathe. Knees buckling and hyperventilating, I was brought into the living room to lie down on the couch where my dad and Uncle Ron were sharing popcorn and continuing to watch the basketball game. It was officially nuts in there and I was so spun out from the lack of empathy, I couldn't speak. I was wailing and moaning like a wounded animal. My mom quickly went to her medicine cabinet and brought me a

valium, maybe two. I choked down the pill with water, while she put a cold cloth on my head. I was officially down the rabbit hole, balled up on the couch while the game droned on. I remember hearing my dad say, "Wow, she's really taking this hard."
To which my Uncle Ron responded, "I didn't know they were that close."

The eating of the popcorn was surreal and the fact that they kept the game on was just heartless. I was in a full-blown combo platter of freak out. Josie remained by my side stroking my head, reassuring me that everything was going to be okay. My mom put another cold cloth over my forehead, because that's the cure for just about everything. The valium started to kick in and I was able to weakly say, "He.. was.. supposed... to come home... tomorrow."

Thankfully, because Matt was with Josie's cousin Frankie, Josie instantly knew that something was not right in my *interpretation* of *what had been said*.
Through my weeping and the fog of death I heard Josie say to my mom, "I think Keene thinks it was *Matt* that you're talking about."

Keene is the nickname that Matt gave me when I was a baby. My parents used to call me Kathaleeny, which Matt, as a two-year-old, couldn't say, so he christened me "Keene" (pronounced key-knee: the middle *k* is silent :). I created the spelling when I decided to write my name in crayon all over my brother's closet. I was busted pretty bad for that one, but at least I was learning to create words. Keene still sticks to this day with family and close friends and of course all of this was running through my tortured mind as I was thinking of all the things I wanted to say to Matt but now I couldn't because in my mind, for an excruciating forty-five minutes, my brother Matt was dead.

The TV went off and my dad came over to me and he said, "Kathleen, it wasn't your brother, it was the dog, *Mack*. Mack was hit by a car, not Matt." Mack was a Cairn Terrier dog that we had given to my Aunt Shirl a year prior.

Are you fucking kidding me?! Where's that other valium?! In fact, I think everyone has earned a valium or *three*. Now my parents and Uncle Ron and Josie were all crying. I went into a new tailspin of relief and grief, all super fuzzy and creamy. It was the worst and the best day ever. Something I never want to repeat and yet it was something I will never want to forget.

Listening is an art form of communication. We need to actively listen more and repeat to each other what's been said. Choose our words and our delivery with care. When someone is overreacting to "Please pass the salt" it might be because they heard "Sneeze mass at malt" which might have some deep hidden meaning to the listener.

Epic Fail ~ Thinking my brother was dead without getting all the facts.

Epic Save ~ Greeting my big brother at LAX with a sign that read "Welcome Home Big Bother!"

Lesson Learned ~ Repeat back to someone what you think they've said, as you could be misinterpreting or not hear it correctly.

"The best way to persuade people is with your ears - by listening to them."
    ~ Dean Rusk

CHAPTER 30

~ on hats

I've worn so many hats in life. I was born a daughter, sister, cousin, niece, granddaughter. I became a friend, wife, stepmom, aunt, mom. I have been a student, actor, hostess, waitress, secretary, horse wrangler, yogi, writer, producer, director. We all wear many different hats to get through life and establish our own identity, but one of the more memorable hats I ever got to wear was Johnny Depp's brown stocking cap that I had on my head for about three and a half dazzling minutes.

My second marriage was to an actor that I knew from Mammoth Mountain. He was from Boston and has enjoyed a good career playing the snarky bully type. His kids also lived in Mammoth at the time and when we got married, his three young teens moved in with us in LA. It was the instant family I was yearning for after the loss of my first marriage to Lorenzo and the painful departure from his young children.

Being a stepparent is one of the most difficult and tricky hats to wear. Ever. It's a fine line of being supportive, know your place and don't over-parent. And for the love of God and all of humanity, don't ever tell the biological parent how to do it, unless you want a full-blown fight. The best thing to do as a stepparent, is be a buffer. That cool, easygoing friend that says, "I'll do my best to help you, but ultimately it's going to be your parents' decision." Or, just simply stay out of it. Of course, this is a lot easier said than done, especially when everyone is living together like a cute little instant family. The stepparent will eventually get kicked to the curb when the real stuff goes down. Blood is thicker than water and a stepparent in my book is the steam that barely gets acknowledged when it really comes down to 'family'.

It's true that we will naturally feel closer to our own children because we were there from the get-go. You can feel close to step's, but in the end, they aren't yours and loyalties should remain with birth parents and the kids should remain loyal to their folks, no matter how much they're screwed.

My stepdaughter, Gillian, from my second marriage was a beautiful fourteen-year-old when I met her at the studio lot where her dad was working on a sitcom. She hated me immediately, which made me wonder where the comedy part was in this situation. I had never experienced being that instantly disliked. I think all she saw was a tall blonde threat. She had become quite accustomed to having her dad's full attention through her parents' divorce and now here I was a sexy, early thirties, *actress*. Her eye roll was palpable. I remember her dad saying to me as he walked me back to my car, "That would be the cold shoulder of my lovely daughter."
"Cold shoulder? That was more like freezer burn."

I had more work cut out for me than I could've ever imagined with his family, but I put my new hat on and dug in with two shovels.

One day in the middle of her new school year, in her new home, with her slightly used stepmom, she was not feeling great, or good or anywhere near wanting to go to school. Her two younger brothers, Jake and Luke, had already left for the day and her dad was not around. It was apparent to me, as her stepparent, that she was just feeling emotionally out of sorts. I told her we would play hooky and go get lunch somewhere fun, just the two of us. She and I had a few words and altercations in the months prior, so I was determined to let her know that I genuinely loved and cared about her. Plus, I was damn hell-bent to score some cool stepmom points, even if her dad screamed at me for ditching school. Besides, everybody needs a break from 'burn out' now and then.

I took Gilly to The Ivy By The Shore, a gorgeous restaurant right across the street from the Santa Monica Pier. I did my best to shut up and listen to her open up about her life, her friends, her fears, her family, her drama. She said one thing at that lunch that sticks with me to this day. She said, "If my dad wasn't around, I could do anything I want and be a success." Her dad's natural approach to life was to be overbearing and opinionated to the point of exhaustion. He was a true East Coaster with an above it all, know it all, went to University attitude. That kind of character created a stifling mixture of insecurity and self-doubt with me, and his kids, especially his daughter, who just wanted to find her own way without being constantly told how to do it. Of course, those pieces of awareness and observations did not fly well whilst in the marriage.

I listened intently to Gillian's problems as we enjoyed our corn chowder and crab cakes at a casual, languid pace, when I suddenly noticed a very familiar form at the bar. It was his silhouette that I instantly recognized and especially the brown stocking cap that I had seen in numerous press photos. Yes, right there, making eye contact with me through a mirror above the bar, was the one and only, Johnny Depp.

"Shut up and finish your soup, sweetheart. We have to go," I encouraged.
"Why, what's wrong?" my diminutive, little blue-eyed doe of a stepdaughter worried.
"Please, for the love of all that's holy, don't turn around."
"Why?" she smiled, feeling my exuberance.
'Yay, she's smiling!', I thought to myself.
 "Johnny Depp is about twenty yards behind you, at the bar *and* he keeps staring at me. We are going over there so I can introduce you," I surmised.
"You know him?" she blanched.
"Not yet," I confidently smiled.

I was also wearing a hat that day. It was a blue beanie that my beloved hairstylist of many years, David Dru, gave me. David is not only a hair stylist, he's also an inventor. He is determined to live the longest and look the best without anything other than minerals and high-powered nutrients found in crystals and other things that I never really understood but always found tremendously fascinating. He designed a line of clothing made from tachyon beads which stimulate energy, healing and brain function. The lapis lazuli colored hat had the word '*FOCUS*' sewn in on the side and I'm pretty sure that's what Johnny was looking at, being a man of many, many hats.

"Check, please," I pleaded to the nearest busboy.
Gillian and I checked each other's teeth, the way good friends do. I loaned her my lip gloss, the way a buddy does. I told her she looked beautiful, which she always did, but it's still always great to hear, and we waltzed over to where Johnny Depp and his business-suited colleague were sharing day drinks at the bar. It was probably his agent and they were most likely toasting the inking of his first *Pirates of the Caribbean.* That's the backstory in my mind anyway. I knew as I was walking over that I had already mustered the best ice breaking line ever.

"I love your hat," I said to Johnny Depp.
"I love *your* hat," Johnny Depp smoldered. (A Meisner enthusiast, I'm sure of it.)
Shit, now what? I was already out of material!
"Thank you!" I joyfully remembered, as good manners kicked in.
"Do you want to trade?" Johnny Depp asked sincerely, with his yummy Johnny Depp voice.

I looked at my stepdaughter whose blue eyes were sparkling like sapphires and her smile was just as beautiful as a swan taking flight for the first time. There was such joy in that moment of us not believing what was actually happening. It was an encapsulated moment of pure bliss. This is what heaven is going to feel like, when Johnny Depp wants to trade hats. I can die now.

"Sure," I said as I yanked my treasured hat off my head, ready to see it placed on one of the finest heads on the planet.

Johnny Depp took his hat off at the same time and we traded, right there at the bar at The Ivy By The Shore. In an instant I could smell the salt in the air, the Caribbean breeze brush past my skin and hear the ocean rushing through my ears. My body was electric with excitement as my stepdaughter watched me transform into the most supernatural amazing stepmom of all freaking time.

Standing next to Johnny Depp, with my hat on his head and his brown stocking cap on mine, was in a word, **amazing**. I didn't know what the day would bring, but never in my wildest dreams could I have imagined this dazzling moment in what was determined to be a Debbie Downer day. Then I remembered something important about Johnny Depp. We had a very good friend, colleague and employer in common, the incredible Stephen J. Cannell.

"We have a common friend," I said to Johnny Depp as we admired ourselves and each other in the massive mirror above the bar.
"We do?" Johnny Depp looked at me with genuine interest.

"Yes, Stephen J. Cannell. He put us both in our first TV series," I concluded.

"Yes, he did," Johnny Depp nodded.

"I was on *Renegade*, and you were on..."

"*21 Jump Street*," Johnny Depp said with a wry smile.

Pinch me, kick me, shoot me with an arrow, I'm literally bantering with Johnny Depp! I was so proud to know my Johnny Depp facts and that we shared not only a friend but also the same experience with a career launch by one of the greatest TV Creators of all time. *Renegade* and *21 Jump Street* were both creations of the talented Stephen J. Cannell and even though Johnny Depp wanted out of TV, it did sufficiently put him on the map.

"I'm Kathleen and this is my stepdaughter, Gillian," I thankfully remembered her name, and mine, a very proud moment.

"I'm Johnny and this is my agent... blah, blah, blah," Johnny kindly introduced. You couldn't pay me enough to remember the other guy's name. He might as well have been invisible. In fact, was there another guy? I only remember a suit.

"My hat looks great on you," Johnny Depp complimented.

"My hat looks great on *you*," I responded in touché-like fashion. Deep breath.

"Are we going to trade?" Johnny Depp asked.

"That's entirely up to you," I said, doing my best poker face in the cool zone.

Of course, I wanted to say, 'Hell yeah, just try prying it off my head, Johnny Depp!'
But I didn't say that, as wearing his fine chapeau was already enough.

Johnny Depp looked at me and then at himself in the mirror and then I saw that beautiful transformation of thought grace through his actor mind. He looked back at me and his beloved brown stocking cap on my head and he said the most beautiful Johnny Depp thing ever...

"That hat... she's an old friend."

Gillian and I looked at each other and we knew we were in a magical moment of love, friendship, loyalty, comfort and couture. I was not going to be the one to ever take an old friend away from Johnny Depp. Who knows? That hat might be part of his Merlin, a timeless piece of his magic that he wears to the set for 4am calls when his hair is still wet from his early morning wakeup shower in slo-mo, and he needs comfort and reassurance that the day will be okay. His brown stocking cap hat got him there and will be there at the end of a long, arduous shoot to ease him back to his five-star hotel, while on location to raw and faraway places. I knew in that instant that even having it on my head for this short, random moment was a gift. It was enough. Besides, *my* hat was an old friend too, given to me by my dear friend who takes great care with every hair on my head. I took off Johnny Depp's hat and gently handed it back to him.

"I understand about old friends. We need to hang onto them," I said as Johnny Depp handed me back my own beanie.

"Yes, we do," Johnny Depp nodded and smiled.

He knew that I got it and was probably relieved that I didn't turn into a petulant child.

We placed our hats back in their proper place, shook hands and smiled from the warm and meaningful interaction. Plus, I was now officially the most rad stepmom of the Universe and basking in Johnny Depp inertia.

"It was very nice to meet you," Johnny Depp said to us both.

"Yes, it was very nice," Gillian said as her sparkling bright blue eyes turned every shade of girl like wonder.

I was done talking, which is also known as speechless. We walked out the door, waited for the valet, got in the car and drove about twenty yards before we both let out a scream only The Beatles have heard.

Epic Fail ~ Ditching school is not a good habit but every once in a while, we need a break and sometimes we get immediate joy from that choice. Yay! No fail on this day.

Epic Save ~ Summoning the courage and proper timing to meet and greet a shooting star.

Lesson Learned ~ Wear a cool hat. It's a great way to be mysterious *and* keep the sun off your face.

"There's definitely healing properties to being in proximity to the ocean and that breeze. There's something about that Caribbean climate and humidity."
~ Johnny Depp

CHAPTER 31

~ **on photography**

I hate math. I hate it so much I believe I might have dyslexia with numbers. I have to repeat phone numbers several times before I'm assured I've written them in the correct sequence. I had to take Algebra 1 three times before I passed that f-ing class. Eventually I stole the final exam out of the copy room. One fine day, I had the great fortune of making copies for class and saw the discarded blue ink sheet of the final. Thank you, God, I knew you cared. Sorry Providence High School, I had no choice. That class did not come with a twenty-four-hour tutor drilling theoretical formulas into my brain and making sure they didn't seep out the next morning. Give me a poem, a sonnet, or a three-page monologue, and I'll have it memorized in a day. If it involves numbers, then I'm generally screwed. But I can photocopy the widow maker, and then memorize the damn thing.

One great truth about numbers is that they don't lie, just like a camera. A camera notices everything within a frame, from body language and comfort level, to the contagious joy of a genuine smile. It can be manipulated to a certain degree using smoke, mirrors, shadows, light, filters, lenses and angles, and the eye can be distracted by shiny objects reflecting light in wardrobe, background or foreground. But the truth for every frame, and the natural gaze that we follow in a subject, is what's going on in the light of the eyes, a.k.a the window of the soul, and that cannot be manipulated.

One single-frame photograph can capture an entire story. It can also destroy a career, a relationship or self-esteem, so be mindful of what you photograph or what you allow others to capture. A likeness can be used as a weapon or an image maker depending upon the responsibility of the subject and the integrity of the photographer. A portrait can move a mind or a heart forever, which is a powerful tool for exploring humanity, and for communicating with the world at large. A snapshot can bring a distant event right into your living room or follow you on the train to work via your smartphone. It allows for human connection where before there was disassociation and separation. Photographs travel across continents and traditions and bring us closer to each other as a species. Observing the world around us through a camera's eye trains you to notice the intricate details within *everything* and *everyone* around you. This form of communication allows us to see just how woven together we all are in this multi-dimensional masterpiece.

My passion for photography has been an ongoing love affair. I'm on a constant quest for beauty, nature and truth, in whichever expression that transpires. A gorgeous cloud with a sunset banking on it; a reflection of disproportionate trees in water; a petal falling in mid-flight; a rose that looks so beautiful in color and then manipulating the hues and adjusting effects to see what else you can get out of it. The possibilities are endless.

Mostly, I love photographing people. I love getting deep in their face and seeing their soul through their eyes, observing their body language and what's going on inside a person in his or her own relaxed state. Bringing out the best in people with a gorgeous photograph to be shared with family, friends and social media, is an everlasting gift that will last long after I'm gone. Taking photos is a way to put my stamp on the planet without leaving a carbon footprint.

I was hired to photograph female entre-preneurs at a networking event. Hours of uneventful 'photo booth headshots' paid off when I noticed a captivating young woman busting her balls across the room. She was a college student and an unpaid intern in charge of everything that no one else wanted to do at this gathering. There was a bushy, bright-eyed quality about her, facial features of perfect geometry, and a certain gravity in her demeanor that revealed strong values beyond her years. The perfect muse. I was instantly drawn to her and offered to take her picture outside this setting. When she arrived a few days later, at Paradise Cove, one of my favorite Pacific Ocean settings, her face was covered in so much makeup, it irritated her eyes to the extent of unstoppable watering and raw, sore skin. I lifted the camera and watched her disappear inside herself with the look of a deer in the headlights. No matter the aperture, the subject ultimately controls the exposure - and this muse dimmed her own light. I was taken aback by the transformation. I desperately wanted her to 'relax' and allow herself to be seen. Fortunately, her watering eyes got rid of most of the makeup that her face was rebelling against. She honestly is the type of beauty that never needs makeup. Her skin is flawless, with natural rosy cheeks and sparkling eyes. She's so naturally beautiful, she could stay up boozing on an all-night bender and still arrive looking dynamically better than most people with twelve hours of sleep. When I told her this, it made her laugh. Laughter is truly the best equalizer to get people to relax. My personal photo goal for the day was to mimic the iconic photo of Farrah Fawcett in the red one-piece bathing suit with the Navajo blanket in the background and her engaging, dynamic smile in the foreground. My poor muse, wiping her tears from her face, was finding her joy in the ability to be totally game and roll with it. Who knows what Farrah was smiling or laughing about in that photo but you can absolutely see and feel her true spirit in that one single frame. I did my best to crack every stupid joke I had in my camera bag that day and through her sodden eyes and the rolling fog, we captured a multitude of amazing shots.

As a photographer it is up to me to take in the person that I am photographing and find what they identify with so that I can direct them into a state that brings out the best in them. Everyone has a relaxed center within. Everyone has strength, power and a superhero pose beneath whatever shyness or self-consciousness is keeping them 'safe' on the surface. Having been in front of the camera myself for so many years, I am highly sensitive to people's experience while being photographed. I do my best to direct them through what I have learned works: relax the shoulders and breathe, soften the jaw and release the forehead, close the eyes and *feel* the environment. I try to steer them away from all mental efforts and the pretense of having to pose, and guide them towards a place of *feeling,* instead of *thinking* their way to what looks good. I encourage the subject to focus on what their senses are experiencing. It's not always about the angles or the clothes, it's about attitude. It's about bringing *you.* It's about who you are beneath the exterior. It takes a relaxed body and a relaxed mind for attitude and truth to come through. Think of clouds and flowers; they're not trying. They're *being.* If you can switch off the mental noise and relax into your innate centeredness, you *become* the cloud and the flower. Let the colors pass through you, let the wind blow through you, let the feelings be there, the material of your clothes, the warmth of the sun – simply be with whatever *is* – that's what nature does. Nature doesn't *try,* it simply *is* beautiful, brave and present.

With some simple direction, my muse slowly eased into the intimate exchange that was happening between her, the lens, the environment, and myself. Gradually, she opened up some more and allowed a glimpse into the deep well inside her. I was able to capture some very candid shots of her soul that day and I will never forget how her green eyes once again filled with tears when she saw her photos a week later. I watched as she took it all in. It was as if she met herself for the first time. That was the beginning of her new career and journey into becoming a successful model, actress and a dear friend - all from one innocent, valiant day with a camera.

When you are able to capture the essence of a person and hand them a photograph where they can see themselves in a way that they may never have seen themselves before, they will embrace this part of their person as, "Yes, I have this in me. I am this person. I have strength and beauty. I have focus and emotions. I have sex appeal and I dare to show you my vulnerability." One single-frame photograph can change how a person feels about her/himself forever. I love the powerful transformation that takes place when someone sees themselves as something more. It's the truest part of math. When all the numbers line up and you discover exactly what $E = mc^2$ actually means. Units of energy, meeting units of mass, meeting the speed of light. It all adds up to a beautiful photo to me.

Epic Fail ~ Algebra I... thrice.

Epic Save ~ Learning another skill that has everything to do with math.

Lesson Learned ~ A photographer's work is to capture the *truth* of a person, a situation, a place or a moment in time in the best possible light.

"Photography is a way of feeling, of touching, of loving. What you have captured on film is captured forever... it remembers little things, long after you have forgotten everything."
~ Aaron Siskind

CHAPTER 32

~ on electricity

My dad was in the electric supply business. He owned a company he started with his dad, Coast Wholesale Electric. It was a very successful company, which he ended up selling, allowing him to retire in his mid-fifties. My brothers and I worked for him at one point or another during our summers, or once we were out of school. The business had three locations, one in Burbank, Oxnard and Chatsworth. In the early 80's, my dad combined locations into one big building that he built in Burbank. He wasn't an electrician, but he knew a lot about electricity.

One evening, when I was about thirteen, I was helping my dad string tiki lights in the backyard for a party. These lights had seen way better days. They were worn out, faded and must've been following my parents around from the Beach Blanket Bingo era. However, my dad was determined to get them out, plug them in and start decorating the back brick wall for my brother's birthday. I was more than happy to help, as I loved helping my dad and I really loved a good party, especially parties for my brothers, which meant more boys around that weren't my brothers.

I was barefoot and the grass was wet, and the very long string of very tired tiki lights were plugged into the house. Dad was at one end of the lit lights and I was at the other, about thirty yards away. He picked up his end and I reached down to pick up mine to anchor on the nail on the wall and I got grounded. Not the kind of grounding that doesn't allow you to go out with your friends for the weekend because you got busted for stuffing your bed with pillows and snuck out the bedroom window and didn't come home until 4am to find your dad waiting for you outside with the sprinklers running. That kind of grounding would have been delightful. No, the grounding I got was sparks flying, hands burning, teeth chattering, electricity coursing through my body and not being able to 'let go' kind of grounding. My exceedingly strong and terrified father couldn't pull the cord out of my hand, that's how powerful the current was scorching through my body. He tried knocking me down to break the current to no avail. He bolted to the house and pulled the cord, and in the same instant all the lights went out. I dropped to the ground, smoldering and shaking. My hands and teeth felt like they were on fire. Of course, I had braces, which I'm sure wasn't a big help. There were significant burns on my hands and I could smell burnt hair inside my nose. A few seconds longer and I'm sure I would've been toast. Melba toast.

I was also screaming bloody murder, which I'm sure was a relief to my dad, being that my hysteria was his assurance I was still alive. My mom and dad got me into the house at the same time the paramedics arrived. I was beyond electrically charged and the only release from the pain, terror and trauma was to use every expletive that I had ever heard from every parent or George

Carlin album. That means I was cussing an impressive blue streak while the paramedics wrapped my smoking, burned hands. It was like I had turrets and Richard Pryor was my speech coach.

"How does it feel?" the kind paramedic asked.
"It fucking hurts is how it fucking feels!" I immediately shrieked.
I didn't even give the poor hero a chance to absorb my tween dialogue before I launched into my next angry manifesto tirade.
"Does it fucking hurt? What the fuck do you think after being fucking electrocuted in your own fucking backyard with a fucking worn out set of stupid fucking idiot fucking tiki lights? Fuck, shit, piss, plumber it fucking hurts!"

I remember my younger brother, Johnny, coming into the living room at that point with a flashlight saying, "There's burn marks on the grass where Keene was standing."
"You're fucking A right there's burn marks! My feet were on fucking fire while I'm getting burnt to a shit fuck crisp out there! What the fucking shit do you think about that?" I was on a serious roll and not giving a rat's ass about my audience.

My poor dad was shaken to the core. My mom was impressed at the wordsmith I was becoming. The paramedics told me to take a few days off from school which I kindly told them to 'fuck off', as I had a basketball game that week and I was not going to fucking miss just because I had several fucking hundred bolts of current race through my body like a fucking runaway train. I was obviously quite tweaked and probably should've gone to the hospital for some sort of evaluation and more shock therapy. The paramedics graciously left, as my dad replaced all the fuses in the box that I had burned out. What a night.

By the weekend, my hands were mostly fine, and we had the party with a brand new set of red chili lights strung across the back yard. The grass took longer to recover, as my burn marks stayed for months. I fouled out of the next few basketball games and over time, I learned how to control my newly acquired sailor potty mouth so I wouldn't get expelled.

Epic Fail ~ Bare feet, wet grass, worn wire, plugged into an extension cord attached to a house with an endless supply of juice.

Epic Save ~ Pulling the extension cord out of the house with the endless supply of juice.

Lesson Learned ~ Wear shoes with rubber soles whenever dealing with electricity or call for grip and electric.

"Electricity is really just organized lightening."
　　~ George Carlin

CHAPTER 33

~ on lying, cheating and stealing

I remember when I was a kid my dad announced, "I hate liars, thieves and cheats." My dad rarely used words as strong as 'hate' so I knew he was serious.

Of course, I had to try all three. I lied, I cheated, and I stole. These are not good things; the outcome is always unfavorable. I put my parents through the wringer with some pretty 'out of control' moments in my late teens and early twenties. Most of the bad behavior had to do with experimenting with the boundaries of my newfound freedom, which landed me in not so great places, quite a few times. There were times I was way out of control and hit serious emotional rock bottoms with an extreme close-up to how bad life can become. There's nothing more sobering than seeing someone drooling at a bar at last call when the lights come on. It's one thing coming out of the dentist chair after Novocain and wisdom teeth extractions, it's another when someone has fried and/or pickled their brain to a stump, and they can no longer control their saliva or their bowels.

It's pretty simple, live a clean and simple life and your life becomes pretty clean and simple. Live a complicated life based on lies, cheating yourself of the world around you and stealing your health, focus and trust of those who love and care about you, and your life will become a freaking shambles.

We have an obligation to our bodies to live a balanced and flourishing life. We owe it to ourselves to take care of our one and only vessel that gets us around on this planet. We can't exchange our body for a newer, less used version. Everything we do to and for our body leaves an imprint; sometimes temporary, sometimes permanent. If you're getting plenty of sleep, eating health consciously and exercising regularly, you're banking wellbeing points into your present and future health. If you're not doing these things, then you're depleting your longevity and creating havoc on your system, causing stress, mortification and disease.

There's a *Scared Straight!* site that I randomly frequent for a gentle reminder of 'how bad shit can get' titled: rehab.com Look up the horrors of methamphetamines. It's perfect for anyone wondering what hard drugs and abuse can do to your mug shot. It shows progressive portraits/mug shots of beautiful, young, vibrant hopefuls and their accelerated decline into the underworld of the devil's dandruff and exploitation. It's truly one of the saddest things I've ever seen. I think it should be a mandatory class in middle school to observe the aggressive aging of these sad, youthful faces and their swift plummet when they fall into the trappings of hard core, habit forming drugs. It looks like the wall of fame from *The Walking Dead*. I'm sure makeup artists around the world study these photos for zombie films. This path in life is a real horror film with no wrap party, but a lifetime of misery and eventually death. And by the way, alcohol abuse will do the exact same thing, only the misery can last much longer. It's not just the skin picking, rotten teeth and malnutrition; it's the despair, confusion, remorse and pain behind those sorrowful eyes. Fear of facing the day, or prison time, is the worst feeling ever. The high anxiety from nagging, sleepless nights is like a steroid fueled mixture of "I don't have my homework done <u>and</u> I have a test" or "I don't know my lines and <u>everyone</u> is going to know I'm a fraud and a fake and lousy at life." It's a feeling that sucks way worse than giving it your all and failing on life's terms. At least with life, we already know going into a game that someone will win, and someone will lose. Losing something or someone does not give you a free pass to lose even more. Nor does it mean that when you win, you are given sanction to party your brains out. It means that if it didn't happen this time, know you did your best and if you keep trying it could happen the next go round. If you have great success, celebrate that as well, in moderation, because that team you beat today, is getting ready to kick your ass tomorrow.

Can you imagine if you went to a baseball game and saw your favorite team lose and they refuse to leave the field after the last inning? What if they sat on the field did drugs and drank themselves into a blackout because they lost? They would instantly no longer be your favorite team. You love your team because even when they lose, they humbly go down to the locker room, shower off and prepare for the next game. That's why you love them, they don't quit. Our body is our own team that we need to coach, discipline and motivate every day. We need to be kind and

281

considerate to this ride that we have been given. We don't take care of ourselves as a responsibility to others and their expectations, we do it because it is our duty to our team of cells that is constantly working overtime to get our butt from one location to the next.

There's nothing more awesome than seeing a racehorse come from behind to take the checkered flag. It's equally inspiring to watch those who continue to go for it, despite the odds, endure the hard work and tireless competition involved. Welcome to life, it stops for no one. There will always be another competitor on every side, but we are all on the field. I believe we are all racehorses going for our own personal checkered flag of dreams. When we get distracted by something that can derail us, we need to tell the person offering the lie, the cheat and the robbing of our soul, "No thanks, man. I don't do that shit." Then quickly trot away.

I believe most cheating and stealing begins with a lie. If you make a habit of always telling the truth there will rarely be an occasion that you will have to cheat or steal. The thing is with lies, is that they just get bigger once they've been started. It's a snowball effect and before you know it, there's an avalanche of false narrative chasing you. I've told some pretty mighty fibs in my day, but one particular moment stands out from my senior year religion class. We had an assignment on the communion. It was an oral report, which I took literally, and took it upon myself to serve wine to the class. I bought two single gallon bottles of milk and immediately poured them out in the kitchen drain, rinsed them and went straight to my parents' wine rack and filled those empty plastic jugs with some mighty fine *Falcon Crest Reserve*. I thought out loud, "Boy, my class is so lucky to be drinking the good stuff and not some two-buck chuck for their first foray into the high life at school." I gave everyone a healthy Lakeside pour into their dixie cup as I went through the motions of the Holy Sacrament, pausing to give my own interpretation of how this ritual is still holding up today. Which I muttered to myself, "No wonder all churchgoers enjoy this Sunday morning ritual." I had already given a 'heads up' to my classmates to know what was what, but the teacher had zero clue. When it came time to bottoms up, I glanced at my unsuspecting teacher who had already drained his glass. He looked at me with a tremendously knowing smile and said, "What's in this grape juice again?"

I looked at him and boldfaced lied in the middle of my oral Eiger Sanction of free-falling fibs and said, "Vinegar."

"Aaah, yes. I can taste it," he nodded approvingly, "may I have another?"

"Of course!" I exhaled and dutifully poured another for him and the rest of my rosy lush friends.

Everyone got two shots and one saltine. The class was remarkably quiet and reverent while we prayed over the sacrament. It was probably one of the first times that rowdy all girl religion class filled with seniors was calm. The red wine brought the mood to a sweet hush. It felt like a real spiritual experience.

Most of my class was getting thoroughly tipsy. Some extreme lightweights were already toasted. It was right before lunch, so stomachs were growling by communion time. I timed it perfectly, the same way you're supposed to receive the sacrament, on an empty stomach. I was pleased as I looked around at the cozy smiles of my little congregation in their first venture into breakfast day drinking. Noticing the relaxed grin on my teacher, I was more than sure I would get a resounding 'A' for my efforts and high jinx.

Our next class was lunch, where everyone was sobering up with a sandwich, chocolate milk and some laughs. I looked up from my bologna and saw my somewhat wasted religion teacher trying to walk a straight line in my direction.
"Oh shit, he's a teetotaler and I'm busted," I muttered to my fuzzy friends.

I was right, I was more than busted, I was suspended. The next day I had to apologize to the class (wink, wink) for unsuspectingly serving them wine (wink, wink) during religion class (wink). My teacher was standing directly behind me, so he couldn't see all the winking.
I told them, "Just because church is generally held in the morning, does not mean that we should be drinking real alcohol at communion - even though it is meant to be had on an empty stomach and happens to be wine and they only give you a little bread."

It was the most ass over tea kettle back-handed no sense whatsoever apology of all time.

The teacher couldn't even wrap his brain around it, since he was probably trying to figure out what the hell I was thinking to begin with. I'm sure he was just more than grateful that it was just a little wine and not a report on anything else that kids can get on the street these days. My lie got me in trouble, with a solid ripple effect. Lying, cheating and stealing are usually a combo package that don't come with any promos or joyful results. Live in truth and worry less.

Epic Fail ~ Serving wine to your teacher and underage kids at school, not a good plan.

Epic Save ~ Embracing the many highs and lows in life, as they come and go.

Lesson Learned ~ Moderation is the key to alcohol, stay away from hard drugs and when you need to get help, call a friend, family member or a treatment center hotline. 844-296-8495

"I realized I wasn't going to live up to my potential, and that scared the hell out of me."
　　　~ Bradley Cooper

CHAPTER 34

~ **on spirituality**

I attended parochial school all my life, except for the one year in public school where I got into a few scrapes. Those ugly and unfortunate moments were not a fine example of my faith-based upbringing. I've been to many different churches, in several different countries, and enchanted by many different organized religions. I understand the need for spirituality in life and the one thing I know for sure, is that it's about relationship not religion. Faith is a private experience yet a personal mystery that brings us together to worship, sing and oftentimes war over.

My Godmother, Victoria, is an atheist. She takes it very seriously. I think part of her reasoning to deny that God exists is because her mother died when she was only two years old. How truly unfair and cruel is that? A little baby girl, growing up in Hungary during WWII, and her mother dies before she has a chance to really know her? Come on now, God. That's just starting life off with a load of bricks in your baby backpack. Sometimes loss, tragedy, adversity and just fucking shit luck are too much for a human heart to bear and the heart gets hardened to the point of denial, rejection, closed, no vacancy.

I feel compassion for those who experience loss. I know the pain of losing someone you loved so much that you thought you would die with the loss of losing them. Somehow that doesn't work, as the pain of a broken heart will not always kill you, but it definitely can stifle and give stress that can cause many forms of sickness. Another reason for my Godmother's lack of belief system is the constant pondering of, 'If God is the Great Creator, then who created God? What was here before God and deeper than that who, what, why, and how did He start? And why He? Why not She? Why Mother Earth and why Father Time?' Why?

It's a lot to think about, that's why faith is born in the heart, not the brain. I can't fathom the universe and its vast holes of non-explanation and wide-open interpretive story. I have read the Bible numerous times. I occasionally go to church with my dad, but I'm not a member, although I have great respect and admiration for those who become one. The one place I know where I can always find God is through prayer and meditation. I find a tremendous amount of comfort and calming from my Daily Prayer. It's a booklet I receive in the mail from the mail fairies at Daily Word. It's a unique little non-denominational Christian daily dose of goodness. My bestie, Miranda, will call me in tears saying, "Did you read the Word today? Oh my God, He nailed it! Again."

I know God has a sense of humor when I look at the animal kingdom. I mean, what the heck is that blob fish about? The one that looks like a very old, white guy who works in a bakery. And what about a baby hippo? Most adorable thing ever!! Or a baby panda might top it, all pink and hamster-like and then grows up to be a big 'ol bear. I don't know how it happened or why, but we're here and it's all for the same reason, to love and be loved. "The love we take, is equal to the love we make," so saith The Beatles, and it was so, so right on.

I had a faith healing moment happen to me in the 80's when I broke my wrist in three places. I was roller skating at Venice Beach and zigged when I should've zagged. I wiped out and fractured my wrist dancing to *Boogie Wonderland* with my old pal, Crazy Peg. At the time, I had just completed my first film, *Hardbodies*, and was scheduled to do my very first press tour with the lead of the film and also my boyfriend at the time, Grant Cramer. I did not want to have a cast on my arm during the experience, so I talked my orthopedic specialist, Dr. Vergess, into sufficing with a Velcro splint until I returned to LA. I promised him that when I returned, I would get a real cast for my seriously broken wrist. I was nineteen and most definitely had a crush on Dreamy Dr. Vergess, also a Lakeside member and a marathon runner. He had the quiet demeanor of someone very accomplished and excellent in his field, and the stealthy stare of someone who spent long hours alone. When he showed me the x-rays of my wrist, he was thoughtful and direct.

"This is going to hurt more if it's wobbling around, plus it will not heal properly," Dr. Vergess wisely instructed.
"I pinky swear promise, I'll be back to get a cast as soon as this trip is over," I assured, once again.

My role in the film was 'Pretty Skater' not 'Skater With a Broken Arm' so I had to do the right thing and sacrifice the healing of my wrist for vanity. Duh. That same day I came back to my condo and started praying for a miracle. Dr. Vergess was right, it was hurting, a lot. I had some information about faith healing and the most important part was to list the reasons why the miracle was necessary and what I would do with the miracle once it happened. The truth is, miracles are happening all around us all the time. In fact, so many miracles are happening so quickly, that we are barely geared up for the next one as soon as the last one is over. There are just too many to document, but people talk about them all the time and give witness, as I am about to do now.

I began to pray. When I pray, I pray to God. God is Love to me. I believe in the Eternal, Universal Power of Love, and that truth is in my heart and in some phenomenal way, this belief calms me down and gives me comfort, peace and unbounded strength. Knowing this, I prayed for the healing of my wrist. I prayed that I would be able to do many good things with my wrist once it was healed. I would be able to wave to people, sign my name and carry my own luggage, all in the name of God. It sounds superficial, but at the time it made perfect sense. I just wanted to be able to do the things I was doing before, however, if my wrist was healed, I would do them with more meaning. I promised that I would spread the Word of my healed wrist to anyone willing to listen and that it would be a very good thing for everyone. It went on and on like this for a few tearful moments, as I really was in pain. Suddenly, I felt a wave of heat traveling through my body, something I had never felt before, then a wash of cool air down my neck. I heard a vibration from my heart say, "It's okay. You can take it off."

I figured the voice was talking about the splint, so I removed it and started moving my wrist back and forth. The pain was gone, and I was instantly scared shitless. I was alone, with no one to witness to, or anyone to witness what was going on. I was instantly terrified of what was happening. Terrified. I ran outside into the courtyard of the condo area with tears running down my cheeks. I was flushed and frightened in the middle of the day. I looked around, but no one in sight. Too afraid to pray anymore, I sat down on my steps, frightened to go back inside the house. It was just a very freaky experience and I was completely confused. Was I talking myself into a faith healing? All of a sudden, an elderly woman walked by and glanced in my direction. She saw the look of terror on my face and asked, "Are you alright?" With a leap of faith, I told her what I had just conjured up. Through my tears and own amazement, I worked my wrist back and forth to show her that it was real, and she looked at me with pure love shining from her eyes.

"I have been crying in my home all morning," the elderly woman's voice cracked.
I began to feel the same wave of heat and cool air on my neck.

"My husband just passed, and I've been so lonely and so sad. I just begged God to let me know... that I'm not alone." She began to cry.

"You did? Really?" I could feel the sting of more tears.

She nodded and said, "Then I stepped outside to get some air and I saw you."

We both stood there in the swirl of two very fresh miracles, comforting each other in our awareness and presence of one fine Holy Spirit.

I went back to Dr. Vergess the next day, almost certain that this was real, even though I needed a night to process. I wanted to quell any doubt in my mind. I wanted x-rays to prove the miracle and they did. Dr. Vergess, a real 'docs do it by the book' doctor of science and medicine could not believe what he saw. He reassured me that there *were* once hairline fractures and that maybe I *should* keep the splint with me, just in case. However, these hairline fractures were no longer showing up on the x-rays, nor did my wrist hurt.

"There had been three fractures, so why wouldn't at least one show up if they were still there!?"

"I can't explain that to you," Dr. Vergess said with his definitive bedside manner.

"No one will ever be able explain this to me, because it was simply a miracle. Which means, no explanation necessary," I reassured Dr. Vergess, as I jumped off the white crumpled protector paper that left a very impressionable ass print on his exam table.

I had never seen that elderly woman before that day and I never saw her again. I don't even remember what she looked like, other than kind and sympathetic. She was there for me in my fear of the known and unknown. She was there for me to bear witness of a freaky phenomenon that scared the crap out of me. She lovingly reassured me that my heart was in the right place and my prayer was going to the right source. My witness was for her witness. It was the flow of energy heading directly to the Origin. It was truly God in action, and I will never feel alone again.

I pray all the time, wherever I am. It gives me great comfort to throw all of my problems right at God. He said to do it. "I am God and I am here for all your problems today" says a plaque that hung in my Aunt Evelyn's home. Aunt Evie was one of the most amazing, loving, positive influencers of my life. We had a deep connection in spirit and in faith. She was my dad's older sister and I truly thank God every day for her. Maybe meeting that elderly woman was a premonition of things to come. Whatever it was, it happened, and I don't need an x-ray to prove it. Although I do wish I had a copy for those who need *proof.*

Epic Fail ~ Roller skating without wrist protectors is taking your wrists into your own hands.

Epic Save ~ Not questioning how miracles happen or deciding why.

Lesson Learned ~ Use your best judgment and listen to your heart.

"Life is full of happiness and tears, be strong and have faith."
    ~ Kareena Kapoor Khan

CHAPTER 35

~ on Esther

Esther Williams, from Inglewood, California was an iconic movie star at MGM long before I was born. At seventeen, she was already a National Swimming Champion in the 100 meter freestyle and went on to become the most famous swimmer on the planet. In 1939 she was assured a spot on the United States team for the 1940 Summer Olympics which were going to be held in Tokyo, Japan. Unfortunately, the summer games were cancelled due to the outbreak of World War II. Oddly, she did not receive a swimming scholarship to the University of Southern California, so she took the next best offer, stardom.

She worked with numerous legendary actors and directors and her movies are something that no one has even come close to replicate. Nobody else has ever had the skill, athleticism or beauty that Esther possessed. She was one of a kind and she was my mentor. I simply loved her and unlike an adoring fan, I had not seen many of her movies. I loved her spirit and her wisdom and the generous way in which she shared both. She called me her 'other daughter' and when Lorenzo and I split up, she refused to let me go. We remained very close throughout the rest of her life.

Esther was America's sweetheart, and a real-life mermaid. The camera loved her and so did all the men. Why wouldn't they? She was in a bathing suit in every movie she made. There was always water around her, so it actually made sense. She was smart, brave and articulate. She was way ahead of her time in the feminist department. She stood up for herself in a way that I'm sure gave several folks at the studio pause. Who was this young bathing beauty with a point of view and brass huevos? It was Esther Williams, the five foot eight mega star who could level you with a single glance and a few parting remarks that would leave you breathless and bewildered. Did she just insult me? I must go thank her for even noticing me. She never minced words, but she certainly put a lovely lilt to the delivery. I'm sure there were very few, if none, who could ever say 'no' to that gorgeous face of hers. She had the ability to lay down the law for her films, as there was really no one on earth who could ever replace her. She was dominant in a swamped field of stars being the *only* swimming movie star. No one else came close, and there will never be anyone like her. The Golden Age of Hollywood is long gone and been replaced by special effects, CGI and computer stand-ins. We will never have someone who did her own stunts and then swam away at the height of her career to raise a family. She was beyond unique or special, she was legendary, and I miss her dearly. Her photo remains at my bedside and I speak to her often, listening for her to give me a clue on what to do next during any given problem. She was a practitioner of the Science of Mind and her thoughtful, positive attitude towards life is something that I've always strived to emulate.

Esther free styled away from the business at the height of her career and like several other women in Hollywood, she got ripped-off blind by a gambling, alcoholic husband. After all that hard work of early calls, freezing water, Vaseline in her hair, bathing suits up her butt and lecherous actors making moves under the water, she was financially broke. With three very young kids and a failure of a husband, she still persevered. She created her own swimming pool line; her own bathing suit line and she did numerous television specials that featured her still amazing form in and out of the water. When she met Fernando Lamas, she knew that there was room for only one star in the family, so she hung up her bathing suit for good and traded it in for a kaftan, and never looked back. She still swam daily, but it was always in the nude, except for when church members or family would come over. She loved the water and was always instantly smiling when she was submersed. The Tiffany blue pool was her old friend and stabilizer. Splashing and spraying, she was her perfect self, light and neutrally buoyant.

Esther loved to cook and gather her chosen few around to tell her stories. Her food was as delicious as the mermaid tales she would tell, rich with flavor and spiced with just enough sea salt and peppery dialogue. She loved to reminisce about the old studio days and how the heads of the studio would fawn all over her when she entered their office, as she was one of the very few who held the reins to her own career. She loved to talk about her male co-stars and how they would try to do something naughty under the water when they thought no one was looking. She would shudder thinking about the dangerous stunts she did in her films and how a few of them almost drowned her. She was a woman filled with enthusiasm for life and reflective for the life she had so voraciously lived. She gave me tremendous insight into my own career and instilled in me that even though relationships and dreams may come and go, we must stay afloat and 'just keep swimming.'

I modeled her line of swimsuits for catalogues and many magazine shoots. We did one photo shoot for *National Geographic* titled, *A Day in the Life of Beverly Hills.* It was shot at The Beverly Hills Hotel and I couldn't believe that I had made it into such an iconic international magazine with one of the greatest legends of all time. It was otherworldly. I eventually became Esther's photographer and producer for many shoots of *Esther Williams Swimwear* alongside Esther's devoted husband, Edward Bell. I hired just about every beautiful family member and friend of mine to model her swimsuits at her home and on their houseboat, *The Million Dollar Mermaid,* named after one of her films and the title of her autobiography.

Esther was honest and she did not suffer fools. If you bothered her, she let you know it. She knew immediately when someone was a fan. I never saw my own mother ever be a fan of anyone, until she met Esther. My mom would get all giddy and have a goofy perma-grin when she was around Esther. It used to annoy me, until I saw the depth and sincerity of my mother's awe and admiration. I eventually found it quite endearing that my mom actually looked up to someone, which rarely happened. Esther and my mom are both Leo's, as are Lorenzo's mom, Arlene Dahl and my godmother, Victoria, both of whom never really hit it off with Esther. That's a whole lot of dominant cats, not interested in sitting around and purring over each other. As a general rule, there is usually only one Leo allowed to a group, but Esther loved my mom and she knew she was a fan, so she endured it.

One great story that I would have Esther tell over and over again was when she was honored for an award that was to be given to her at a well-known country club in Los Angeles. Let's call it, *Los Angeles Country Club*. She was already in her mid-sixties and mostly wearing pant suits due to the relentless aging condition of when stunning legs are not considered as stunning in the good way. Esther had great style, and the money to have great style, and she took tremendous pride in her appearances. She arrived at this gala event in a stunning *Oscar de la Renta* ensemble of black silk pants and a multicolored brocade jacket from a Japanese obi. She was immediately informed by the staff that *pants* for women were not part of the *dress code*. She assured them that she was the 'honoree' of the evening and no one had given her the rulebook for the women's dress code. Then the horror of all horrors, that poor lackey handed Esther a balled up, black skirt, pulled from the female staff's clothing line.

Esther looked at the skirt, and the pathetic fool holding the skirt, and she said in her most alarmingly calm voice, "Hold onto that filthy skirt, dear, I'll be right back."

She then turned to her husband, Edward, and said, "Where's the microphone, darling?" Edward led her up to the podium, knowing something thrilling was going down and that he'd better get his valet ticket ready.

Esther got up to the mic and announced to the anticipating and thrilled audience, "Good evening, I'm Esther Williams." Huge applause.

"I want to thank you for honoring me tonight for my lifetime of achievements."

More applause.

"But I have just been informed by your less than delightful staff that I'm not dressed properly for your event, so I will be leaving now due to the archaic dress code of 'no pants for women'."

Boom, drop the mic. The hush and shameful, "Oh no's!" from the audience were the only thing she heard on her departure. She had her press agent immediately get the *LA Times* on the phone where she released the gauntlet on that tired old golf club with its shitty old skirt they wanted The Mermaid Queen to fashion. How dare they. That stodgy, stuffy old club will never be the same.

Epic Fail ~ If there is a dress code, **always** let your guest know ***before*** the event.

Epic Save ~ Not being pressured into wearing someone else's balled up skirt.

Lesson Learned ~ Having the guts to instantly recognize a wrongdoing, say something immediately, gracefully walk away and call the press.

"Fashions fade, style is eternal."
	~ Yves Saint Laurent

CHAPTER 36

~ on kissing

My first kiss was immediately followed by a loud fart. It was the end of summer, in the caddy tunnel at the club where my dad has a membership. I was twelve and so was Tommy. I had a crush on him for most of my life, up to that point. I had just returned from a six-week trip to England with my British uber nanny, Mary Rogers. It was 1977, the year of The Silver Jubilee, which marked the Queen's 25th year in reign. The entire country was in a parade for a solid year and it was magical. Everywhere we went were banners, celebration and everything and anything you could stamp the Queen's face on. It was tchotchke heaven. I decided the best gift to bring back to The States for Tommy, was to collect patches from every place I went and sew them on a pale blue Oxford shirt. I decided that an even better idea would be to collect patches for both of us, and sew them onto matching Oxford shirts, so we could be twinsies. (Note to self, twelve-year-old boys are not looking to be twinsies with twelve-year-old girls. It messes up their image that they're desperately trying to discover.) Nonetheless, I painstakingly bought, collected and sewed over twenty patches on each shirt. When I was done, it looked like two blue oxford shirts covered in travel hell. It was really just a memento of all the places I had been, and it gave me an opportunity to learn how to sew. It went over like a fart in a caddy tunnel during your first kiss.

Tommy looked at the shirt, then looked at me and said, "Do I have to wear it?"

"Of course not, but if you want to kiss me, you should," I replied.

That clinched it and we immediately went down to the place we were never allowed, in the dark curve of the tunnel. We kissed, and then I farted. Really? Yes, really. That's what happens when excitement builds and you're doing several things you're not supposed to be doing, in a place where kids are not allowed. He hated my shirt, so I told everyone that *he* farted when we kissed. That fixed it. Not.

It was quite a while before I kissed anyone again after that. I'm pretty sure I waited until I was in eighth grade. Then all the hormones broke loose, and it was game on. By the time I got to high school, I had kissed quite a few. When I started dating Lorenzo, at seventeen, in my senior year, I was no longer a virgin. Kissing does lead to sex; the same way alcohol can lead to drugs. Although, I have to say, and several of my girlfriends agree, kissing is by far more intimate. Unfortunately, not everyone is good at it, nor do they take the time to learn. First base is followed by two more bases and then home plate. It's just not the place where guys want to dwell, because there are so many other fun things to conquer on the field to get a score. However, first base is the most important, because without it, you're striking out or just sitting on the bench. Tommy got a 'walk' to first and then I literally 'blew' it and got sent back to the dugout/penalty box.

Kissing is an art form of; build up, eye contact, fresh breath, good hygiene, confidence, hand placement, body pressure, head tilt, soft lips, tongue (but <u>please</u>, not too much). Most important, you've got to like the person. I have liked a lot of guys, but there were very few who knew how to kiss. Sometimes, you need to tell them how to do it, as in what you want and how you want it. That moment will define the likability factor, as some people are easier to direct than others. If you can't vocalize what you want because you're too embarrassed to verbalize your desires, or maybe you don't even know what you want or how to say it, go to the Internet. There are several sites that will direct both willing partners to the best kiss possible and learning together is a great thing. The Internet has a lot of information on sex, but stick with the kissing as long as possible. There's no rush to do anything else, as the kiss will usually define how everything else will turn out. If someone rushes a kiss, then chances are everything else will be rushed too. Why would anyone want to rush the most important part of an intimate moment?

One of my favorite works of art is *The Kiss* by Gustav Klimt. It truly tells the story of utter collapse in someone's arms as they embrace and crush you with their kiss. In this timeless piece of art, I find absolute surrender and bliss surrounded by flowers and gold. The details in Klimt's painting are far more than the eye can understand in a single viewing. It hangs high in my home in a gilded frame and is a constant reminder to the intricacy of intimacy. We all have a need to feel connected, vulnerable and open to this part of the dance, which is the beginning of affection and togetherness, so make it last as long as possible.

Fairy tales end with a kiss, they don't start with one. That's where the happily ever after part begins. Let the adventure of getting to know someone be the buildup and let the kiss define if the journey will continue. So, on behalf of every Cinderella, Mulan, Belle, Snow White, Tiana, Jasmine, Ariel, Pocahontas, Aurora, Rapunzel and Giselle, we like to kiss. So please for the love of God, *learn.*

Epic Fail ~ Rushing sex before enjoying the kiss.

Epic Save ~ Slowing the roll and enjoying the brush of one's lips.

Lesson Learned ~ A good day starts and ends with a kiss and a prayer of gratitude.

"A kiss is a secret told to the mouth instead of the ear; kisses are the messengers of love and tenderness."
~ Ingrid Bergman

CHAPTER 37

~ **on reality**

I am so stupid for Bravo. I love Andy Cohen and every bit of programming on his network. I have always been a huge fan of James Lipton's, *Inside The Actors Studio.* I hang on every word in every interview, just like the youthful sponges' in his audience. The draw for me with Bravo's Reality TV is that it feels like a familiar glimpse into how I grew up; glamorous, intoxicated, and at times prettier on the outside then on the inside. Everybody has their hefty bag of problems but the rich and enfranchised carry steamer trunks. The greatest part about these shows, are the things they don't discuss. They stick to their relationships and stay out of the daily grind of the god-awful news in the world. We are all inundated with such an onslaught of the world terrors that to be able to enclose yourself in a fantasy bubble is actually good for the senses. It is for mine anyway. I know about the reality of the planet and there are times I just need to turn it off and go watch a comedy, a documentary, a rockumentary, or just some good 'ol Bravo reality. I find the anthropology of it all very fascinating and entertaining. Beautiful people in stunning places, wading through all the bullshit of their entitled life. One of my favorite pastimes is to get caught up with all *The Housewives* and sit back and thank God that isn't me. Although, I do secretly wish I was on the show, I'm just not rich enough or married enough to compete with anyone in Beverly Hills. If they had The Single Mom Valley Girl version, I'd be perfect. I think the fans all fantasize about sitting around and dishing with Erika Jayne and Lisa Van Der Pump about the best place to get your face on. These hard-working ladies are works of art. I love 'em and just like The Housewives, I love some more than others. Such is life and flip the table.

My reality growing up, and still continues to be, comprised around famous people. I am forever bumping into someone I know who is generally some kind of celebrity just through proximity. I didn't know too much about reality TV until I met Gretchen Rossi and Slade Smiley from *The Housewives of OC*. I was shopping my pilot, *Hollywood Bump and Grind*, a half hour female *Entourage*, that became re-titled to *Fame Game*. Apparently *Bump and Grind* had other connotations and difficult to translate into foreign languages. Slade and Gretchen were sharing space in my EP's downtown studio for Gretchen's fashion line, *Gretchen Christine*. After I met the dynamic duo, I had to find out more about their show. Then I got hooked and became emotionally invested in all of them. Now I run into my favorite reality stars all the time, just because of the city I live in, my dad's club, the place my brother works and the Ralph's where I buy groceries. I'm a total fan girl sometimes, I can't help it. I get excited to meet people. It's fun talking to famous people when they've done a good job and letting them know that the people in the audience (me) are really enjoying it. I think it's good to give compliments. I believe people like it. They don't like it when they're biting into a big fat hoagie, or telling a joke to their friends, or on the phone in the stall next to you. Timing is everything with compliments, comedy and baking a cake.

I was at my first *U2* concert, with my rocker friend, Jim. We were pretty close to the stage, in the standing General Admission area. I was crying at the end of the concert, while Bono sang *Amazing Grace*, a cappella. It's astounding to me that something so beautiful can bring you to tears so spontaneously. It's quite a special feeling which doesn't happen every day. Before I knew it, some kind of amazing human handed us two backstage passes and took off. Who was that heavenly being and why did he just give us two passes with that sticky back that you plaster to the leg of your jeans? Thank you awesome person, whoever you were! Jim and I stuck those things on and waltzed right back into the most dreary looking, folding chairs and rectangular table with big bowls of craft service junk food and no glamour whatsoever, backstage roadie area. I had nothing to compare it to, since this was my first exceptional backstage moment. I decided to give the folding chairs a try since we had been standing for hours. My butt had barely hit the hard plastic when Bono came around the corner and walked right over to me and gave me a great big sweaty hug. Yes, this really happened. This was my reality for that most amazing, graceful moment in time. Like, this has got to be what heaven feels like. You cry at Amazing Grace and you get to go to heaven and Bono gives you a sweaty hug and you're in! Plus there's lots of Cheetos, jellybeans and folding chairs, which I sat in for about an hour and a half, not believing what just happened. That's when you really want reality TV following you around to document.

Another great reality moment was when I got to introduce Tom Hanks and Rita Wilson to Esther Williams outside Pavarotti's dressing room. I had gone to the opera with Esther, to witness the great Luciano Pavarotti, in *Othello*. As luck would have it, we all had the same thought to go backstage to tell him, "Well done, Pavarotti." So that was a fun one, because I used to date Rita's brother, Theo, who I will eternally feel bad about how it ended, as it was <u>totally</u> my fault. Tom had cast me in his writing and directing debut, *That Thing You Do!*, so there was that thing in common. Esther was my ex-step-mother-in-law through Lorenzo, so there was some rich history there. It was a relief when Pavarotti brought us into his dressing room, as I remember the hallway being quite close with all that mega-watt star power.

When I first met Arlene Dahl, Lorenzo's gorgeous, movie star mother, we were in Palm Beach, Florida. We were standing outside a lovely restaurant awash with twinkling white lights in the balmy sway of palm trees. The banyan trees out front were dancing in the wind as Arlene said, in her most magical sing song voice, "Close your eyes, darling."
I dutifully did.
"We could be *anywhere* in the world right now."
Arlene has a mystical and honest approach to the world of astrology. She knows the solar system, star power and following the lights that guide her. She loves to read astral charts and enjoys the insight that surrounds the time of one's own birth and how that forecasts their life. She did many positive astral readings for me which gave me great

comfort and validation for a life that was already well charted.

I was like, still with my eyes closed, "Well, we're in Palm Beach, which is pretty amazing. I'm not sure if I need to astral travel anywhere else."

"We are already there, wherever you want to be," she cooed.

I love that about Arlene, she's in Palm Beach and possibly reimagining it as St. Tropez. I've never been, so Palm Beach was good enough for me.

The most difficult reality is being somewhere that you don't want to be. In a place that doesn't feel safe and you're not feeling respected or appreciated. It's an awful feeling to feel like you're a hostage to a relationship or situation. Sometimes the thought of having to change our reality is so daunting and overwhelming, that we stay and 'hang in there' just because it's too paralyzing to move and rock the boat. Here's the truth: if you want your reality to change, you have to change it. You have to find your voice and scream, speak or write a letter. Share your reality with friends, family, co-workers, teachers, cops and/or the court to make a shift in your reality. If your reality is mental, physical or emotional abuse, telling someone is a great first step to a reality change. Secretly imploding and scared to death of an outcome serves no one. Be brave, like Bravo, and let the fur fly. Everyone has a right to a better reality and saying something about a narcissist who is trying to control you will help ignite the change.

Our reality is up to us. We can ignore things that matter, or we can address them head on. We can let things go that aren't a big deal or we can make matters worse by throwing gas on a spark. We can give ourselves a break from all the world's hardships and find a time to decompress from things that feel out of our control. We can cry at concerts, we can give compliments and we can pretend we're in Tahiti, when we're really in Santa Monica. Just close your eyes and imagine your perfect life, then do something to make it your reality.

Epic Fail ~ Staying in a place that doesn't feel safe or where you are unappreciated and disrespected.

Epic Save ~ Recognizing your true reality and doing everything possible to make a change for your wellbeing.

Lesson Learned ~ Creating a life that feels safe and self-respected, so that astral travel is unnecessary.

"Reality is merely an illusion, albeit a very persistent one."
~ Albert Einstein

CHAPTER 38

~ **on bullies**

Bullies are like old mold. They were already stale and nasty, and over time, they become carcinogenic. Bullying is about an imbalance of power between the bully and the victim and is intended to cause harm through repetitive action. Some of the people most difficult to forgive are repeat offenders. It's one thing if someone continues to hurt you and you're able to create a boundary and/or remove that person from your life, but if they are a family member, or someone at school, or the workplace, it becomes a real dilemma. When someone continually picks on you because they think they are cooler, smarter, stronger or better than you, you know you're dealing with a bully. We've all had at least one in our life. I've had a few.

I've been picked on and made fun of for so many things. My height (too tall), my weight (too skinny), my teeth (buck and braces), the color of my hair (dumb blonde). Blonde jokes have always been an easy target. I was forced to learn a few for self-preservation. You know when you're dealing with a bully when at the end of putting you down and hurting your feelings, they end with a deflecting, "I was only joking."

Guess what? They weren't *only* joking. They were also searching for your weak spot to see if you flinch and buckle under their obvious putdown humor. They are lying when they say they're 'only joking' because what they are really trying to do is make you cry, not laugh. If something makes you feel hurt from something someone says, respond with a quick and affirmative, "That was mean." If they respond with, "I was only joking" then strongly proclaim, "It hurt my feelings." If they say something so lame as, "Oh my God, you're so sensitive!" instead of "I'm so sorry", then you know for sure, you've got a bully on your hands. Walk away and don't look back.

Restraining, or cease and desist orders, are very difficult to keep in place when you are dealing with a bully on a regular basis, especially if you have to co-exist with that person on any level.

If a bully is tormenting you in school, tell your parents <u>and</u> tell the school administration. The responsible parent should immediately contact the school, talk to the teacher and the principal, and be specific about the problem. A meeting should be arranged between school administration and the parents of the bully and if that doesn't get resolved, then the parents should duke it out on the playground or in the courtroom.

If a bully is tormenting you in the workplace, go to your boss <u>and</u> Human Resources and be specific about the problem. What if the bully is your boss? Speak with your boss and record the conversation, then go back to Human Resources and give them the proof exposing what a tireless jerk your boss is and start looking for another job.

If a bully is tormenting you in your family, you're not alone. It's very difficult to get away from a family bully, as there are so many ways to be a nuisance, cause harm, create stress and encourage low self-esteem. Bullies like to cause self-doubt by pointing out every mistake by offering criticism, over and over again. This kind of criticism is designed to make the bully feel better about themselves, rather than helping the victim. There are ways to deal with and hopefully minimize the effects of dysfunctional family members. Bullies like to see a reaction, so don't give them one. Remain calm and unemotional. You can control your reaction, you can't control the bully, but it will make a difference if they continue to get a zero response. Write down the time, place and type of incident, as this will help you identify any patterns of behavior. This will help to alleviate any future problems down the road. If the bully is more grumpy on a Wednesday than a Friday, make yourself scarce on that day. Find people you trust and turn to them. It can be another family member, or a friend, or a teacher, or someone in authority. Share what's going on and give them details. It helps to get it off your chest and it allows for some help to come into the mix.

Establishing boundaries, asserting yourself and remaining confident sound easy, but when you're being bullied, it's tough. If you are currently being bullied and gathering the courage to make a change, be sure to recharge from being stressed out. A long walk, a good book, yoga, music, or a good movie can be useful tools to help you get back on track and reboot. Taking a self-defense course of any kind is a great way to get your body and mind in a 'ready to respond' and 'stay the hell away from me' mode.

I have had the great pleasure of being in quite a few action films, conditioning myself for fight scenes and playing tough characters that take no prisoners. I've throat punched, karate chopped and pulled guns on massive brutish men. I've clothes lined, spinning heel kicked and double barrel shot-gunned more than I can count. In *CIA Code Name: Alexa,* I played the title role and had the great opportunity to head butt O.J. Simpson in an interrogation scene. We filmed this movie three months before the horrific murder of his estranged wife. OJ was definitely showing signs of angst during our filming. One day, he arrived to the makeup trailer and was very agitated. I gingerly asked him, "What' going on?"

He never looked at me as he studied himself in the brightly lit mirror. He finally responded, "I saw my wife jogging in <u>my</u> neighborhood."

I thought maybe that was odd, because they were separated and why would she be jogging in *his* neighborhood.

"That's kind of strange, where does she live?" I questioned.

"About a mile away," he said with no emotion.

"Oh, so it's really, like, y'all's neighborhood," I assured him, doing my best sunny side up impression in an attempt to lighten the extraordinarily chilling weirdness in the air.

He didn't like that retort at all and for the rest of the shoot he was a grumpy, moody actor guy. In hindsight, it was possible that something was brewing. I'll never forget watching that white Bronco speeding through the streets and freeways of LA, trying to sprout wings and fly away from one of the most despicable and heinous bully acts of all time.

I've played out the scenario of being questioned by O.J.'s "Dream Team" regarding his moody behavior on set many times in my head. Stepping forward to get involved in that mishigas would have been a very lame fifteen seconds of fame. This is the only way I imagine it would've played out.

Robert Shapiro: Please state your full name to the court.
Kathleen Kinmont: Kathleen Kinmont.
Robert Kardashian: Please state your occupation.
KK: I'm an actor.
Johnnie Cochran: Ahh, an actor. Actors like to act, don't they?
KK: I believe so. For money. Yes.
RS: What kind of role was Mr. Simpson playing in this straight to video movie?
KK: A detective.
RK: What was your role in the film?
KK: I was playing a turned CIA Agent running for my life.
JC: Who was chasing you?
KK: Mr. Simpson's character.
RS: Being an actor yourself, have you ever heard of preparing for a role?
KK: Uh, yeah, sure. Yes.

JC: Do you think Mr. Simpson might have been preparing for his role in finding something deep inside his actor mind to get himself girded up to chase you?

KK: Maybe.

RK: Yes or no, please, Ms. Kinmont.

KK: Yes, he could have been preparing his role.

RS: So, while he was in the make-up trailer, where most actors are preparing and getting ready to step on the set, he was possibly having a moment of *reflection* in anticipating his film work. Would you agree that that is a normal thing that actors do when they are on the set?

Long pregnant pause of 'Why did I come forward with this?'

RS: Ms. Kinmont?

KK: Yes?

RS: Is that a yes to the question?

KK: No, I mean, yes. Yes, that's a yes to the question, I guess.

JC: Thank you, Ms. Kinmont. No more questions.

KK: (Look of bewilderment and regret.)

RK: You can step down now, Ms.Kinmont.

The one good thing about a bully is that the majority weren't born that way. They were born nice little babies who just wanted love, but somewhere down the road, they got bumped, kicked and bullied by someone else. As we've witnessed form the in-depth backstory of *JOKER*, they might have experienced massive head trauma as a child in a crib or as an adult on a football field. Child abuse, trauma and neglect are tremendous factors in the creation of a bully. If a parent has abandoned their child or killed themself, this will create confusion, despair and angst. These components become a major factor in the making of a bully. Through someone else's doing, a bully becomes mean and nasty and wants to hurt someone else the way they were hurt. Or a bully was just born a sociopath. Either way, however we can muster up the ability, we need to feel compassion for that person, as they probably didn't intend to be a hateful jerk when they grew up. They are definitely and definitively hurting somewhere deep inside their heart. Pray for them, as it's only become a deplorable habit to be a narcissist, and trust me, they will end up dealing with someone bigger one day. You can count on it.

Epic Fail ~ Allowing someone to bully you.

Epic Save ~ Speaking up for yourself and establishing boundaries.

Lesson Learned ~ If you suffer an attack, the best ally is to remain calm, get help and go live your best life.

"No better relation than a prudent and faithful friend."
　　　～ Benjamin Franklin

CHAPTER 39

~ **on humor**

O ne of the biggest challenges in my professional life was when I decided, while pregnant, to give stand-up comedy a try. That job really takes some gonads and a dedication to fail. The ones that succeed are tirelessly writing new material and relentless in their pursuit of a laugh. After I did a few open mics at The Comedy Store, I realized a lot of comics are pretty screwed up and depressed. It's by far one of the toughest gigs out there. Standing alone on a stage with a bright light in your face and your balls in your neck, can be a major high or a soul crushing fail. I believe it was the great comic genius, Woody Allen, who captured the phrase "Comedy is tragedy plus time." Which means when you've got your rental car stuck in the mud on your Hawaiian vacation after it just hit a tree, one day you'll be able to laugh about it. It's true, some things that aren't at all funny at the time, one day will be. Not always, but sometimes.

It's the way people can laugh at a funeral when they think of something wild and crazy their loved one used to do that still cracks them up. My beloved Aunt Shirl's memorial was filled with tears, music and laughter. We all went around the room sharing our cherished memories about this fun-loving, wildly creative and beautiful spirit who we all adored immensely. She left her imprint on all of us with her contagious laugh and her love of imagination and the absurd. She was my mother's younger sister, so naturally, there was some competition in their relationship, but they always bonded over their diabolical, wicked, derelict sense of humor. They knew how to get a laugh and they knew timing. Sometimes they went for the jugular but as women learn early on, we can get away with a little more because of our gender. Somehow it becomes shocking when a woman is funny, as with men it can just be offensive. Unless you're Kathy Griffin who held up a bloody Trump head.

My brother, Matt, one of the funniest people I know, said that if Kathy had just turned that around and had Trump holding up her bloody head, it would have been a completely different statement. Maybe it's not too late for that. Kind of gross for my taste, but that's the point of comedy, you have to go to a very raw, edge of the cliff if you want to stay current, crotchety and provocative. If you want to get noticed and asked back, you have to dig deep and do and say stuff that's going to make your parents cringe. You have to be willing to say to yourself, "I don't care what anybody else thinks, I think it's funny and I'm going to say it."

Howard Stern has created an entire empire based on that concept. I remember the first time I was a guest on his show, and he was begging to see my underwear. I was initially shocked and then terrified of having to show him my very stupid and not sexy, nor prepared, underwear. It was the middle of a New York winter for Gods sakes! In my lame deflection I said, "What would your wife think?"

Howard, without even flinching or a nanosecond of hesitation, replied, "My wife has leukemia, so who cares."

His trusty sidekick, Robin Quivers, gushed, "Oh Howard," through her bewildering laughter, "your wife doesn't have leukemia."

"Well, she could," he said.

More hearty laughs, followed by a swift uncoupling.

I still didn't show my lame ass underwear that day, though he tried. I explained they were winter panties and so not hot or sexy. When I came back to do his show for the second time, in the summer months, I wore a kick ass Calvin Klein underwear ensemble complete with thigh-high riding/dominatrix boots. I graciously gave him a memorable eye-full upon arrival. Always good to be prepared in case you have to show up and show your underwear. I thought let's get this stripping nonsense out of the way so that he can bear witness to my charming personality and willingness to be fodder for his feast.

I came back a third time for Howard's show and I was so willing to let loose, it got me fired from *Renegade*. That was not funny, but a great reminder that some humor can most definitely hurt.

I don't like making fun of people who can't defend themselves. I don't like making fun of people who can defend themselves. I don't have steel cold balls to throw at anyone or poke fun at those who are obviously suffering. Mean and aggressive humor can cause job loss, weight gain, weight loss,

329

drug use and disease. People that have been relentlessly picked on will sometimes even take their own life to get away from the abuse. So don't pick on kids, the handicapped, old people or each other. There are plenty of things to find funny without potshots at people who are just trying to find their way and get through life with a smile.

Make fun of yourself and point out all your own foibles and mishaps and get those around you to laugh at themselves too. You might end up with a talk show!

Epic Fail ~ Thinking that you can say anything you want, without thinking how it will affect others.

Epic Save ~ Self-deprecating humor is a way for everyone else to laugh with you at something they recognize in themselves.

Lesson Learned ~ In a public forum, when you don't want to say something bad about someone, just plead the fifth.

"It's your outlook on life that counts. If you take yourself lightly and don't take yourself too seriously, pretty soon you can find the humor in our everyday lives. And sometimes it can be a lifesaver."
    ~ Betty White

CHAPTER 40

~ **on forgiveness**

I remember something my mom said to me so clearly the day I got married to Lorenzo. She said, "Marriage is about giving and forgiving." Since we marry ourselves to so many people and things in life without a marriage certificate, I believe this giving and forgiving concept should really start with ourselves. I've sufficiently beaten myself up for the many dumb things I've done and it's time to give some forgiveness. I think these years alone, without a man by my side and in my bed, has been a deep reflective time looking at all the choices I've made, and I've finally come to this ~ How do I trust myself to choose, when all my choices have ended with grief?

It's a very tricky thing, love. You want to believe that someone is going to be there for you, yet you also want that person to be independent. You want to be part of somebody's world, yet you don't want to be the only thing they live for. It's like calling someone your Best Friend, it really is a ton of responsibility to be the best of anything. Ask Clayton Kershaw. The guy is so hard wired for strict routine in his performance because of the pressure to perform as the world's best. In his quest, there will be no straying from a strong habit of humility, regimen and unearthly focus. He is unfazed. Do you think he has a lot of time for small talk during the season? Probably not, but I'm sure his wife forgives him for it.

There are some things that happen in life that feel absolutely unforgivable. The problem with that is that it inevitably catches up to the person as a resentment and can cause all kinds of stress related disease. Nelson Mandela is a great example of someone who lost his freedom without just cause. He sat in a jail for many years, only to be released decades later and shake hands with his prison guards on his way out. He decided somewhere through his prison sentence that he should forgive the situation, and he did. It made him even more of a hero. He was so humbled by the experience that people were just amazed at his fortitude and strength of spirit. Somehow, being able to forgive puts that person back in the driver's seat of their own life. They are no longer fueled by anger and their brain is no longer working on overdrive on how to get even. We can't get even when someone has done a wrong. If someone has murdered someone you love, you can't go out and murder someone they love. It's not legal, and the repercussions of taking someone else's life for someone you lost is a huge karmic debt and chances are, there will be many repercussions that follow. Even jail will never feel fair for a murderer, as it does not bring the person back that was taken. It takes time but eventually forgiveness will have to settle in, as the weight of anger becomes too much to bear.

I was so furious at the world when Lorenzo and I broke up. My life was going so great. We were working together on a great show. I was only twenty-eight and looking forward to having kids with him. I had waited so long for him to be finally ready to have a life with me. It seemed like everything was in place for a wonderful life together with the man of my dreams. I was a loving stepmom to his kids. I took good care of our home. I was contributing financially, spiritually and emotionally. I kept asking myself the same three questions: "What the hell? How did I fail? Why me, God?" I was so angry. I was on the floor for about three days. I fell asleep on the living room floor, crawled to the kitchen, ate on the floor, crawled to the bathroom etc. I was literally floored by the whole thing. When I showed up to work, I had to endure the sad faces of all the crew members. They knew what was happening and did their best to console me on this inconsolable state of affairs. Several of them told me about their own personal divorce drama, which is not the thing anyone wants to hear about when they are in the throes of their own painful demise, I mean divorce. I finally had to grow up and take charge of the sad sack of shituation and forgive Lorenzo, plus tell the *Renegade* herd to stop with the long faces. I had to show all, including myself, that I was resilient to this loss and move on or quit the show. I was not in the mood to lose everything, including my paycheck, so I eventually pulled it together, forgave all the bullshit and carried on.

Forgiveness is a daily ritual. The anger will try to sneak back in, so like a mantra, a golf swing, an at bat or a yoga pose, forgiveness needs to be practiced over and over. Then there will be something new to forgive in every day, allowing forgiveness to become more like a predisposition, a tendency, a habit. The more you practice letting go, the more your body will respond in that manner to several other situations. It's a conditioning process. You can recognize the people who practice letting go and you can sense the ones who don't practice that concept, as they are quick to go to their very happy, angry place. There are those who enjoy rage, in a way that anger makes them happy. They are quick to ignite and get puffed up and loud with a sense of righteous joy, which emulates from them as they position themselves on a throne of displeasure. I know a few people like this and even though they may be super creative, it holds them back from certain wonderful moments in life. I try to steer clear from folks who can't forgive, as it feels like something bad will happen when people can't see straight from their indignation. They aren't as aware of the world around them, rather looking at it through a pinhole. I've been there, so I know. The world becomes very small when you're angry and feel wronged. It feels like you want the planet to stop spinning so you can kindly remove yourself from the ride. I think quite a few people get so caught up in the swirl of life and its overwhelming amount of pain, loss and trauma, that they say, "I just can't do it anymore, I'm out." People take their own life when they can't forgive themselves or someone else, or they think someone won't forgive them. It's a dire, vicious circle when you can't forgive and feel the need to cling onto something that no longer serves you.

Remember this, no matter how heinous the crime, no truer words were ever spoken than those from the incredible human being, commonly known as the Son of God, who, without resentment, hung from a cross and weakly said, "Forgive them Father, for they know not what they do." Now that's strength.

When we pray for someone, it naturally releases us from the burden of having to be angry at them. The weight of anger is real. It's like the weight of depression, which to me feels like the lead vest they put over you when you go to the dentist to get x-rays of your teeth. That substantial vest must weigh about fifteen pounds. I've only been seriously depressed a few times in my life and that's the feeling. You wake up with a corpulent vest attached to your whole body. It's a physical and emotional leaden, burdensome, dense feeling. You just want to sleep and do nothing. You're dragging your tired ass from one dark, dank depressed room to another. It's a miserable, lonely solicitude deep inside your bones. The only way to shake it, without drugs, is to go outside and go for a walk and talk with a friend. Crying is also very good to get out all the old, pent up junk and allow new oxygen to enter the body. I also recommend any and all Jim Carrey movies. He's just so ridiculously funny and great in everything. Thank God for Jim Carrey and his ability and fortitude to get out of his own funk to show up for work and make us laugh. I'm sure he has his bad days too. Thankfully, we can find the laughter in between the tears. We all want something we don't have. Success in life is being grateful for what we do have and making the most out of what's working for us and forgiving what doesn't.

Epic Fail ~ Carrying around a footlocker of anger in our hearts.

Epic Save ~ Finding ways to forgive on a daily basis to heal ourselves from resentment.

Lesson Learned ~ Prayer, meditation, therapy, yoga, friends and family will bring us back to a life of gratitude, if practiced.

"Forgiveness takes place in our own mind. It really has nothing to do with the other person."
~ Louise Hay

340

CHAPTER 41

~ **on repetition**

The definition of bad 'crazy' is mentally deranged, especially as manifested in a wild or aggressive way. Good crazy is defined as extremely enthusiastic. Bad crazy is known for repeating the same stupid thing over and over and expecting different results. I have done the 'bad crazy' in many ways thinking things would turn out differently. In the end, I got the same results from things I already knew did not serve me. I have also done the 'good crazy' with things that I know do serve me, and the results are the same, something good arrives.

Repetition works well with exercise, good food habits, being early, paying bills, returning calls, answering mail, healthy hygiene, getting a good amount of rest and being kind. Repetition does not work well with staying up late, drinking too much, doing drugs, missing appointments, calling in late, or not calling in at all, ignoring mail, bills and being mean.

It's pretty simple, healthy habits bring healthy results. Nasty habits bring nasty results. The more you do, the more you bring. The less you do, the less you have. Kindness is a habit, just like sarcasm. If you continue to look at life like everyone has it out for you, then life will feel like it does have it out for you. If you continue to look at life like what can I bring to make the experience better, then you will find something to make life a better experience.

One of my favorite acting exercises is a Sanford Meisner exercise titled 'Repetition.' I know, I'm already repeating myself, but just in case. I love the way this exercise brings us to a basic awareness of the person in front of us and how they genuinely make us feel just by what they are wearing, how they are standing, the tone of their voice and what they are noticing. It's very simple and wildly complex. The few rules are; don't ask questions, don't talk about yourself, only notice the person in front of you, tell the truth, if in doubt repeat and don't stop playing the game. Repeat the same phrase until something changes and move on to the next phrase, if it's an organic shift. It's amazing where the exercise can take someone.

I think as a species we become conditioned to repetition, just like Pavlov's dog. After a certain amount of time repetition becomes comforting just like the monotony of donning a uniform. I don't need to think about what to wear when I have something that's already been established. A uniform removes the guesswork, as it's already been decided that this is what I put on to represent that thing I do. It's very similar to what a chosen costume feels like for an actor who is getting ready to embrace the character they are creating. Many actors say once they are wearing their costume, that's when the character becomes alive and present. What we wear on the outside, helps to create the interior of an emotional experience. We also have several emotional uniforms that we wear to help us through the day. Sometimes we wear a smile to help us get through a situation. Sometimes a smile is not appropriate, and we should just show compassion, or if all else fails, RBF a.k.a. resting bitch face.

My dad and I were out looking at memory care facilities for my mom. My mom's new habit has become repetitive sleeping. She has become very sleepy in her twilight years and part of her brain is turning towards dementia and slowly shutting down. I don't know how to stop it, because I can't. Doctors don't know how to stop it, because they can't. There's a phrase in the world of professional sports, "So far, Father Time is undefeated." Which means, at some point, no matter how great of an athlete you are, you will get old and you won't be able to play anymore. No matter how many sit-ups, lunges, squats you can muster, you will become too old to compete with the youth who is taking over the locker room. However, don't stop exercising because that will be the death of you.

As my dad and I walked through the circular floor plan, through the calming sage colored walls of the facility, I quietly smiled to several patients who looked very lost and lonely in their imaginariums. (This is a word I created when my beloved Esther Williams began to mentally slip away; it's the imagination that takes over when you're swimming in an aquarium bowl) It's always been disheartening when I smile at someone and get absolutely no smile in return. I assume the person is terminally depressed or must have had a debilitating stroke. My smile has always had a pretty good response for most people. In fact, my smile is so toothy big and dimply it's the equivalent of having a baby horse right up in your face blowing a raspberry. When someone does not smile back, it becomes a kindness challenge. In fact, I believe my smile could challenge Dwyane Johnson's smile in a 'Smile Off.' I believe I just threw out a challenge to The Rock. :-)

So, my dad and I are walking through this mental facility and I'm smiling like a loon, because that's my repetitive habit when I try to make sad people feel good. I actually got a few people to smile in return as we passed through the rooms of people moaning and yelling at caregivers. We were almost at the end of the brief tour, when an old woman in a wheelchair yelled down the hall to me, "You're a pretty girl!"

"Thank you," I said, "so are you."

"You're smiling like a real asshole!" she responded.

"What did she say?" my dad asked.

"I'm smiling like a real asshole," I repeated in dutiful Meisner tradition.

"That's what I thought she said," he smiled. "I think we found your mom a new roommate."

We shared some pretty good bent over laughs for the rest of the day from that one.

Repetition is great for prayer, meditation, food, water, work, play, sleep, love, laughter. Repeat.

Epic Fail ~ Thinking everyone will always smile back.

Epic Save ~ Smile, even when your heart is breaking.

Lesson Learned ~ Repeat the habits in life that make you feel good about yourself.

"We are what we repeatedly do. Excellence, then, is not an act, but a habit."
    ~ Will Durant

CHAPTER 42

~ **on entitlement**

I was in fifth grade when I got cast in a commercial for the Fisher Price toy set, *Little People*. Little People were a ton of fun, as you could make them do all the things that big people did, only in the palm of your hand. You could make them ride a bike, a horse, drive a car, ride a plane or hop on a bus like a big person. Little People were always going somewhere fun like the beach or the mountains. They had families that stayed together and never divorced, and they did things a happy family would do, like picnic, sleep and play. It was a chance for a kid to feel like God and maneuver the Little People from one fun spot to another, always joyful and never in danger. It was a lighthearted toy with very few moving parts and nothing to choke on. It was just a simple slice of life that was colorful and engaging and I was 'the star' of the commercial (with another girl) in Little People nirvana.

I thought I was the absolute massive bomb for being cast in such a monumental commercial for such a world-renowned toy. All my friends would see me playing with the Little People. My youthful face filling the screen while my long blonde hair cascaded down my back, as I created wonderful scenarios with my blossoming, visionary imagination. The director was so nurturing and encouraging me and my brand-new sidekick brunette 'friend' to smile at each other and play together like lifelong besties. I had to share the spotlight with this 'other girl', as commercials like to see kids playing together and not necessarily alone.

You never see a kid grab a toy out of another kid's hand during a commercial, although this is exactly what happened during the filming of our magnificent spot. I was effortlessly smiling and playing while the camera dollied through the well-lit world of Little People when all of a sudden, brunette 'other girl' yanks the toy horse right out of my hand.

"Cut!" yelled the director, trying not to shout in my face.

Too late. The shock of the toy being snatched and the look of horror on the director's face at the 'other girl' were too much. His two progeny artistes burst into tears. Actors.

My nanny, Mary, was with me that day and I immediately ran to her like a fool kid who had just her hand slapped. Now I 'hated' that 'other girl' and I did not want to play with her at all anymore, in real life or in the commercial. I ran off the set and cried by a tree and really wanted her to know just how bad she hurt me by yanking that horse figure out of my hand while I was just about to make it do something special! I couldn't remember what that was anymore, but it was going to be good and they were probably going to use that part in the commercial and she wrecked it! What a horrible person she was to do that! I did my best to make her feel like hell because I was not the one who took something out of her hand during her ECU! (extreme close-up :-)

Funny how I can still remember everything about that very old moment, but that's entitlement for you. It's the birth of justifiable anger and the thought that you are absolutely in the right from every angle since the beginning of time. I felt so justified and deserving of the moment which she tried to steal by taking 'my toy' and crying even louder on the other side of the set. I remember throwing my hairbrush into the grass and Mary just stood there and gave me 'the look.' I instantly knew I had gone way over the top with this and she was looking at me like, 'Girlfriend, puh-lease. I've seen you endure way worse from two brothers who take your toys all the time.'

I quickly picked up the brush and started to reel it in, as I was a professional and not accustomed to tantrums like this. I remember the director coming over to console me and asked if I could do my best 'pretend face' in order to be 'friends again' with the 'other girl' as that would really 'make his day', figuratively and literally.
I said, "I guess so," the way a diva in a training bra would respond.

Everyone was thrilled to see the two little 'darlings' approach the set and begin our cautiously optimistic 'fake play'. At one point, right before they called for lunch the 'other girl' said, "sorry" which prompted me to hand her the beloved horse toy to her in the spot. They fortunately captured this genuine moment on film, and it became the highlight they used in the commercial. I think it was the pure look of sweet shock from 'other girl' that sold the moment. It would have just been an ordinary commercial with two non-reacting kids playing, smiling and not really connecting on any level other than just happy to be in a commercial with pretty new clothes and adults fawning all over them. With the previous episode of tears, entitlement and having to suck it up and accept an apology in front of grownups, it became a real moment. I remember everybody looking at each other like, 'Thank God we got through that one' and 'Is there any possible way to shoot a toy commercial without actually having to cast kids?' The truth is, these moments happen all day long on sets with Big People i.e. adults with larger egos and stronger feelings like someone else deserves everything just a bit more, because they worked just a bit harder for it.

We are all entitled to kindness, forgiveness, and peace. With time we learn to let things go and take our place in line like the rest of humanity and when in doubt, give up, give in and have some fun with it.

Epic Fail ~ Making a problem worse when you have the power to be part of the solution.

Epic Save ~ Creating a safe environment for someone to apologize and start over.

Lesson Learned ~ If someone offers a sincere apology, accept it and move on.

"What separates privilege from entitlement is gratitude."
~ Brene Brown

CHAPTER 43

~ on hostage to the outcome

One of the great truths came from a good friend /mentor / manager/ producing/ writing partner. He said, "Out of one hundred percent of your meetings in the business, only five percent will actually pan out and mean something. The bummer is, you will have to actually show up to all one hundred to get to the five." No truer words. How many times have I been in a situation where I felt that this moment is going nowhere? In an effort not to burn a bridge, I feel obligated to do the prerequisite niceties. Only God knows where this human will be in ten years and I certainly don't want to be the wench remembered down the road for being a stuck up 'better than' who didn't give someone the time of day; we all know where that got me. I do my best to listen to others, even the dull and ignorant, they too have their story. (Thank you, *DESIDERATA,* as for there, by God's grace, go I.) Sometimes I'm truly flabbergasted at how someone will listen to my umpteenth idea, watch my sizzle, short film, or pilot. The biggest compliment is when someone actually takes the time to read something I've written. Thank you, reader! In a world of technology and *CliffsNotes* by an animated voice (no offense Siri, I'm sure that's a stage name) we've lost the fun of finding a book and doing our homework, which was actually a worthwhile venture.

The most painful part of being an artist is being hostage to our outcome. The allure of an endgame, a pot of gold and an easy street keeps us tethered to a brass ring just out of arms reach. We endure all the hard work, sacrifices, commitment to our craft and the endless surroundings of fame and fortune to those who 'made it', only to be reminded of how most don't have what they have. And oh yeah, "If I could only win the lottery, I would be the greatest job creator of all time."

One of my best conversations that is forever crystallized in my memory bank, is with Tom Hanks the night he won his second Oscar® for *Forrest Gump.* I was so lucky to be a part of this incredible night and it was a dream filled with humble excitement. We were all so reverent in the limo on the way there, as you never know what the outcome will be. Tom had won the year before for *Philadelphia* and seldom do actors get an opportunity to win again, in the same category, the following year. I mean, it is one of the more political awards where they like to spread the wealth and there is a ton of entertainment revenue at stake. Welcome to the world of, 'We have favorites, but we do our best not to show it.' Anything could have happened that night, but Tom remained in the joy of being in a great film and happy to be part of the nominations. Well, he won anyway, Mr. Happy To Be Nominated. Again. Deservedly so, as *Forrest Gump* remains one of my three favorite films of all time. After the awards and back in the limo, I asked Tom if I could hold his Oscar® as we got ready to hit every amazing party for the night. Tom graciously let me hold his Academy Award® as I gushed, "I want one of these."

Tom replied, in his most truthful voice, "Well, you know, Kathleen, you're only one movie away."

He meant it and I believed it. Soon after that monumental Oscar® evening, Tom cast me in his writing and directorial debut, *That Thing You Do!* So, he was right, I was only one movie away... from working with an Oscar® winner.

We are all just one moment, one meeting, one connection closer to the steppingstone of achieving our dreams. However, the journey we have embarked upon is truly the grandest part. The deepest question we have to ask ourselves is, did we take the time to acknowledge how we got there? Or are we doing it just for the money or to hold a trophy as the end all and be all? No doubt, it's great to win, but it's also about doing what we love, regardless if there's a gala, red carpet, nominees and an almighty winner. Granted a paycheck is also highly important, especially if we're doing something we don't love.

There are times when I'm really wanting for something to happen and it doesn't, but something else takes its place and it's often better than the thing I was striving for. Stay positive and do your best and the outcome will be your income. Be hostage to nothing and let your conscience, experience and faith be your guide. Listen to your heart and keep the smoke blowers, derelicts and grifters at bay.

Epic Fail ~ Missing the joy of experience because you're so stuck on the result.

Epic Save ~ Follow your dreams and enjoy the journey.

Lesson Learned ~ Being gracious as a winner and a loser, is the true nature of a champion.

"A winner never stops trying."
　　　　~ Tom Landry

CHAPTER 44

~ **on players**

There are so many different kinds of players in this town. Tall, short, unassuming, unedited, entitled, nondescript jerks who prey on innocence and dreams. I'm pretty sure I've met most of them, at least the ones in LA. There are always going to be new ones in training that aren't interested in a fifty something 'ol lady, but dang, they are lining up in droves for unsuspecting youthful prey. All you have to do is let someone know via word of mouth, or by lightning speed of the internet, what you want in this town and there will be someone on the stand-by, promising you the planet, with strings attached, usually to a place in their nether region.

I recently had someone stalk me on *LinkedIn*. This is a site dedicated to connecting people specifically to job related information. This is how it works, you check all of the boxes for your special skills where you're remotely capable, and pray that the people you've asked to 'endorse' you will say, "Yes, I've worked with this person, and they are capable at this particular job function." Then, before you know it, you're being considered for a number of job opportunities that almost have nothing to do with your previous skill set, but at least you are now in the running. Certain skills lead to other skills in this town and just like the old story about starting in the mail room, a few years later you could be running a studio, and/or retired in Pittsburgh.

A vast majority of this town has and always will be about control and manipulation. As the diversity card continues to lay claim on certain parts, there are no real 'types' anymore. It's just either they are looking for a male or a female version of the character and it comes down to either a man or a woman or transgender of both. Finally, an open playing field!

The person who stalked me on *LinkedIn* is a married male director and has probably seduced hundreds of women in this town and globally through his long list of domestic and international credits. In truth, I believe he doesn't even like women. His misuse of power as his mode of operation was so skeevy and smarmy, it screams, 'Women are like paper towels, to be used once and then quickly tossed.' He hunts on this particular site looking for a female to his liking, who is branching out into his own distinct career path and then he promptly goes in for the kill. I'm assuming he's grown tired of the competition in the work force and looking to take out one wide eyed hopeful after the next. It all starts with a cup of coffee and a lecture on how difficult the business is and how incredibly difficult it has become. Before you can even say, "I need to put more money in the meter," you feel like one of the immigrants that's been latched behind the iron gate as the Titanic is swiftly sinking into icy water. People love to be the gatekeeper in this town because more often than not, at one time they were the one behind the iron curtain, and now they hold the rabbit foot of impenetrable luck and good fortune of a resume that says, "I worked on *MacGuyver,* so I know how to get you out of this wishing well and into the field of dreams with some chewing gum, a blow torch and a hair net." It's all such a tremendous amount of horse crap it makes me want to hurl.

This is how it really works. You do the work. You get up early. You read, write and grind your guts out. You get out of your comfortable place and put yourself in a place to meet people and share ideas. You say yes to things that don't compromise your ethics and self-esteem and for God sakes don't sleep with married people or people who are committed to someone else, for they are **players**. They like to think that everyone else is out there cheating on someone, so it makes it okay for them to scandalize and utilize the planet for their own greed. What they are really doing is taking advantage of a situation with their own dirty agenda and doing their best to derail and tarnish something they wished was them. Misery loves company and it doesn't engage in joy.

The second I told this fool that I was on my way to directing, was the same second he put the moves on me. It was like he grew six more arms and I started getting inked by this nasty sea monster. The swirl of bullshit was immense and the "Let me be your mentor" dialogue was a joke. I have hundreds of mentors at my fingertips through TCM, Netflix, Hulu, Amazon and my own private collection of DVD's. It's called studying the greats at your own pace. Read, watch and listen, not just the films on your 'must see' list, but to the body language and the amount of times someone references their own resume and the famous people they knew or once met. The truest sign of a player is when they talk about themself to themself in third person and haven't even noticed if you're still in the booth or casually left with a doggie bag.

Epic Fail ~ Giving someone who has not earned your trust or respect the opportunity to make choices in your life.

Epic Save ~ Recognizing someone eager to attach themselves to your career with their unsavory agenda and removing yourself from their radar.

Lesson Learned ~ The only way to learn something new is to actually take the time to invest in acquiring that particular skill.

"In a narcissist's world you are not their one and only. You are an extension of that person and last place in their mind, while they back up narcissistic supply."
~ Shannon L. Alder

CHAPTER 45

~ on moving

Moving sucks. There's no way around it. Some people move so many times they actually become good at it, but it still sucks. I have one friend who has moved forty-nine times and she's only fifty-two! I for one have never had an easy move. It's always work and just like childbirth, once you get into your new place, you forget all about the difficult and painful labor. Until, oops you do it again. I've lived in California my entire life. I've never been a resident of another state or country or galaxy. I've never traveled out of the earth's atmosphere but I know one day I will, and for that journey I won't need to call to turn off the utilities or have the cable guy meet me somewhere to hook me up with the Dodgers. The worst part of a move, besides the blood, sweat, tears and endless bruises, is the ramping up in your brain beforehand. The logistics are a killer. Who do I call to help? Where will all my stuff go? Do I really need to keep saving this shit from grade school? The things that meant something to me ten years ago are the things I'm ready to trash and burn today. Like my vows. They are currently sitting in an old rusty hibachi that I left at my old place. I should really go get those out of there, as they didn't light properly, and somebody might think I'm weird for leaving them behind. Oh well, they might make the new tenants' s'mores taste better, or s'not.

My first home was in Toluca Lake for about nine years. My second home was three streets from the first house in Toluca Lake for about nine years. My third home was a boyfriend's house in Brentwood for about six months. My fourth home was my dad's 'chick pad' condo in Burbank for about a year. My fifth home was a boyfriend's house on Wonderland Avenue for about a year and a half. My sixth home was back to my dad's condo for another year. My seventh home was in Burbank Rancho for about eight years. My eighth home was in San Diego, while we filmed *Renegade.* My ninth home was in Studio City for about five years with my second husband. My tenth and eleventh homes were in Studio City for about four years, as I moved from one apartment to the slightly bigger apartment next door. My twelfth home was in Valley Village for about two and a half years. My thirteenth home was in Burbank for less than a year. My fourteenth home was in La Crescenta for eleven years. That's the longest I've ever lived in one spot! Wow. No wonder it's been such a monumentally difficult move.

Everything I owned was in that last home. I didn't have a storage facility, so this last move has been a terrific bi-atch! I am thoroughly thrashed and still dealing with it. Plus, the added landscape of having a kid who outgrows stuff every six months, and wanting to save every piece of kindergarten art and not having another 'adult decision maker' to help has really put me over the edge of what to keep and what to give away. Forget selling stuff, as the stuff I already had was mostly hand-me-down crap that I found on someone else's yard. At this point I just want to put a sign on my yard that says, "Free Crap, Tell a Friend." George Carlin does the greatest monologue on *Stuff*. I could hear his droning voice every time I would start to pick through my *stuff* and wonder, "Why? Why am I keeping this stuff? Does it bring me joy? Does it? Really?" Most of the answers were a firm, "No!" I've since whittled my stuff down to 'need' or 'don't need'. If I had to run with my kid and our dog from a burning home, what else would I grab? The answer is nothing because I already have my hands full with my kid and my dog. Everything else can be replaced, except for photos. Fortunately, since we would still be alive, we could take new ones.

I am now in my fifteenth home, back in the San Fernando Valley. It's a great relief to be filling our new home with things we love and letting go of all the old and tired furniture, clothing and memories. We kept the photo albums, as they only depict the happy and joyful times. My daughter had the best foundation for a young education a kid could have. The Learning Castle and La Canada Preparatory were impactful parts of her life that we will remember fondly for the rest of our lives. My next-door neighbors, Lana Marie and Dennis, were the best of the best. Before I got the Dodger channel, I would watch the game on their big screen through my kitchen window. They were like family. I will miss the bubble we lived in on 'The Balcony of Southern California'. I will miss walking through Descanso Gardens a few times a week with the absolutely stunning, Elizabeth Gracen. I will miss our Vons, our sushi place and dry cleaners. I will have to find those new people and create new experiences through being a 'Val' once again. It shouldn't be too hard, since I basically grew up in NoHo neighborhood. I will miss being inconspicuous, as I would meander through town unnoticed. Being back in the Valley means I will be running into more people I know, or better yet, more people that know me. My daughter will be in a new school with new teachers, new friends, new environments and I will be able to drive her through many memories of my life, while getting her to her new one.

Bottom line, moving is good. Moving is pain. Moving is effort. Moving has a payoff, as it is something new and it forces us out of our comfort zone. Ask Danielson from *Karate Kid,* he knows. Trying something new is a very good idea, but putting it into effect scares us, as we don't know what the outcome will be. I have such respect for people who pack up their life, family and dreams and jump into another country, not knowing the language or their bearings. How do they do it? What guts it must take to move to a foreign country without a single friend or family member to greet you. I do know what it's like to be desperate enough to get out of where I am and put forth the energy to move on. I have taken risks in going to places I've never been, in order to have a better life in the unknown. We must take a leap of faith and we must have faith to take leaps. And we must dance, the greatest form of movement there is.

Epic Fail ~ Staying somewhere where you're not happy, because you're afraid to move.

Epic Save ~ Have faith you can get out of anywhere you don't want to be.

Lesson Learned ~ Once you arrive to your next destination, find the local dance studio and start dancing.

"It doesn't matter how slow you go, just as long as you don't stop."
    ~ Confucius

CHAPTER 46

~ on education

I barely graduated high school. I never went to college. I never had a meeting with a college counselor or even toured a college campus. It wasn't even really part of my thought process, or my alma mater's for that matter, as I knew what I wanted to do (act) and I was already in training outside of school. Immediately after my high school graduation, I was cast in a film, *Hardbodies,* so basically, I was set. Or more importantly, on a set. I always wished I had had that collegiate experience, as I'm sure it would have helped me in some way, shape or form. Or maybe I would've just partied a lot, cranked up some serious debt and received a degree in something I'd never use. You never know until you give it a try, unless it's something that you're already familiar with the outcome. The beautiful thing about scholars is that they are eager to know more, which is the key to maximizing everything we can from life; a willingness to learn.

There's a tremendous amount of pressure to go to a great college and earn a degree for the highly competitive job market on the planet. It's even more dynamic if you can learn another language so that you can compete on the international playing field of life. If you become fluent in Mandarin, have a doctoral degree in business, and you play golf, chances are you're going to be in a great position to call the shots. If you drop out of school, have no interest in anything and don't enjoy the process of learning, or you think you know it all, life is going to be difficult.

I did show up at Santa Monica City College for about a week. The drive from Toluca Lake to the west side every morning was brutal and for a Valley girl who only had to drive a mile or two to get to any given school, this new commute was torture. I don't even remember why I decided to go there, maybe because I wanted to be near the beach, and I had always wanted to go to Pepperdine University and SMCC was the next best thing. I was almost into week two of my 'college days' before I bailed and ended up driving to the exact same location for a few fun weeks to shoot *Hardbodies* on Venice Beach. It was such a poignant roller skating turn in furthering my career, and at the time I felt like I had made the best career decision ever. USC Film School was not even on my radar. Or Barnard, or Juilliard, or any other 'ard' school. At the time of my high school graduation, 1983, no one was telling me, a tall blonde with entertainment aspirations, to go to theatre school or film school and learn all the crafts and mechanics of production, just in case I'd like to write, direct or maybe even produce something of my own one day. I mean Quentin didn't go to college, he just started doing it. Which was kind of the whole, "Go live your life and have experiences, so you have something to draw from and for the love of God, don't get fucked up and waste time in a theatre school so they can strip you of all your natural, spontaneous choices." University is a lot of stage work and was in a way frowned upon by everyone in 'the

372

business' who didn't go to a University. I would have loved to have been there for the networking, friend making and 'off to college' experience. I'll always regret not going.

My ideal situation at the time, which I was more than willing to create, was to be available for every audition that came down the pike. In the interim of waiting for my agent to call me with the promise of another possible job, I waited tables like every other compliant actor and model waiting for something else better to happen. I learned menus, drink orders, waiter's names, manager's names, owner's names, shift times and how to screw up an order so that the wait staff always had a plate of fries or Szechuan dumplings in the back. My 'college experience' became Hampton's on Riverside Drive in Toluca Lake, Chin Chin on Sunset and Paty's in Toluca Lake. Paty's was really more like 'finishing school', since I only worked there for three days. The owner back in the early 80's was a stickler for uniform, which consisted of a very starchy, white linen shirt and black, ill-fitting polyester pants. This short lived posting was in the blistering heat of an LA summer and I was like, "Oh hell no." Hampton's and Chin Chin were amusing and merrymaking as the wait staff were primarily young and the new go-getters of Hollywood, which meant there was a considerable amount of shenanigan's and shagging going on between filling orders. It was basically the 80's version of *Vanderpump Rules*.

I learned a lot in the days of 'I should probably be in college right now.' I was studied in pushing things to the limit, i.e. alcohol, drugs, staying up late, or never going to bed at all. I schooled myself in rushing to get somewhere, making excuses for being late or not showing up. My tuition for the 'University of Hard Knocks' definitely came with a price with no offered scholarship or financial aid. I paid for all of it and weathered though with no diploma or degree to show for my investment. Just a ton of wasted, wasted time, and a couple of greasy aprons that I ceremoniously threw in the trash. It lasted a good four years and by the tender age of twenty-two, I had already been in a few films and ranked up a few TV credits and ready to receive my bachelors by marrying Lorenzo.

I did continue to study acting in-between wait shifts with my group at James Best Theatre. Throughout my career as an actor, I've realized the value of being in class and my teachers have been some of the greatest coaches and advisors LA has to offer. I would like to give a special, "Thank you!" to all of the incredibly talented and gifted instructors that I have had the prodigious opportunity to work with throughout my career: Jack Lucarelli, Tracy Roberts, Geno Havens, Roy London, Stanley Zareff, Larry B. Scott, David LeGrant, Richard Lawson, Howard Fine, Sandy Marshall, Margaret Medina and Courtney Gains. Their guidance and watchful eye helped carve my confidence, craft and create a process to continually do what I do; create a believable character formulated from my own personal truth.

Thank God for fabulous books that are made into stunning films like, *Little Women*. Such a lovely reminder of how far gentlewomen have traveled and the sojourn journey that languidly stretches before us. #Gratitude for today's Gen Z women in training to quietly take over. They are thoughtfully in line to celebrate the current concept; the more we educate and encourage each other, the more balanced this planet will become. They understand that if we embrace all genders to the power of learning, training and research, the closer we will be to problem solving all issues. I am not man-bashing or trying to take anything away from hardworking men in the job force. It's just that I was raised with the archaic notion that women are encouraged to attach themselves to someone rich to take care of them. This concept has been flushed from today's mindset and thankfully, my own young and career-minded daughter will have her own vocation, make her own money and God willing, never fall hostage to someone else's paycheck.

As an actor, dancer, singer, musician, producer, writer, director, crew member or anything else in the arts department, you are basically self-employed. It is a highly inconsistent, undependable, erratic profession. There are so many variables in getting and keeping a job, which only lasts as long as someone else continues to invest in the production. When the production is complete, you are now jobless. It's heartbreaking, mind-numbing, soul-selling work. It's also one of the greatest money-makers, influencers, and overnight rocket stardom to global fame. I can't imagine where we would be without music, dance and entertainment? Our world would be lost without all the lunatic artists who tirelessly create in an attempt to shine light, camera and music on all the crazy things we do, say, and feel as a human race. I didn't need to go to college to learn all this, but I do know that having an excellent education gives you an edge in the career pool. So, if you are considering stepping into the world of the arts, learn as much as you can, in order to make your best, educated decision. Then find a really fun restaurant with creative people that will give you good hours. A journey into the arts is your own, into the unknown. The relationships created along the way are what remain.

Epic Fail ~ Failing to realize how beneficial it is to further an education as far as possible.

Epic Save ~ Hanging up the graduation gown to 'UHK' - University of Hard Knocks

Lesson Learned ~ Learning is a constant, as long as we keep an open mind.

"Education is what remains after one has forgotten what one has learned in school."
~ Albert Einstein

CHAPTER 47

~ on moms

"Hi mom!" One of the greatest go-to lines when a camera is suddenly in your face and you have nothing else to say but the automatic acknowledgement of the self-sacrificing person who brought you into this world and took care of your needy butt. Whether you were adopted, in-vitro, C-sectioned, vaginally delivered or dropped off at the fire station, someone took care of you and it needs to be appreciated that 'moms' are something else. They are the toughest race and, sorry fella's; a mother's love is uncompromisingly above all things on the planet. Moms will fight to the death for their young. I honestly believe that 'motherly love' could change the world into a peaceful planet, because 'brotherly love' has so far not done it.

When a mother nurses her child, the environment needs to be calm for the milk to drop. It's physically impossible to nurse while stressed with hectic noise and chaos around. The need to feed and bring forth life is something so miraculous and instinctual that the thought of anything happening to that precious babe is paralyzing. Moms are quietly amazing and guess what, men can't do it. They can't give birth, make milk produce from their nipples and they generally don't have the patience or capacity to nurture in the way a woman is naturally available. Men mostly come into the baby picture when the kid is walking, talking and grabbing the remote. I'm using broad strokes here and I know some men are very maternal. I also know that dads love their kids to death and will fight to protect them too, but it's usually the mom who is the one to deal with all of that super high intensity of bringing a life into the world and keeping it going, thriving and making the crying stop. Babies want their moms, it's natural, since she's the one they were used to and also the original cord of food supply.

The best moms are the ones who know they can't do it alone and they get some help from dad, books, family, friends, chat rooms, therapists, pediatricians, God and nannies, who also might know a thing or two to get a baby stress free and give mom a break. In today's world, being able to be a mom and raise your baby is a luxury, as most moms only have a few weeks or maybe a few months break from work before they have to take their breastfeeding equipment into the public restroom. I know that there are a lot of dads out there now doing it on their own, and I applaud them, but I'm praying that they also know the value of having a woman's touch for their child is vital. Women have something special that says, (cooing mom voice) - "Everything is going to be okay. I will comfort you when you're hurting." The same way a child needs a dad's influence to say the exact same thing.

Women also know the importance and necessity to cry and feel pain. It's natural for us because we usually do it daily. We are touched by good things and bad things equally. We don't judge our tears as weakness but as a sign of feeling and connecting. We identify the needs of others and we go to them on instinct. That's a mom thing and my mom has it in spades.

My mom has been such a tremendous influence and a great giver of everything. She is the most incredibly funny, beautiful, generous, glamorous and 'full of love' support system I've ever known. She made the perfect match for herself with my dad and she has loved him in a way that I've tried to emulate in my own relationships. She got very lucky and she knows it. She has shown me how to navigate the pitfalls of despair and how to celebrate life in the most simple of things. Her attention to detail in language, body and spirit is remarkable and acute. She has a vast knowledge of random information and can kick ass at *Jeopardy* or any other word game known to man. She's a voracious reader and her command of the English verbiage and word play can slay the most adept competitor. She is not the person you want to engage in for a pithy chat. She is extremely deep and does not suffer fools for a nanosecond. Before I really knew her or what she did, she had been on TV for many years of her life playing the role of 'wife' to some great actors and comedians. In 1959, she played Jackie Cooper's wife for three seasons as Navy nurse Lt. Martha Hale on *Hennessey,* in which she earned an Emmy ® nomination in 1961 for Outstanding Supporting Actor. In 1962 she played Joey Bishop's wife, Ellie Barnes, for four seasons on *The Joey Bishop Show.* In 1967 she played Jonathan Winters wife for three seasons in *The Jonathan Winters Show.* Playing opposite these major actors and heavyweight comedians honed her chops for lightning speed repartee. She was the beautiful straight woman to these clowns, and they loved her. She adored the attention and they glowed in her success. Above all her acting roles, she was a mom who loved her kids. She did her best to always put us first and occasionally she brought us along for the ride.

I remember so clearly when she was stopped one day at the grocery store by some gregarious buffoon who shouted across the market, "Abby Dalton! Is that <u>really</u> you?"
"That depends. Who's asking?" she deadpanned.
The dude was just dumbstruck. She wasn't wearing any make-up, fresh off the tennis court, with her three rambunctious kids in tow.
"I just can't believe it! I've had a crush on you since I was twelve," the poor fool gushed.
"Well, thank you," she graciously replied.
"You're so much prettier in person," he said while simultaneously nodding and shaking his head.
"Aww, thanks. I guess I'll have to have a chat with the DP," she said, as she coolly glided her cart away.
"Who was that?" I asked, mostly unaware that my mom actually had a career other than us.
"A fan," she said.
"Of what?"
"My acting."
"In what?"
"Good question."

She had taken a bit of a sabbatical, or enforced hiatus, from her career to take part in raising us with our nanny, Mary, but she definitely hit the pavement again after that moment. She performed in numerous plays and dinner theatre across the country which led to several trips for us kids to visit mom on the road. She couldn't manage three kids while working, so it was a great time for one kid to travel and be with her, mano y mom.

My most memorable excursion was a trip to New Orleans where she was playing the craziest character, Opal, in *Everybody Loves Opal*, opposite Bob Crane, the lead actor from *Hogan's Heroes*. While my mom was playing an old nutty cat lady, I was making friends with the local kids who had a pony in a field of poison ivy. I loved watching her prepare in her dressing room and transforming herself into something I never imagined she could embody. She had crafted the perfect effect of 'saggy boobs' by cutting out the nipple area of a bra and sewing in knee high nylons where she hung lead fishing weights from the toes. While she was crafting 'swinging tits' and rehearsing, I was riding that little poison ivy pony in my red satin Farrah Fawcett shorts. It was magical to be with her when she was working, but it was also a lot of fun being outside and making friends and acquiring the worst case of poison ivy rash between my inner thighs. Okay, that last part was not fun at all, it was heinous. My gorgeous and adoring working mom had to tend to my debilitating fever and swollen body in the middle of her workweek. I don't know who tended to that freakin' little poison ivy pony who'd been rolling around in that shit for its entire life, but at that point I stopped caring. My mom took great care of me during that special trip and nursed me back to health in record time. In other words, she knew her most important role, her stage life came in second place.

God, she really loved to work though. It got her out of the house, gave her a sense of purpose, self-worth and a paycheck. I always wondered why she loved it so much, until that trip. I was able to witness every aspect of the process that she embraced. My mother was kind and available to every person involved in the production. She loved the accolades from people noticing her work and she really knew how to receive a compliment. She made it look effortless and fun. She was never stingy with the experience, as she always encouraged me to go for it, if acting was something I wanted to pursue.

When she landed the role of Julia Cumson on *Falcon Crest*, I pretty much knew that acting was something in my blood too. She didn't play the, 'Oh God, it's the toughest business in the world' card to try to discourage my interest. She encouraged my enthusiasm by giving me insight and the direct number to her theatrical agents, Pervis Atkins and Edgar Small. She wrote me checks for acting class, vocal lessons and head shots. She would run lines with me for plays, auditions and scene study. She gave me notes and compliments simultaneously. I never felt a hint of jealousy or competition from my mom. She was my biggest cheerleader and my mentor. She felt pure joy every time I landed a part because she knew firsthand how difficult it was.

I have such great respect for my mom and her career. She worked very hard for a very long time and no matter what age she stopped working, or attempting to get back out there, she left a mark. She will be remembered by many as a beautiful, funny and dynamic actor who made a few funny guys seem even funnier. For me, she will always be **mom** first, Miss Dalton second.

Epic Fail ~ Wearing short shorts on a bare back pony who's been frolicking in poison ivy.

Epic Save ~ Mom's love.

Lesson Learned ~ We have many roles in life, but it's apparent that becoming a parent will supersede everything.

"A mother is she who can take the place of all others but whose place no one else can take."
~ Cardinal Mermillod

CHAPTER 48

~ on dads

My dad is my buddy and my best friend. I have never known a man to have my back more than my dad. He has never failed me or let me fall. Of course, I've fallen down several times and failed miserably at many things, but I have never felt like a complete and total failure for any length of time because my dad has always been there to help me back up. I am so naturally like my mom in the way I look, talk and my career choice, but I strive to be like my dad. He is the greatest guy on the planet and every person who knows him agrees. His work ethic and code of conduct is unparalleled and true. It is truly mind blowing how consistently kind he proves himself to be day after day, year after year. He is a gentle man with an alarming sense of humor and a vast spiritual awareness. He has a strong and quiet faith and his presence instantly puts even the most agitated and anxious at ease. He has a 'people person' gift which would even astonish Jesus. My younger brother, Johnny, has inherited the attribute, which gets tested daily in the maze of personalities and conflicts at his high-level studio job. Whenever my brothers and I get into any type of situation that requires doing the right thing, we all use the tried and true reference of "What would Dad do?" It has never failed us as a barometer for our next move or decision in this game of life. We are profoundly aware that our dad has somehow become the Chosen One for many of our friends, and his, and if I had a quarter for every time someone told me how wonderful our dad is, I would be taking the entire family, including all the cousins, to Bora Bora on a private yacht for a year. Maybe two.

My dad started off like any other carefree five-year-old kid that got abandoned by his mom and adopted by his aunt and uncle. He never looked at his adoption as being 'unwanted', he considered himself 'lucky' to be wanted by someone else. He even endured his own biological father's suicide when he was a young man returning from his Navy service in WW II. I never knew or met my biological grandparents, Vern and Katharine, but my great Aunt Myrtle, Vern's sister, became my dad's mom and her husband, Burt, became his dad. They were wonderful grandparents to me and my brothers. Myrtle, God bless her soul, lived to be a hundred and one.

Burt was a major influence on my dad. He sadly passed away when I was only four. I remember his gentle kindness vividly and it's the same personality trait that makes my dad stand out from the rest. A man cannot be gentle and kind without thoughtful patience and attentive listening. My dad is the most remarkable active listener I've ever encountered. He takes it all in and patiently waits for the opening to present itself. He's not sitting there with what he has to say as an interruption but something that will help progress the dialogue into a solution or a worthy anecdote. He is wise and judicious and has 'sage' written all over him.

My dad was seventy-five, when I decided to gently cram yoga into his life. My mother was already a yoga enthusiast and my dad, someone who is always pretty much up for anything, was nothing but willing to join us in our practice. It became more than our weekly yoga; it was a place for us to collectively pray and brought us even closer. Our openhearted talks after yoga was what I was really showing up for. There's nothing like doing a bunch of sitting, stretching, standing and falling down in balancing postures to bring a family together. It became a communal prayer of praise for the body we were given and greeting the day with a healthy acknowledgment for what's in store. My dad got the whole yogi concept immediately and has taken to it like a duck in a pond of lotus flowers. He is consistently serene and accepts the fluctuating abilities of what he can and cannot do. He does not judge or condemn his body from one day to the next, instead he allows himself to feel good in his talent to show up and be present. He understands that yoga is not about points or a trophy for who's the most bendy, flexible Gumby in the room. It's about breath, and the pure joy of being able to breathe and the ability to release all the stale air and thoughts from the tip of your toes to the top of your head. It's about prayer and listening to the deep wisdom of, "Ow, this hurts." It requires the skill to notice when to back off and find your breath again. It's about challenge, involvement, completion and gratitude. Yoga is an opportunity to breathe compassion and kindness into your central nervous system. Most of all, it's a practice, which means there is no end game, it's just something we practice as a practice. The only way we become good at it is by continuing the practice. I've never seen anyone so naturally able to enjoy this aspect like my dad. He is a golfer, so he understands the mental concept for application. Most golfers will take a practice swing to remind their body of how to do it right without any points deducted or added. I believe yoga is that great practice swing before you get ready to launch your balls into the flow of life. For my dad, yoga is a great way to make friends with the ground and say a prayer before you kiss your ass goodbye.

I did quite a few things that would qualify kissing my own ass goodbye as a teenager growing up with a ton of options and friends who like to sneak out and party. One fabulous night, my dad had given me and my neighborhood pal, Shanlee, tickets to *The King and I.* We were fifteen, too young to drive but not too young to be taken in a limo to The Pantages and dropped off to see an epic musical. This was way before Uber and Lyft but nonetheless, considered a safe ride for a couple of teenagers who were just getting their feet wet with grownup moments. Shanlee had an eighteen-year-old boyfriend at the time, Mario, who her parents despised. He had a friend or was it his cousin, who's name I can no longer recall and who my parents never met. Since we were already soaring on a solid super high from being whisked around in a limo and seeing Yul Brynner sing his bald head off, we decided to kick it into higher gear by stuffing my bed with pillows and sneaking out to meet 'the guys.' Meeting up with 'the guys' consisted of watching them smoke cigarettes around the corner from my house and wondering what the hell we were doing out at 3am. It was lame and exciting all at the same time. The rush from sneaking out my bathroom window finally wore off around 4:30am and I told Shan I was pretty tired, and we should get back before we got busted. Too late. My dad was already up and waiting for us on the front porch with his trusty metal device used to turn on sprinkler heads. Given the right mood, that thing could be a real weapon. He reminded me of Gregory Peck wielding the harpoon at the end of *Moby Dick*. He had already used that thing to turn the sprinklers on, which were blasting our walk of shame like a fountain of 'yute'. As in Joe Pesci's version of, "Yute better get your asses inside now, girls." I was so busted and ashamed of letting my dad down, I couldn't even look at him as we skulked past him into the house. Although I do remember him saying, "Hope you enjoyed the late show." He didn't come in for a while, probably stayed watch until the sun rose, thanking God we were safe, sound and home.

When I was a kid, my dad and I had this special thing of trying not to laugh. We are both very quick to smile at life and when he tried not to, it always cracked me up. The same applied for me, when I would try not to smile or laugh, it always got him. What kind of crazy is this? Two people trying to crack each other up by not smiling or laughing is just the best game ever. It would start as a stifled snort laugh, the kind you get in school when it's really quiet and someone just cut one and you're doing your best not to lose it, but you end up getting in trouble with the teacher anyway. The kind of laugh that builds from an inside giggle that you're desperately trying to stifle but only builds from the inability of not being able to hold it in. It's like a bottle of champagne that's been shaken so hard the cork blows. No matter how bad, sad or angry I felt at anything, my dad could bring a smile to my face with this game of simply trying not to laugh. He never used it as an inability to not listen to what was going on with me or to minimize any real feelings that I was having, but he knew that he had this wild card and when the time was right, he would play it to bring me back to zero. The opportunity to smile again, through my tears, is one of the greatest gifts my dad has given me.

No matter where I am in my life or who I'm with, my dad will be the mainstay of the greatest man I've ever known, and I am forever grateful to be put on this planet as his daughter and his friend. He has shown us all what a really great dad and friend is all about.

Epic Fail ~ Thinking you can sneak out of the house with a very aware parent at the helm.

Epic Save ~ Having a kind and forgiving parent to greet you when you finally call it a night and go home.

Lesson Learned ~ When you have a parent who trusts and respects you, pay it forward.

"My father gave me the greatest gift anyone could give another person; he believed in me."
    ~ Jim Valvano

394

CHAPTER 49

~ on heroes

I believe we all have the capability to be brave, courageous and lionhearted. It is in our DNA to survive and do all that we can to live. I don't think that we arrive on this planet with the need to kill, but with the desire to live. This deep-rooted instinct is stronger than anything else we endure in this life. I have seen little babies with 'hero' written all over them in their fight and struggle to stay alive. At some point in the journey we learn to hate, judge and dismiss other life as meaningless. The truth is, all life has meaning. As a planet, we need everyone who has joined us to complete the current cycle of a very intricate dependency. We need the shoemaker and the podiatrist equally. We need the saddle maker and the horse breeder equally. We need the baker and the farmer equally. We need clean water and fertile land equally. We need all races, religions, and colors of the rainbow equally. We need light and dark, day and night, work, play and rest equally. This is the combination that brings out the best in all of us and allows us to be heroic for each other. If the balance of the sea creatures and marine life is so intricate to our well-being on land, then we need to do the same for them.

Heroes are not just our first responders receiving a paycheck at the end of their selfless day of saving lives, homes and futures. Modern day heroes are simply regular people who perform random acts of kindness out of the goodness of their heart just because. Not just because it feels good to help and be of service to mankind, but because on some level we are cosmically aware that we all need to be rescued. When we help without hesitation by jumping in and saving someone in any way, it is an automatic deposit into the Karmic Bank of the Universe. We all have our hand out, that's how we arrive. We are born with our mouth open and a shit ton of needs. If someone doesn't start caring for us from day one, it could be a very dicey future for humanity. We need others to step in and help in an unflinching, fearless and valiant way. We need heroes for children, parents, family, friends, teachers, and world leaders. The only problem with being a hero is that it comes with accolades that have the power to inflate egos and make us mere mortals self-absorbed.

I used to be the proud owner of a black, Cabriolet Porsche, which is a very expensive convertible car that makes you look like you're somebody special and rich. I was neither, well maybe a little bit, but not much. Driving that car around LA was a lot of fun and I remember fitting in in a way that I hadn't before. With the perfect shades and blonde hair flowing, I was like a Hollywood *Post Cards From the Edge* in motion. Like most metropolitan big cities, we have our fair share of those who have hit upon bad times. Our streets are lined with homeless and those who are struggling with all kinds of problems. Like most compassionate humans, my heart has always ached in a deep, hopeless place when I encounter the homeless. They are not all drunks and drug addicts, a lot of them are good people who have hit a really bad turn in life and unfortunately did not have a hero to rescue them. For me, it was a tremendously sad and guilty feeling driving by a homeless person in a convertible Porsche. I decided since I did not have a bottomless pit of cash to give out at every street turn in my wildly hip car, instead I would buy countless bags of street corner oranges for a dollar from another guy who really needed it, and hand one out to each homeless person I encountered as a gift. This way they would get something to eat that was filled with vitamin C and healthy fiber. What a genius and heroic move on behalf of the Blonde Ambition Tour! I was a solid week into this genuine act of kindness and feeling mighty proud of myself in my efforts to stop scurvy amongst the downtrodden. Until one day...

I had a few oranges left in my bag and I thought I would be extra generous to one really gnarly looking dude covered in filth and rage. He had crazy eyes times ten, so I graciously gave him the rest of the bag. He looked at me like I had just spit in his face and blurted, "Crazy bitch! I don't want your damn oranges! I want money!"
'Uh-oh,' I thought. 'This is definitely not going according to plan and I'm feeling like my right foot wants to step on the gas and orange peel right out of here,' which I did. I burnt rubber and he hurled those oranges at me like a rapid fire, laser-pitching machine right into the back of my adorable pricey convertible. That guy had an awesome arm and amazing aim. Where's a Dodger scout when you need one? I will never know who he was, or if he got traded, as I didn't use that off ramp again for a

very long time. Just another heroic Hollywood save followed by an epic fail.

Being a hero is sexy, hence the tights, mask and cape. Everyone wants to get a photo with a hero and have the hero hold their baby. We give parades, sculpt bronze and carve marble all in admiration of our heroes. Our heroes are the winners and the underdogs. They are the hard workers who do what it takes and don't complain about doing it. They are the ones that look for trouble only to make it stop. They don't heighten conflict by adding fuel to the blaze. They are problem solvers and contributors. They are those who we count on in dire need. They are sometimes people we know and love and sometimes complete strangers who we pass on the street. They lift us up in life with their commitment, strength and spine. They are among us and we are among them. We need them for every epic fail in life to remind us that as long as we are here, we survived it, together.

Epic Fail ~ Not caring about those who need help.

Epic Save ~ Acknowledging that there are countless ways to help and do what you can.

Lesson Learned ~ You can't save them all, but one at a time, we can make a difference.

"A hero is someone who has given his or her life to something bigger than oneself."
    ~ Joseph Campbell

CHAPTER 50

~ **on dance**

My daughter is an amazing dancer. She was born with the most graceful hands I've ever seen. Her body is strong, limber and full of joy when she moves and bares her soul. From the beginning of her ability to walk, she has always felt the music. Her talent is deeply rooted in her ability to interpret emotion into movement. I watch her and cry. Every time.

Her very first dance class was immediately followed by a trip to the ER. We were at a local *Creation Station,* ink still drying on the Release Form, when she tripped and fell during a 'ring around the rosy' moment while holding a massive circular parachute. She was simply going faster than the rest of the toddlers trying to get that parachute up in the air where it belonged. She lost her grip on the rubber handle and went chin first into the hardwood floor, splitting open her little perfect baby face. I scooped her up and had her chin wrapped in ice and paper towels while my dear friend, Lisa, sped through Studio City to St. Joe's in Burbank. Lisa kept a cool demeanor behind the wheel while I speed dialed the plastic surgeon who had recently sewn my third husbands thumb back on from a skill saw mishap days before our wedding. Aah, the tangled tango of real life.

I never knew what a papoose board was until I entered the hospital that day. It's just like it sounds, a little board to strap down your little papoose. Seeing my precious tiny innocent bleeding and screaming two-year-old, strapped in like Hannibal Lecter, was a dance of demons in my heart.

"Mama, mama, mommy, mommy, mama," she tearfully cried over and over again.
"It's going to be okay, baby. You're going to be okay," I whispered, choking back tears as Dr. Stone dutifully numbed, cleaned and sutured.

The whole process was mind throbbing and traumatizing as I gasped and gagged on fight or flight hysteria. All I could think was, "Why the hell would you have a spin out, snap the whip moment with brand new walking kids in ballet slippers?" I really wanted a copy of that Release Form to use as Kleenex, or something else. I also remember that sinking feeling of, "Well, there goes her dance career."

By the time her twelve stitches were removed, she was already pirouetting. She has dance so ingrained in every part of her DNA, there is truly nothing that will stop her from moving and creating to the music. She has performed in numerous recitals with dance companies and schools. She embraces tap, ballet, jazz, contemporary and lyrical like they are long lost friends. She finds the coolest music (which I love to *borrow)* to choreograph her intricate and emotional dance numbers. She finds herself and simultaneously loses herself in her spontaneous interpretations that she performs in our home.

More than anything, she loves to dance and more than anything I love to watch her. It's a perfect, symbiotic relationship of performance and admiration and because it's never the same, it never gets old.

My mom got her start as a showgirl in Vegas. She had limited dance skills, but she did know how to roller skate. (I'm sensing a full circle of life here with my own roller-skating initiation in *Hardbodies*.) At the end of the feather wearing, leg baring roller skate 'dance number,' they did a mesmerizing, crowd pleasing 'crack the whip.' (Another full circle of life moment) This 'finale' move would launch one fearless 'dancer' flying around the stage and hopefully into the waiting arms of a heroic, burly stage tech. My mom picked the short straw that night and got placed at the end of a very scary line of worn out skaters and when they cracked her off that human whip, she went zip-lining to the front of the stage, instead of off to the side. All she saw was bright lights and the look of horrific fear on the front row before she was snapped down at the ankles by the brass bar at the end of the stage that encased her skate like a bear trap. She tried every which way to get her skate out from under that railing but it was so wedged in there, she did the only thing a dancer can do at that moment. She did a lot of smiling and arm stylings as she unlaced her skate, removed her swollen foot and gracefully danced off the stage and cried. She decided acting was going to be a lot safer. What a rube!

Singing, dancing and acting have long been the mainstay triple threat of Hollywood. If you are capable at all three, chances are you'll have more chances in getting a job... at Disney. It doesn't guarantee anything other than being a well-rounded performer who truly knows how to get the most out of their instrument. I highly recommend studying all forms of artistic performance to understand body placement, vocal control and the ability to emote all forms of emotional stylings. We are deeply sensitive creatures who are inspired by sound, movement and the percolating of our own cells. Nothing is more true than when you are swept up in the presence of dance, especially on *Dancing with the Stars*. I have wanted to be on this show since its inception. I'm perfect. Barely recognizable, limited dance ability and a shit ton of enthusiasm and nerves. I yearn to be a cast member competing with other 'stars' getting spray tanned and bedazzled for a two-minute moment of emotional, physical and spiritual freedom. And then while you're catching your breath and sweating off your sequins alongside your professional dance partner, you get judged! It's just the most grueling and beautiful clinical study of performance art around and I love it.

I finally got tired of dreaming, wishing and thinking about learning how to ballroom dance, and took my own bull by my own horns, and waltzed into Arthur Murray Dance Studio in Sherman Oaks and demanded lessons. I am an actor after all, commanding myself to perform at all hours and at all costs. So why not learn the fine art of ballroom dancing to round out my TV karate chopping? The gift of dance has been one of the great treasures I've given myself. I have glided into the waters of rhythm and smooth dancing and it has become a baptism of determination and discipline. Ballroom dancing is unlike any other form of dance as it is a coupling of trust, sensitivity and equal amount of exertion from one partner to the other. It is ridiculously intimate, and the end game is when the music is finished, and you're swept up in the afterglow of completing the number and you move on to the next number and/or partner. I love how thoroughly physically and mentally challenging learning a dance can be, and the spiritual lift received when you nail it. At my age, I will never be a professional dancer, but I will be a very competitive amateur. For someone who has always enjoyed taking the lead, I have finally discovered the reward in learning to follow. Dancing also has science-backed benefits proven to fight dementia. Sign me up! Oh, that's right, I've already signed up. See? It works!

I have the utmost respect for dancers and athletes, in general. They understand and enfold the discipline, the pain, the upset, the glory, the wins and the losses in every part of their body. Tired, achy, cranky and broken, they continue to show up, stretch out and give their bodies energy to the tireless wheel of enthusiastic moms, dads, friends and fans who cheer them on. I never knew what bunion pain was until I started dancing. The truth is there is no pain that will keep me from continuing the practice of dance as it has become my therapist and parishioner as I leave all my stress, anxiety, problems, sweat and tears on the dance floor. I walk away flushed and fueled from the tremendous amount of endless exertion. "Dance it off" has become our mantra at home. I have such an overwhelming amount of appreciation for what my daughter puts her body through on a daily. She is a without a doubt a *real dancer* and I *AM SO* dancing for Life.

Epic Fail ~ Forgetting that ballet slippers and roller skates need ample room for freedom.

Epic Save ~ Always having a plastic surgeon on speed dial.

Lesson Learned ~ Take the leap and sign up at a local dance studio.

"You don't have to be great to start, but you have to start to be great."
~ Derek Hough

CHAPTER 51

~ on when

"Are we there yet?!" my brothers and I would simultaneously shout from the back seat of our 70's station wagon. Mom, riding shotgun, and dad behind the wheel, would share a colossal eye roll as they pulled out of our Toluca Lake driveway for yet another fun weekend of skiing in Mammoth. Three hundred miles of, "Are we there yet?" became the anthem that started every excursion.

"Enjoy the journey!" mom would sing, as she popped a valium and cracked a beer. Dad, dutifully behind the wheel for six hours, would crank up the Frank Sinatra, or John Denver or better yet, Vin Scully. Nothing was as amazing as drifting into a deep, driving slumber from a Quarter Pounder w/ cheese, fries, chocolate shake, Dramamine (thanks Dr. Mom?) and the rhythmic tones of Vinny commentating a Dodger game through the Mojave Desert. That's about where we'd lose the game on the radio and that's about where we'd all pass out. You're welcome, Dad. I would usually wake up around Crowley Lake, sensing snow and Davey McCoy (my teenage sweetheart/love of my life) in the air. Some of the best journeys happen when you don't know what's going on, and when you finally arrive, bewildered and half asleep you wonder, "Now what?"

Welcome to the moment of, "What's next?"

Why we love routine, is the same reason why we love spontaneity and adventure. It's the yin and the yang of, "I got this, and I don't got this." Routine allows us to know what to expect, as we've already done it. Spontaneity is like a first dance, which can also be very amazing. How will we ever know if something could become an astonishing routine for our self and possibly something in which we might become adequate and enjoy, if we don't simply give it a try? I'm talking about stuff that's good for us, not necessarily burning high falls off skyscrapers, but a new exercise or eating something healthy in a new and unusual recipe, or above all, being open to love. If not right now, then when? When do we give ourselves permission to change and embrace the unknown? When do we say I _can_ wait for the next great thing to happen and I _will_ work very hard for it? In the meantime, while I'm experiencing 'the happening', I'm going to _enjoy_ every nuance that surrounds this plan that I have for myself. For me, I know I don't do this enough. I've been very impatient at times and it does not serve me well. When I react indignant and super charged to 'my way or the highway', there's usually some kind of backlash. I always feel horrible after I yell these days because I don't do it as a routine. It feels mean and I don't want to be that kind of friend or mom or coworker who yells to get their point across. Sometimes it happens because, hey, welcome to the human race, we have volume that goes up to eleven.

From the moment I was born and able to walk and talk, all I ever wanted was a horse, or a pony or a donkey or a zebra. I fell in love with mules later on in life, appreciating the great majestic working breed with their soft fawn coloring and smoky eyes. So sexy and compliant. Every Christmas and/or birthday during my very early years, I would race through our family home to the front yard, expecting to find a great four-legged creature tied to a tree with a bright red ribbon around its neck. Just like the car commercials at the holidays. Who are these people that have a shiny new Range Rover waiting in the driveway without any warning? Are they really that surprised? Really? Really. Why isn't it *ever* a pony? Stupid.

Anyway, it never happened. I got jipped from that super-entitled spoiled brat moment of finding something so beyond extraordinary happening in my non-horse-zoned area. I had to deal with the fact that my parents were never going to move out of their luxe home in Toluca Lake to reside in the Burbank Rancho in a smaller house with horse poop and flies in the back yard. So, I gave up, poor me. However, when I was fifteen, more of a responsible age to take care of a horse and also about the same time I started noticing boys, they deftly sidelined my fascination with _two_ beautiful Moab horses. They were full brothers, Julius and Caesar. Moabs are a cross breed between a Morgan and Arabian horse. They were both completely black, typical of a Morgan horse and full brothers, which meant they had the same dam and sire. They were two years apart. Julius, the older horse, was

411

the better horse, magnificently gaited and well-mannered with a large, strong head. Caesar was the more adorable horse, with the classic Arab face and mannerisms, which translate into unpredictable. They bought two horses, one for me and one for my mom, so that we could ride together and have a relationship during my independent teens. I pray that will be the case for me and my daughter one day too. I remember screaming my lungs out when they both stepped off the trailer and into their plush digs at Circle R Stables in Burbank. I couldn't believe that **"When?!?"** had finally arrived. And quickly on the heels of 'when?!?' arriving did **"Now What?!"** kick into gear. I was immediately immersed into the care and handling of not one but TWO HORSES!! 'Be careful what you wish for...' No truer words.

During the time of wishing for what we want, we should be aware of the care and handling of receiving that great thing on our want list. Kids don't arrive with instructions and neither do pets or relationships. Jobs arrive in the way of 'landing' something and then we have to dig even deeper to execute that which we assured we could deliver. If we think we can 'wing it' to the point of passing tests that we haven't prepared for, we are going to be disillusioned to the point of failure. There is a fine tight rope balance between thoughtful realist meets blind idealist. I walk into as many situations as possible with the notion of, "We'll see." It allows me to feel positive in other people's presentation's, including my own. I don't have all the answers and neither does anyone else, unless you're the teacher with the answer handbook. Nothing will ever beat preparation, studying and executing your best. Other than that, we have to depend on the climate of the room and the ability to show up and be there, even when we don't feel like it. That's what separates the thoughtful achievers from the wishful pipe dreamers. You have to be willing. Willing to work, willing to fail, willing to pick yourself up, dust yourself off and get back in the saddle every time you get thrown.

When your kid is sick, or your animal wounded, or your partner upset, don't question them with, "When will you be better, already?" You nurse, doctor, and show compassion to allow healing and recovery to take place. You *give them time*. The more we allow ourselves to find the natural timing in life that's presented, the less we try to shove our needs ahead of mother nature and a moment that just might not be the right time, *yet*.

"Are we there **yet**?" said the Sherpa to the mule up the trail to Mount Everest.
"Eee-ahhh," replied the mule. Translation, "Don't forget to look at the view, and where's the beer?"
Horses love beer because of all the grain, barley and hops. I love beer because it puts me right to sleep so I can get my 'beer-ty rest.'

A little girl runs into the yard on her birthday and gasps when she sees the lawn covered with poop.
"Oh mommy! Oh daddy! Thank you! Thank you so much!!" she squeals, sniffing the pungent air.
"For what, honey?" they cringe, looking at each other perplexed amidst their annual fertilizing.

"For the pony that's got to be around here somewhere!!"

Epic Fail ~ Missing the journey by only focusing on the pre-determined destination.

Epic Save ~ Appreciating and nurturing the time and focused energy it takes to bring dreams to fruition.

Lesson Learned ~ Be generous with your compassionate kindness and the Universe will respond to all your dreams and hard work.

"The two most powerful warriors are patience and time."
    ~ Leo Tolstoy

CHAPTER 52

~ on religion

I t's complicated. There's a very strong passage in the Bible that says, and I'm paraphrasing, "The church will come down on the four corners it was built." So, make a round church! Problem solved. Or just have church at the beach, mountains, desert, field, back yard or in your heart. There are a lot of great churches out there and sadly some have created a discord for the rest. Church is not just about being at a place, it's about being in a community and sometimes it's functioning well and sometimes not. I believe religion is about the relationship we have with ourselves and those around us. Just like in a family, a relationship, school, workplace or circle of friends, if a person gets turned off by another person or when trust is broken and safety compromised, yes, it all falls down on every corner it was built. I believe religion was created so we could have structure in all things as a solid guideline to goodness that helps get us back on track. We need to feel good about being governed and religious faiths are the templates that bind us all together. I've seen it happen numerous times in the Baptist, Protestant, Lutheran, Catholic, Christian, Buddhist, Jewish and other religious smorgasbord offerings I've sampled, where someone is an asshole and it turns someone off to that religious sect. But here's the truth, humans are not God, they make mistakes, and fortunately if it happens to be someone attached to an organized church, then they are already being judged, by God.

What about when we judge God? What happens when we feel so let down and angry when He rips someone we love out of our life? What about when horrible, heinous, hideous things happen on this planet and we are left to wonder, "Why God? Why?!? Why would you create so many diseases and allow stupid thoughtless drunks behind the wheel?!? Why does the drunk driver get to walk away and not the beautiful innocent's?!? Why would you let anyone with a burning rage to kill, show up with a gun and not let that fucker get hit by a drunk driver on their way?!? Where are you God? What is wrong with You?!?" The truth is, I don't know but I do know that a lot of the survivors of every imaginable trauma, disease, loss and abandonment lean on their faith to get them through. I don't think God has it out for us but we do have it out for ourselves. If *hope* is the source of my strength that keeps me going and believing/*hoping* that 'everything is going to be ok', then that *hope* is *God*.

The most painful and profound moment I have experienced God was during a Shiva walk for the most unimaginable loss a family can endure. This beautiful family lost both of their children at the hands of a drunk driver. This tragic and horrific loss became a paralyzing anger, sadness and overwhelming guilt from still having my own daughter by my side. Everyone who knows this family was experiencing the same crippling and imploding grief. I didn't know what a Shiva walk

418

was, but after attending the funeral for these two gorgeous and beloved young teens, I knew I had to do whatever else was asked of me to be a part of their parents grieving and my own. Shiva is the week-long mourning period in Judaism for first-degree relatives. On the seventh and last day of Shiva, the mourners are required to sit for a small part of the day followed by a walk around the block, symbolizing the return to the regular world, a world which will never be the same. After many stories, prayers and songs honoring their cherished children, we gathered outside their gate for the Shiva walk. There must have been at least a hundred of us, silent and still, waiting for their courageous and faith-filled parents to take their first steps into the world without their loving daughter and son by their side. Those steps were a crystallized moment of what faith, religion and community are all about. There was a gentle breeze that evening that felt like angel wings. We were being guided and led by faith and companionship, on this earthly plane, and the heavenly realm. It was quiet and somber at first and then came the whispers of communication and quietly shared stories. I could hear people begin to talk about plans and maybe a laugh or two and before you knew it, we had completed a quarter mile walk through their hilly neighborhood and there was *life* amongst us. It was not the life they were used to, but it was the life they were embracing and honoring with their family, friends and those who barely knew them but came to support out of love, loss and respect. I will never forget that evening Shiva walk that said, "We are here for you, you are not alone in your pain and we will comfort you in any way we can." And there is God.

I've been to many different church gatherings and I do love the ones that happen outside the most. The kind of church you have when you're not in church. The kind of religion that embodies human kindness, gratitude and compassion. When we embrace the things that are free and cost nothing but time, that's when spirits recognize kindness/God in action. A smile from one person to the next. A feeling of "Hey, I just met you, but I believe your life is worth something and I want to show you respect." This doesn't work if you're running from the cops, driving drunk or pulling tomfoolery's at school. Respect, like the circle of trust, is earned. I think you earn respect when you give respect and it's the same with trust. Religion is that concept. Trust and respect yourself and *I* place *My* trust and respect in you. It's also good to give when you meet at these gatherings, whether it be money or giving of yourself. It shows reciprocity to how much we are given in grace.

'Namaste' translates into 'I recognize the Divine in you, as you recognize the Divine in me.' We need religious beliefs to remind us of why we need to walk the line. We need something bigger than ourselves to keep us in check, morally, physically and above all, spiritually, which is a direct line to keeping the mind in check. When we are right with God/the Universe, we are right in our mind. I have never heard God ask me to kill anyone. I pray and meditate daily, and I don't adhere to killing in the name of God. Those who do, have someone else on the line. Either way, there are a lot of different cell phone numbers, a few carriers, and only one Universe in which we are ricocheting all the calls. God is Love. That's all. When we all go to that Source, we realize how tolerant we must be of all calls to God. Nobody owns His number, but He has ours. When we pick up the phone all we have to say is, "Hello God, it's me, you know, you're **favorite**." He's right there listening. He was even listening before you picked up the phone.

I've always felt that it's about relationship and not religion. I'm not a member of a church but I do frequent different church gatherings with my dad because I love the sermons, the music, the message and praying with others. I like the outfits and hairdos and smiling at people. I like the parents and the cooing and crying babies and the scrappy little kids getting up front and putting on a pageant. I do love the feeling after a morning in church. There's definitely a glow that radiates from being uplifted in any spiritual experience. It's **love**.

Even with the fire and brimstone stuff, it's about love. Well, that part is kind of about fear, but it's in an effort to encourage people to love one another before the fire and brimstones take us all out. We never know when our time is up and how we are going to go. So, while we have the chance, let us love one another and be kind to one another. Why not? What have we got to lose? I can't figure it out. Haven't all the lines been drawn in the sand? Can someone please spend all the money on climate control to end hunger and establish peace? We have the technology. We have the solutions. We just need everyone to come together in a great big Kumbaya circle of collective faiths and engage the plan. Enough already with the terror and corruption. I know the heroes are working overtime on breaking codes of diabolical proportions every day. I pray daily for our very special humans who devote themselves to the protection of our good and the safety of others, because the sad truth is not everybody feels this way.

In August of 1990, I was in Israel for a couple of weeks visiting my action star husband, Lorenzo Lamas, who was shooting a film with another super sexy actor, Michael Pare'. Talk about a spiritual experience. Being around those two studs in a buddy movie in a gorgeous location on the Mediterranean. Oh. My. God. Let's just say I'm going to have to spend some time in confession on those fantasies. Anyway, I was on vacation and wanted to have a chaste spiritual experience in Jerusalem. As 'God luck' would have it, our tour group was led by none other than the biggest non-believer on the planet. I could tell he really hated his job. It was comparable to a Hollywood bus tour where the tour guide is completely 'over it' pointing out the same wealthy celebrity homes for minimum wage. Talk about resentment on steroids. Imagine coming around the bend on every part of the path that Jesus walked, and the tour guide is throwing away the information with a totally non-plussed, sarcastic tone.

"Here's where they *say* "Jesus" walked," the tour guide said with the sound of air quotes lingering in his hard-core non-believer tones.
"Here's where "*he*" prayed," he rolled his eyes.
"And the walk of the cross," he dismissed.
This was before cell phones, so unfortunately, he wasn't able to text while talking.

I was so astounded at this guy's lack luster performance; I wasn't even paying attention to the stuff that was whizzing by me on this more than bizarre drive-thru Tour of the Christian Faith. I did buy a Bible bound in olive tree wood, where "Jesus" prayed. Sorry olive tree, but you needed to be a souvenir from the Holy Land. I do love that Bible and I do love that I had that experience. I made it to the Wailing Wall and said a prayer for that tour guide and left a prayer for me and Lorenzo. I also got to see the vast and wildly astonishing Salt Sea. It was an incredibly beautiful place, fraught with discontent. I continue to pray for the Middle East and for all of us who are affected by terrorism and the strife we continue to endure. We are a planet of many religions based on **love**, so I pray that **love** is what rises to the surface.

Shortly after Lorenzo and I returned from Israel to the United States, Iraq invaded Kuwait. I remember thanking God profusely that we made it home safe. In August of 1994, Lorenzo and I were on our way out of our marriage union. I was working with him on *Renegade* and feeling very, very low. I would get up early and take the sacrament to help me feel strong through my day. I would say a prayer, have a bite of bread and a sip

423

of wine from the night before. I guess that great idea I had to serve wine in my morning religion class really stayed with me. Anyway, I was partaking in a communion between me and God to give me strength to get through a day of working alongside my defunct marriage partner. Acting as a strong, kick-ass character in the show, and as an invincible human in front of an entire crew, was daunting to say the least. Continuing to work with each other, while we were going through a very painful and personal divorce, was definitely not in my contract. I was in San Diego and I felt so alone. My brother, Johnny, was also down there working for Stu Segall Productions but the hours were insane, and we hardly saw each other. I was bereft of companionship and friends. I could feel the weight of depression yanking at my soul. I felt such gut wrenching, heart breaking loss. I lost my best friend, my lover, my everything. Yet I still had to work with him and do a good job because people were actually watching the show. Plus, I loved my job and I knew somehow it would save me. During those first few months, I was routinely out of my body, nauseous, head-achy, stressed, depressed, despondent, anxious and broken. I was going nucking futs.

I had to do something that gave me the superpowers it takes to be a warrior of this capacity, so I turned to my spiritual path of what has always given me strength. I never had a first communion like a Catholic girl does. I was invited to partake by different religious sectors and included in the Catholic Church once I converted when I was a junior at my all girls Catholic High

School, Our Lady of Corvallis. I loved the feeling of embodiment. It reminded me of when I embody a character in a role and take on those characteristics. If I took on the characteristics of the Christ Body, which is a communal experience, compelling me to do and say the right things, then I would be able to endure the most painful of walks to the set. Which I did, on the set, not on the Howard Stern Show, which is another story. Guesting on Howard Stern is a whole different kind of religious experience.

Religion is a personal preference and journey. There might be one road you encounter and cling onto, or there might be several. As long as the foundation is built on love, peace, compassion and kindness, you're on the right track to follow a good path. If we really think about it, there is not just one path, as we all have different co-ordinates on the planet at all times. Meaning, no one else has my particular point of view, literally. My POV is my own, and mine only, as I only gaze from my own personal set of eyes and where my ass is currently sitting. My latitude and longitude only belong to me and I have my own view of the sunset and clouds and what they look like to *me*. I know I'm going to get massive doses of hate mail from the hard-core Christians for this, but yes, Jesus *is* a Way but not the only way. Some are saying, "No way!" But I say, "Ya way or Yahweh," pronounced the same. (By the *way*, writing hate mail based on religion preference is a lesson in futility.)

If you don't have a clear picture of what God looks or sounds like, take a nature walk and listen, or go join the army and sit in a foxhole with mortars and shells going off around you. There are so many opportunities to be aware of the presence of Light, especially when you're sitting in the dark. It might be someone's smile when you're feeling down or someone reaching out, when it seems like no one cares. We can be the kind one who taps the brakes and encourages someone on the sidelines into the flow of traffic, when everyone else seems to be speeding by. We can see God by someone helping an elderly person cross the street. We can hear God in the blissful sounds of a babies' laughter. We can feel God in a cool breeze as it whooshes through a pine tree and a sense of calm and peace wash through your soul. There are countless ways to feel the presence of enlightenment through music, art, emotions and dance. There are multiple ways to volunteer and help those on the streets, shelters and suicide hotlines. We have families, friends and strangers among us who are hurting and lonely and all it takes is reaching out to see, hear and feel God within and around us. This is a ride we do together, to love and be loved. And when in doubt, just thank God you're still here, and for the special ones who came before us, who graciously showed us **love** in return.

Epic Fail ~ Believing one's faith is superior to someone else's.

Epic Save ~ Embracing all, including those who have no faith.

Lesson Learned ~ Even in the darkest of times, we are never truly alone when we have God in our heart.

"Just as a candle cannot burn without fire, we cannot live without a spiritual life."
    ~ Buddha

Photo Glossary

1. ~ on *I should've been nicer to Quentin Tarantino* - Getty Image Royalty Free Stock Photo from *Django Unchained* - Special Screening at Shinjuku Piccadilly, February 13, 2013 in Tokyo, Japan (Photo by Adam Pretty/Getty Images)
2. ~ on acting - Kathleen Kinmont - Photo Still from *Stranger in the House* - Canada, 1997 (Photo by Jan Thijs)
3. ~ on *Bride of Re-Animator* - Kathleen Kinmont - Screen grab from the Film - Los Angeles, 1990 - (Cinematographer Rick Fichter)
4. ~ on *Mrs. Sweeney* - Abby Dalton - La Crescenta, 2013 (Photo by Elizabeth Gracen)
5. ~ on *Renegade* - (left to right) Kathleen Kinmont, Stephen J. Cannell, Lorenzo Lamas and Branscombe Richmond - San Diego, 1996 - Episode ~ *Rio Reno* (Photo by Kathleen Kinmont)
6. ~ on Lorenzo - Kathleen Kinmont and Lorenzo Lamas and the *Renegade* Harley – Kern River, 1991 (Photo by Mike Liakos)
7. ~ on birth - Jack Smith and Abby Dalton - Mammoth Mountain Inn, Mammoth Lakes, 1960
8. ~ on organs - Abby Dalton and Kathleen Kinmont Smith - Toluca Lake, 1979 (Photo by Jack Smith)
9. ~ on dating - Kathleen Kinmont - Malibu, 1997 (Photo by Richard Reinsdorf)
10. ~ on valet - Kathleen Kinmont - Burbank Rancho, 1993 (Photo by Mark Mauriello)
11. ~ on almost famous - Kathleen Kinmont - Oak Park, 2018 (Photo by Miranda Frederick)
12. ~ on yoga - Kathleen Kinmont - Leo Carillo State Beach, Malibu, 2015 (Photo by Elizabeth Gracen)
13. ~ on poop - Kathleen Kinmont Smith - Los Angeles, 1966
14. ~ on children - (left to right) Dean Heck, Abby Dalton, Johnny Smith, Matt Smith, Gary Heck, Shirley Heck,

Kathleen Kinmont Smith and Mary Rogers - Lakeside Golf Club, Burbank, 1968

15. ~ on parenting - Kathleen Kinmont - Poipu, Kauai, 2017 (Photo by Matt Smith)

16. ~ on laughter - Kathleen Kinmont - West Hollywood, 1997 (Photo by Russell Baer)

17. ~ on death - (left to right) Johnny Smith, Kathleen Kinmont Smith, Burt Smith, and Matt Smith - Toluca Lake, 1968 (Photo by Jack Smith)

18. ~ on family - (left to right) Marlene aka Abby Dalton, Gladys, Shirl, Sam and Ray - Family Passport - Glendale, 1943

19. ~ on divorce - Kathleen Kinmont - Lakeside Swimming Pool - Burbank, 2019 (Photo by Aubrey Swander)

20. ~ on marriage - Jack Smith and Abby Dalton - Whistler Blackcomb, British Columbia, 1989 (Photo by Warren Miller)

21. ~ on writing - Kathleen Kinmont, Kristanna Loken and Adrienne Wilkinson (in silhouette) on the set of *Fame Game* - Los Angeles, 2014 (Photo by Vatch Karagozian)

22. ~ on baseball - Kathleen Kinmont - Dodger Stadium, September 15, 2015 (Photo by Lisa Marie Wilson)

23. ~ on looking up - Kathleen Kinmont - Santa Monica, 2006 (Photo by Russell Baer)

24. ~ on jealousy - Kathleen Kinmont and Kristanna Loken - La Loggia Restaurant, Studio City, October 8, 2019 (Photo by Danielle Agnello)

25. ~ on change - Kathleen Kinmont - Santa Monica, 1979 (Photo by Troy Freeman)

26. ~ on aging - Abby Dalton - *Falcon Crest* - Napa Valley, 1985

27. ~ on compassion - Kathleen Kinmont and Ayden Grace - Saint Joe's Hospital, Burbank, October 8, 2004 (Photo by Barry J Holmes)

28. ~ on pets - Kathleen Kinmont and Bolt - North Hollywood, 2018 (Photo by Michael Strider)

29. ~ on listening - Kathleen Kinmont - The Brewery, Los Angeles, 1997 (Photo by E.A. Deutsch)

30. ~ on hats - Kathleen Kinmont wearing LA Dodger 'ball catch' hat and Johnny Depp t-shirt from *Crybaby* - North Hollywood, March 28, 2019 - Dodgers Opening Day - **Dodgers** hit 8 Homers in 12-5 win over Arizona
31. ~ on photography - Kathleen Kinmont - Hollister Ranch, Goleta, 2019 (Photo by Gary Heck)
32. ~ on electricity - Kathleen Kinmont - Los Angeles, 1990 (Photo by Doug Dobransky)
33. ~ on lying, cheating and stealing - Kathleen Kinmont - *The Corporate Ladder* - Los Angeles, 1997 (Photo by David Moir)
34. ~ on spirituality - Kathleen Kinmont - The Brewery, Los Angeles, 1997 (Photo by E.A. Deutsch)
35. ~ on Esther - Esther Williams - *Neptune's Daughter* - Weeki Wachee Springs, Florida, 1949 (Photo by Everett)
36. ~ on kissing - Kathleen Kinmont - 18th Hole at Lakeside Golf Club, Burbank, 1999 (Photo by Mark Mauriello)
37. ~ on reality - Kathleen Kinmont - Poipu, Kauai, 2017 (Photo by Matt Smith)
38. ~ on bullies - Kathleen Kinmont - *Phoenix* - Studio City, 2019 (Photo by Tiana Coles)
39. ~ on humor - Kathleen Kinmont - Burbank Rancho, 1994 (Photo by Russell Baer)
40. ~ on forgiveness - Kathleen Kinmont and Antwoine Tuggerson - Liv'Art Dance Studio, North Hollywood, 2019 - Screen grab from *Thunderclouds* Dance Reel - Cinematographer Jonathan Pope
41. ~ on repetition - Kathleen Kinmont - Santa Monica, 1996 (Photo by Russell Baer)
42. ~ on entitlement - Kathleen Kinmont - West Hollywood, 1997 (Photo by Russell Baer)
43. ~ on hostage to the outcome - Kathleen Kinmont - Los Angeles, 2016 (Photo by Jeffrey Byron)
44. ~ on players - Kathleen Kinmont - Hollywood Honeywagons, North Hollywood, 2018 Gown Design - Stanley Hudson - Makeup and Hair - Stacy Rosas (Photo by Michael Strider)
45. on moving - Kathleen Kinmont and Black Jack Gambler - Griffith Park, 1999 (Photo by Mark Mauriello)

46. ~ on education - (left to right) Teal Roberts, Grant Cramer and Kathleen Kinmont - Publicity still from *Hardbodies* - Venice Beach, 1983
47. ~ on moms - Abby Dalton and Kathleen Kinmont - Tracy Roberts Actors Studio, West Hollywood, 1990
48. ~ on dads - Jack Smith and Kathleen Kinmont - Dodger Stadium, June 22, 2017 - the day my dad was honored as, Military Hero of the Game (Photo by Christine Trimarco)
49. ~ on heroes - Kathleen Kinmont - Publicity still from *Night of the Warrior* - Los Angeles, 1991
50. ~ on dance - Kathleen Kinmont and Roman Bykov (background right Tom Antonellis) - Arabian Nights Showcase - Diamond Star Ball at Warner Center Marriott, Woodland Hills - March 1, 2020 (Photo by Maude-Productions)
51. ~ on when - Kathleen Kinmont and Avalon - Griffith Park, Burbank, 1984 (Photo by Kyle Martin)
52. ~ on religion - Kathleen Kinmont - Cover shoot for *Kathleen Kinmont's Restorative Core Yoga - 33 Ways to Embrace the Ground* - La Crescenta, 2012 (Photo by Michael Strider)

Dedication Photo ~ Ayden Grace - Rankin Ranch, Caliente, 2018 (Photo by Kathleen Kinmont)

Back Cover Photo - Kathleen Kinmont - Los Angeles, 1997 (Photo by E.A. Deutsch)

CPSIA information can be obtained
at www.ICGtesting.com
Printed in the USA
FSHW021504300720
71919FS